The Digital Origins of Dictatorship
and Democracy

Oxford Studies in Digital Politics
Series Editor: Andrew Chadwick, Royal Holloway, University of London

The Digital Origins of Dictatorship and Democracy
Information Technology and Political Islam

Philip N. Howard

OXFORD
UNIVERSITY PRESS

2011

OXFORD
UNIVERSITY PRESS

Oxford University Press, Inc., publishes works that further
Oxford University's objective of excellence
in research, scholarship, and education.

Oxford   New York
Auckland   Cape Town   Dar es Salaam   Hong Kong   Karachi
Kuala Lumpur   Madrid   Melbourne   Mexico City   Nairobi
New Delhi   Shanghai   Taipei   Toronto

With offices in
Argentina   Austria   Brazil   Chile   Czech Republic   France   Greece
Guatemala   Hungary   Italy   Japan   Poland   Portugal   Singapore
South Korea   Switzerland   Thailand   Turkey   Ukraine   Vietnam

Published by Oxford University Press, Inc.
198 Madison Avenue, New York, New York 10016
www.oup.com

Oxford is a registered trademark of Oxford University Press

Jacket photograph is the skyline of Dhaka, 1999 © Philip N. Howard.

Library of Congress Cataloging-in-Publication Data

Howard, Philip N.
The digital origins of dictatorship and democracy : information
technology and political Islam / Philip N. Howard.
  p. cm. – (Oxford studies in digital politics)
Includes bibliographical references and index.
ISBN 978-0-19-973641-6; 978-0-19-973642-3 (pbk.)
1. Islamic countries–Politics and government.   2. Information technology–Political aspects–Islamic
countries.   3. Internet–Political aspects–Islamic countries.   I. Title.
JQ1852.A58H69 1010
320.917'6702854678–dc22
2009043565

9 8 7 6 5 4 3 2 1

Printed in the United States of America
on acid-free paper

This is for four men who served in the military and gave me things. Gordon Howard (Captain, 3rd Canadian Infantry) raised a great father for me; Colin Stratton (Sergeant, Australian 3rd Army Division) raised a great mother for me. Although I only knew them much later in life, Fonzie Graham (Seaman First Class, U.S. Navy) helped raised his fabulous granddaughter, and Charlie Moskos (Specialist, Combat Engineers, U.S. Army) helped raise me as a scholar.

Acknowledgments

This project began at the Mendel Center at Glenrock, Australia, was developed at the Whitely Center in Friday Harbor, Washington, and completed at the Center for Advanced Study in the Behavioral Sciences in Palo Alto, California. Support for fieldwork in Dushanbe was provided by the National Science Foundation while I was co-Principal Investigator on a project called "The Effect of the Internet on Society: Incorporating Central Asia into the Global Perspective" (Award #0326101, Beth Kolko Principal Investigator). Support for fieldwork in Dar es Salaam was provided by the Simpson Center for the Humanities at UW. Support for fieldwork by myself and graduate research assistants in Baku, Cairo, Gaza, Istanbul, London, and Sanaa was provided by the National Science Foundation while I was Principal Investigator on a project called "Human Centered Computing: Information Access, Field Innovation, and Mobile Phone Technologies in Developing Countries" (Award #0713074). Any opinions, findings, and conclusions or recommendations expressed in this material are those of the author and do not necessarily reflect the views of the National Science Foundation. This research was conducted with the approval of my university's Human Subjects Division under Application #32381. Within my department, my hard-working chairs Jerry Baldasty and David Domke supported this research through travel funding, coaching on grant writing, and permission to arrange teaching quarters conveniently. Ron Krabill was a supportive writing buddy. The University of Washington is a generous, supportive institution.

Some of the material on technology distribution appeared in "Is the Digital Divide Narrowing, or Becoming a Chasm? Inequality in the Global Distribution of ICTs, 1995–2005," *Information Technology and International Development* 3, no. 4 (2007) and in a piece coauthored with Nimah Mazaheri, "Telecommunications Reform, Internet Use and Mobile Phone Adoption in the Developing World," *World Development* 37, no. 7 (2009). The chapter on cultural management was developed for the "Culture and Power" workshop in Oslo, Norway, organized by Fredrik Engelstad, Wendy Griswold, Anne Krogstad, and Aagoth Storvik. The concept behind the index of digital

Islamic states was developed for Intel's People and Practices group, and their financial support allowed for time to analyze large datasets. Collegial research conversations with Ken Anderson, Maria Bezeitas, Dawn Nafus, and Tony Salvador have led to several fruitful collaborations. Much of what we know about censorship comes from Ron Deibert's research. His project, the OpenNet Initiative, is an excellent example of public scholarship: a high standard of research on a socially significant problem with findings presented in an accessible manner. Charles Ragin was generous with his time in reviewing my conclusion chapter, and with suggestions for weighting the national technology use indicators by economic wealth.

For immoral support I am grateful to Sandy Oh and Declan Hill. Fieldwork cannot be done without generous friends, and it cannot be done without making new friends. For moral support, spending their social capital on my behalf, original insight, and help navigating local institutions, I'm very grateful to: Beth Kolko, Jan Spyridakis, and Eric McGlinchy for assistance with fieldwork in Tajikistan; Tanya Pergola and Simbo Ntiro for assistance with fieldwork in Tanzania; Andrew Buchman, Shannon McNary, and several bloggers who wish to remain anonymous, for assistance with fieldwork in Azerbaijan. Research assistance was provided by Tamara Barnett, Laura Busch, Damon di Cicco, Tabitha Hart, Muzammil Hussain, Courtney Madsen, Nimah Mazaheri, Fahed al-Sumait, Samer al-Saber, Penelope Sheets, and Bo Zhao. For friendly critiques of my ideas, I am also grateful to Pippa Norris, Russ Neuman, Francois Bar, and seminar colleagues at the Center for Advanced Study in the Social and Behavioral Sciences.

Ultimately, this work is for Gina Neff, and is possible because of Gina Neff.

Doha, Qatar

Contents

List of Tables, xi

List of Figures, xiii

Prologue: Revolution in the Middle East
Will Be Digitized, 3

Introduction: Political Communication and Contemporary
Muslim Media Systems, 13

Chapter 1:   Evolution and Revolution, Transition and
               Entrenchment, 37

Chapter 2:   Lineages of the Digital State, 57

Chapter 3:   Political Parties Online, 84

Chapter 4:   New Media and Journalism Online, 108

Chapter 5:   Civil Society and Systems of Political Communication, 132

Chapter 6:   Censorship and the Politics of Cultural Production, 157

Conclusion: Information Technology and Democratic
Islam, 180

Appendix A: Countries in This Study, 203

Appendix B: Annotated References, 219

Notes, 231

References, 239

Index, 261

List of Tables

Table 0.1: Presenting Comparative Data   35
Table 2.1: Conditions—Telecommunications Reform and ICT Policies
            in the Muslim World, 1960–2008   64
Table 2.2: Government Offices Online in the Muslim World, 2008   68
Table 2.3: Outcomes—Remittances, ICT-led Growth and State
            Capacity, 2010   78
Table 3.1: Political Parties Online in the Muslim World, 2000–2008   92
Table 3.2: The Growing Infrastructure for Diverse Ideologies,
            2000–2008   94
Table 3.3: Outcomes—Information Infrastructure for Political
            Parties, 2000–2008   98
Table 4.1: Blogger Arrests in the Muslim World, 2003–2010   113
Table 4.2: Media Concentration in 15 Largest Muslim Media
            Markets, 2010   121
Table 4.3: State Media Ownership and Online Journalism, 2007–2010   124
Table 5.1: Civil Society Online, 2008   138
Table 5.2: Cost of Internet Access in 12 Large Cities, 2000 and 2010   141
Table 6.1: Censorship and the Production of Political Culture,
            2003–2008   176
Table 7.1: The Prominent, Parsimonious Causes of Democratic
            Transitions and Entrenchment   193
Table A.1: Proportion of Population Practicing Islam, Rate of ICT
            Diffusion, and Countries Experiencing a Democratic
            Transition   209
Table A.2: Proportion of Population Practicing Islam, Degree of ICT
            Diffusion, and Countries Experiencing Democratic
            Entrenchment   211
Table A.3: Proportion of Population Practicing Islam, Degree of ICT
            Diffusion, and Countries That Remained Authoritarian   212
Table A.4: Proportion of Population Practicing Islam, Degree of ICT
            Diffusion, and Countries Experiencing an Extended Period of
            Interruption from Foreign Powers, Interregnum, or Anarchy   213

Table B.1:   Study Population: Countries Experiencing a Democratic
             Transition   220
Table B.2:   Study Population: Countries Experiencing Democratic
             Entrenchment   223
Table B.3:   Study Population: Countries Experiencing
             Authoritarianism   225
Table B.4:   Study Population: Crisis States and Other   228
Table B.5:   Study Population: Comparative Case Studies   229

List of Figures

Figure 0.1: Mass Media for Communication and Culture, 1990–2010   17
Figure 0.2: Information Technologies for Communication and
             Culture, 1990–2010   18
Figure 1.1: A Trend Line for Technology Diffusion and
             Democratization, 2010   50
Figure 1.2: Degrees of Membership in the Set of Countries Where
             Technology Diffusion Caused Democratization, 2010   51
Figure 6.1: Cultural Production and Consumption in Muslim
             Countries, 1995–2008   162
Figure 7.1: Conditions, Outcomes, and Consequences   191
Figure A.1: Membership in the Set of Populated Countries:
             Uncalibrated   204
Figure A.2: Membership in the Set of Populated Countries:
             Calibrated   205

The Digital Origins of Dictatorship and Democracy

Prologue: Revolution in the Middle East Will Be Digitized

On Friday, June 12, 2009, Iran voted. On Monday, June 15, Tehran erupted. With implausibly fast ballot counting and high levels of electoral support credited to Mahmoud Ahmadinejad in the dense urban centers and Azeri communities known to back the opposition candidate Mir Hossein Mousavi, the country exploded in demonstrations and violence. Over the next few days, Tehran and other major urban centers saw the largest street protests and rioting since the 1979 Revolution. And the wired world was drawn in.

Domestic politics has often interfered with the administration of elections in Iran, where even competing in elections requires the blessing of the ruling circle of mullahs. The 2005 presidential election that brought Ahmadinejad to power also had irregularities and media blackouts. But this time, civil society groups, social movement leaders, and disaffected youth had access to an information infrastructure largely independent of the state. Armed with mobile phones and the internet, trusted networks of family and friends spread the news of electoral fraud and escalating tensions.

New information and communication technologies (ICTs), such as the internet and mobile phones, have had clear roles both in starting new democratic processes in some countries and in entrenching them in others. Activists in Indonesia effectively used mobile phones to mobilize to topple Suharto in 1998. During Kyrgyzstan's Tulip Revolution of March 2005, mobile phones were again used to organize activists to join protests at key moments, helping democratic leaders build a social movement with sufficient clout to oust the president. Kuwait's women's suffrage movement was much more successful in 2005 than it had been in 2000, in part because it was able to use text messaging to call younger protesters out of school to attend demonstrations. In Egypt, Tunisia and Kazakhstan opposition groups that face state censorship simply move their online content to servers in other countries. Recent elections in Turkey and Malaysia have demonstrated that blogs have a role in entrenching democratic institutions: challenger candidates who blogged on the campaign trail tended to prevail over incumbents from ruling parties who did not run information-rich campaigns.

Civil society in Iran is incredibly wired, but the political impact of digital media there is difficult to assay. Estimates of the number of blogs in Iran range from 40,000 to 700,000. But if the usual ratio of active blogs to registered blogs holds, there are still upwards of 100,000 active sites in the Persian blogosphere. Once the universal character became widely used, Farsi rose to be the tenth most popular blogging language globally. And for several years, the government has been arresting and fining opposition bloggers based within the country. Even the Revolutionary Guard developed a strategy to generate 10,000 blogs, though the Basij militias have not proven up to this particular task. The Bureau for the Development of Religious Web Logs offers blogging workshops to Iran's clerics. During the protests, even the most apolitical bloggers covered the demonstrations, and traffic at the dominant blogs swelled.

There is one mobile phone for every two people in Iran, though in urban areas the vast majority of residents have a mobile phone. There are over 80 internet service providers operating throughout the country. About one-quarter of the Iran's 70 million people have used the internet, around 10 million are regular users, and the large cohort of youth is particularly sophisticated with digital technologies. So the country has one of the world's most vibrant social media communities and the most concentrated broadcast media system in the Muslim world. Why, then, has the digital revolution in Iran not had the type of clear political outcomes or institutional consequences seen in other authoritarian regimes?

The answer, in part, is that while such information technologies have become a fundamental infrastructure for journalists and civil society groups, they are a necessary but not sufficient causal condition for contemporary regime change. So based on real-world experience, what is the causal recipe for democratization, and are information technologies an important ingredient?

For scholars of political communication and social movements, Iran is an interesting case: it is one of the most wired of Muslim countries and has an organized and articulate democratic movement, yet no democratic revolution appears in sight. If new information technologies have a role in democratization elsewhere, why not in Iran? Indeed, much of the research on ICTs and politics in Iran fails to demonstrate much in the way of democratic outcomes, preferring to say instead that the internet is important for providing rhetorical space for dissent. In many authoritarian states, political parties are simply outlawed, while in others they are tolerated but must identify themselves instead as "organizations" or "social movements."

CAMPAIGNING

In recent years Iranians have come to expect their political candidates to be online—candidates without a web presence simply do not appear modern. Challenger candidates usually avail themselves of more than just websites, however. Ahmadinejad's campaign blog (Ahmadinejad.ir) kept his supporters up to date, responded to political spin, and took donations in support of his campaign. Mousavi's use of digital campaign tools was a strategic response to his exclusion from coverage by state-run television and newspapers. He used Facebook (www.facebook.com/mousavi) to reach out to voters, alert them of his public appearances, and help them build a sense of community. Months after the election, he maintained a dedicated YouTube channel and Twitter feed. Iran watchers have noted that women were particularly active in civic discourse during the elections, engaging in political conversations at new levels and in ways rarely seen in offline public interaction.

The vocal Persian diaspora has long been able to express its interests through broadcast media based in London and Los Angeles, but social networking applications have allowed even small enclaves to create content and reconnect with friends and family in Iran. Within Iran, clerics such as Mohammad Ali Abtahi used Facebook to help organize supporters and host political debates. Facebook was blocked by Iranian authorities soon after it went live in 2004. In a move they probably regret, however, Iran's Council for Determining Instances of Filtering allowed site access early in 2009, and young Iranians took to it quickly. They reconnected with cousins overseas, and they used Facebook applications to socialize with friends living down the street. Opposition campaign managers in Iran consistently say that such internet applications allow them to get messages out as never before and thereby organize bigger and bigger campaign rallies. Without access to broadcast media, savvy opposition campaigners turned social media applications like Facebook from minor pop culture fads into a major tool of political communication.

Several days before election day, a group of employees from Iran's Interior Ministry issued an open letter revealing that they been authorized to change votes. These days, "open" means distributed by email and hosted on websites both inside and outside the country. So the ministry's office of internal affairs was unable to recover the leaked documents. In response, former president Rafsanjani developed a plan for ad hoc exit polling by mobile phones. Deliberative democracy theorists argue that independent exit polling is a key logistical feature of healthy election practices. This probably explains why disabling mobile phone services is so important for discouraging any organized measurement of how rigged a contemporary election may be.

VOTING

SMS traffic surged on the eve of the election, but in the early morning hours before the polls opened on June 12, the text messaging systems went dark, and many mobile phone subscribers found service disrupted. Key opposition websites also went offline, including those of the two high-profile opposition candidates, Mousavi and Karoubi. Foreign news sources, such as the BBC website, are usually blocked from access within Iran, but the list of blocked sites grew significantly that morning. The government began jamming the frequencies of Farsi-language satellite broadcasts from the BBC and Voice of America as well.

PROTESTING

Late in the day, government officials declared that Ahmadinejad had defeated his more moderate challenger, triggering massive street protests by Iranians who doubted—or did not like—this outcome. For many, the outcome was sur-prising, and the vote tabulation had been implausibly fast.

People took to the streets of Tehran and Esfahan immediately. There was a flood of digital content from the Iranian street: photos, videos, blog posts, tweets, and SMS messages flowed between protesters and out to the interna-tional community. While this content was flowing, the government closely inspected digital traffic to try to identify social movement leaders. To regain the upper hand in political communication, the government-run Data Communication of Iran disabled internet access for 45 minutes late in the afternoon on the 13ᵗʰ to initialize its "deep packet" inspection system. The process of inspecting the traffic, however, choked bandwidth to the rest of the world, such that Iran was effectively off the global grid for almost 20 hours between Saturday night and midday Sunday.

To support network communications, the Iranian opposition organized a supply of proxy servers unknown to government censors and coordinated attacks on pro-Ahmadinejad websites and state media portals. Free online tools provided encryption, anonymizers, and other secure communication networks. Despite government interference with digital services, SMS, Twitter, and other social media were used to coordinate massive turnout at protests across the country for Monday, June 15. By Monday, the cyber-war was also was well under way. The attacks were launched not only by a few university students well versed in the dark arts of hacking, but by an army of amateurs eager to learn the few basic skills that would collectively over-whelm the government information systems. Parts of the information infra-structure of major government agencies were rendered unusable, from the

Ministries of Justice and Foreign Affairs to the official websites of the police and Supreme Ruler Khamenei.

A few days into the protests, the international community of tech-savvy digerati also began working to disable the government's information infrastructure and support social movement leaders. Volunteers around the world contributed by turning their home computers into proxy servers for users based in Iran, allowing such users to bypass the government's censorship efforts. Pro-democracy activists on the web traded notes on how amateurs could launch denial-of-service attacks on government servers and suggested which targets would be most important. Within Iran, bloggers learned how to get their content around government censors. Tip sheets offered helpful links on how to use Twitter securely and effectively.

Both Facebook and Twitter were used by many young people for street-level communications during the protests. On June 16 the U.S. State Department asked Twitter to delay a network upgrade that would have shut down service for a brief period during daylight hours in Tehran. Over 90 percent of Twitter users in Iran live in Tehran, and 25 percent of the current Iranian user base created accounts during the last three months of political campaigning. State Department spokesman Ian Kelly rejected the accusation that by meddling with the development of Iran's information infrastructure, the Obama administration was taking sides in Iran's disputed elections. "This is about giving their voices a chance to be heard. One of the ways that their voices are heard are through new media," he told reporters.

Twitter was used to help street protesters find safe hospitals, where injuries could be treated without drawing the attention of Basij militias. As these militias moved through neighborhoods and gunshots were heard, alerts went out. When intelligence agents raided an apartment or took a family member, the incident was shared with family and friends. Protest leaders also used Twitter to recruit more international cyberactivsts.

Barely a week after the protest marches had begun, Google fast-tracked the development of a Farsi-language translator, and Facebook rushed out a beta translation of its content into Farsi. Both companies were hoping to serve the Persian—and global—online audience eager to communicate about events in Iran.

On June 20, Neda Agha-Soltan was shot dead at a demonstration, and her death was caught on several mobile phone cameras. Just as in-country protests were cooling, the videos of her blood pooling on the street were uploaded to YouTube. Her death, digitally captured and distributed over the internet. became one of the iconic global images of the protest, turning her into a martyr who inspired (rekindled) protests 40 days later.

Twitter user persiankiwi had 24,000 followers by day 6 of the protests. Mousavi11388 was engaging 7,000 followers. #StopAhmadi kept more than

6,000 followers alert to photos streaming up to Flickr. The Twitter service itself was registering 30 new posts a minute with the #IranElection identifier. Specialty Persian news channels in Los Angeles received hundreds of digital videos daily, and YouTube became the repository for the digitally captured, lived experiences of the chaotic streets of Tehran. #CNNfail let the global audience for political clashes in Iran gripe about CNN's paltry coverage. Between June 7 and 26, an estimated 480,000 Twitter users exchanged over 2 million tweets, with Twitter streams peaking on election day at over 200,000 per hour.

Digital media sustained protests well beyond what pundits expected. Indeed, this new information infrastructure gave social movement leaders the capacity not only to reach out to sympathetic audiences overseas but also to reach two important domestic constituencies: rural, conservative voters who had few connections to the urban chaos; and the clerical establishment. The unprecedented activation of weak social ties brought the concerns of disaffected youth, cheated voters, and beaten protesters to the attention of the mullahs. The result was a split within the ruling establishment on how to deal with the insurgency, how to proceed with counting ballots, and how to credibly authorize Ahmadinejad to take power.

CENSORING

In some ways the regime's response was decidedly old media: expelling foreign correspondents, blocking phone lines, preventing the publication of daily newspapers, and accusing enemy governments of spreading misinformation. They did not count on the large number of Iranians eager to submit their own content to international news agencies, and, perhaps more important, they did not realize that large numbers of Iranians would use social media to share their own personal stories of beatings, tear gas inhalation, and protest euphoria with each other.

Almost as quickly as protesters took to Twitter and Facebook, the government's security apparatus began using these applications to spread disinformation. It is estimated that more than 5 million websites are inaccessible from within Iran. Websites run by the Basij collected digital video and photos of protesters and asked Iranians online to help identify particular protesters. And to the surprise of many technorati, it became apparent that the Iranian government had built a single choke point for traffic to the rest of the internet and a deep packet inspection system that would slow traffic to allow for content analysis. Most countries have such monitoring centers, but their use is governed by some public policy oversight designed to identify the lawful circumstances for intercepting traffic. Once built, however, the owners of such equipment get to decide what those circumstances are and set the keywords that will alert authorities about who is communicating what over the nation's digital infrastructure.

EVALUATING

Overall, it is not clear that the international cyberactivists had more than a symbolic effect on the infrastructure of the Iranian government. It may be in the interests of the ruling mullahs to have opposition venting online, rather than through some other form of political resistance. Many of the tools for attacking government servers, such as BWRaep, also effected the bandwidth available to other users in Iran.

Millions of people took to the streets in the week after the election results were announced and certainly not all were using Twitter. The majority of them, however, were responding to both strong and weak network ties and to the digital technologies designed to maintain those ties. Even with the blackout on domestic broadcast media and censorship of digital traffic, the social movement leaders were able to circumvent the state's choke hold on information flows. Traditional radio and televised appeals did not figure in the mobilization, and they are not very important to understanding what happened in Iran last summer.

With few reporters on the ground, the "technology revolution" was an easy peg for coverage by Western news agencies. Twitter was an important communications tool during the heated days of protest, but an unknown number of the new accounts created in those days belonged to external supporters who identified themselves as being in Tehran; there were also local users who self-identified as being elsewhere in hopes of evading regime censors. Moreover, these tweets reflected the chaos and uncertainty of the time: Iran's supreme mullah Ayatollah Khamenei did not shave his head and attempt to flee in a blue suit. While it is likely that government interference caused disruptions in network communications services, some services would have been crippled by unusually high demand.

Yet, the Iranian government continues to take the threat of digital revolution seriously. On election day, Mousavi had 10,000 fans. A month later he had 10 times that, and a genuinely global campaign. In July the Iranian Parliament began debate on a measure to add websites and blogs promoting "corruption, prostitution and apostasy" to the list of crimes punishable by death. Security officials have detained the webmasters of reformist websites and shut down servers. Several high-profile bloggers remain in prison.

EVOLVING

In the Middle East, elections—even rigged ones—have increasingly become moments of political crisis. Several countries in the region hold legitimate, competitive elections. A few simply ban political parties altogether. Some have elections with open competition at lower levels of office, while the outcome of elections for the executive branch of government are never really in doubt. And even countries allowing party competition can be divided between those in which licensed political parties stand a reasonable chance at achieving electoral victory and those in which official recognition comes with no opportunity to take office. Many ruling elites have managed their country's development for decades. What has radically changed in just the last decade is the information infrastructure of political communication.

At key moments in a political crisis, it is possible for the state to disrupt the supply of newsprint and ink or shut down the broadcast towers of radio and television stations. It is much more challenging for governments to disable networked information infrastructures. Cutting the power to some internet service providers or mobile phone towers often means that information packets flow to other network nodes. Network traffic in and out of a country can sometimes be stopped by disabling the internet exchange points in port cities, but doing so can have broader consequences for the national economy, constraining the capacity of the state organization itself. Regimes that deliberately create choke points in their packet-switching infrastructure are better able to censor, but such points are themselves a security risk for the regime. Technology design can actually involve political strategy and be part of a nation's "constitutional moment." In Iran's case, the ruling elites tried to constitute an information infrastructure that could be closely managed in times of crisis.

NETWORKED EFFERVESCENCE

Street protests are the result of and conduit for collective effervescence, a rare spirit of energy that grips people hungry for change. In contemporary systems of political communication, citizens turn to the internet as a source of news and information in times of political crisis. It is not only that online social networking services are influential as a communications media; rather, they are now also a fundamental infrastructure for social movements. And the internet globalizes local struggles. Authoritarian regimes always conduct propaganda battles over broadcast media. But what is the regime countermeasure for the chilling effects of a plea from someone in your social network who has been a victim of police brutality?

Cyberactivism is no longer the unique provenance of isolated, politically motivated hackers. It is instead deeply integrated with contemporary social movement strategy and accessible to computer and mobile phone users with only basic skills: it is a distinguishing feature of modern political communication and a means of creating the élan that marks social change. Twitter may have been the branded information tool of choice for some of Iran's opposition opinion leaders, and other tools will emerge in the years ahead. The service routes messages from many sources to many users through varied outlets from webpages, mobile phones, and many other kinds of consumer electronics. But it is the networked design that is a distinguishing feature of social media that will be ever more threatening to authoritarian rule.

Information and communication technologies are the infrastructure for transposing democratic ideals from community to community. They support the process of learning new approaches to political representation, of testing new organizational strategies, and of cognitively extending the possibilities and prospects for political transformation from one context to another. It does not matter that the number of bloggers, twitterers, or internet users may seem small, because in a networked social moment only a few "brokers" need to be using these tools to keep everyone up to date. These are the communication tools for the wealthy, urban, educated elites whose loyalties or defection will make or break authoritarian rule. Indeed, it is probably more useful to evaluate applications such as Twitter through the communities they support, rather than through tool features. Twitter communities have leaders and followers, and tweets supply them with information, misinformation, and disinformation. During the protests, the top 10 percent of users generated over 65 percent of the tweets.

Limited by 140-character bursts of content, Twitter would not be the tool for sharing nuanced political critiques. But it would be a mistake to tie any theory of social change to a particular piece of software. In the summer of 2009 the Iranian insurgency was very much shaped by several digital communication tools, which allowed social movements within the country to organize protests and exchange information and made it possible for those groups to maintain contact with the rest of the world. Most important, the internet gave the social movement access to the clerical establishment through weak ties of social networks that connected mullahs to Iranians on the street. Social movement scholars write that elite defection usually marks the end of an authoritarian regime. And in addition, in the West, democracy advocates with an internet connection can support an international social movement by contributing bandwidth and computing resources just by running a piece of software.

If Iranians have grown accustomed to clerical interference in elections, why did they take to the streets in such force? If new information technologies such as mobile phones and the internet provided the communications infrastructure for mobilization, was the lack of democratic transition a technological or social failing?

In the language of fuzzy sets ways, Iran's postelection insurgency was *almost* an example of a digital revolution. In is unlikely that protests would have lasted as long, raised so much international support, and had such an impact on domestic politics had it not been for mobile phones and the internet. The internet did not cause the insurgency, and it is probably a truism to say that no contemporary democratic revolution in the Middle East will happen without the internet. In times of political crisis, banal tools for wasting time, like Twitter and YouTube, become the supporting infrastructure of social movements. As one ethnic Azeri blogger told me, the regime has learned that the internet makes collective action possible.

Technology alone does not cause political change—it did not in Iran's case. But it does provide new capacities and impose new constraints on political actors. New information technologies do not topple dictators; they are used to catch dictators off-guard. Today, being an effective social movement means utilizing social media. However, the world has seen interest in change expressed from within Iran, and this may prove to be the most destabilizing outcome of the protests. The regime's brutalities streamed around the globe. The world saw the dissent; the regime knows the world saw the dissent.

In the summer of 2009 we learned that Islamic democracies will be born digital. The initial conditions for social movement organizing are very different from those of the pre-internet era. Iran's street protests failed to topple their government. But just as important, the world's most technologically advanced censors failed to manage the government's election crisis. And the region's dictators have a new concern: their own tech-savvy, disaffected youth.

Introduction: Political Communication and Contemporary Muslim Media Systems

Is democracy advanced through the diffusion of new information technologies? Among the diverse countries with large Muslim communities, how do such technologies provide capacities and constraints on institutional change? In this book, I demonstrate that over the last fifteen years, technology diffusion has had an important causal role in democratization. New information and communication technologies, such as mobile phones and the internet, have provided new infrastructural conditions, with distinct outcomes for systems of political communication and broad consequences for the institutions of democracy.

I accept two foundational assumptions proposed by many Islamists: that Islam is not inherently incompatible with democracy; and that information and communication technologies (ICTs) have, in the past, played a significant role in the institutional evolution of political cultures in the Islamic world (see Allawi 2009; Nasr 2005; Abou El Fadl, Cohen, and Chasman 2004 for an introduction to these propositions). I argue that the introduction of digital ICTs provides an occasion for significant change in how political culture is produced and consumed around the world. My goal for this book is to present and assess the evidence about the introduction of digital ICTs and changes in the production and consumption of political culture in developing countries with significant Muslim communities.

The internet has had a notable impact on relations between peoples and nations. In particular, ICTs allow people to learn about each other, and often also about themselves. In the West, major news media often peg stories about ICTs on one of two hooks. The "technologies of freedom" peg appears in news stories that celebrate the use of information technologies such as mobile phones in allowing democratic activists to organize effective public rallies. For example, when protesters in Indonesia out-maneuvered Suharto's police and ended his autocratic rule, news stories were quick to highlight the fact that email and mobile phones had significantly improved the organizational capacity of that country's democratic leaders. The "technologies of oppression" peg appears in news stories that examine the ways that authoritarian regimes use the very same ICTs to oppress their populations. For example, news stories highlight the ways that Iraqi insurgents coordinate military campaigns, spread political messages we dislike, and publicize beheadings. When such news stories are specifically about how the internet improves the organizational capacity of terrorists, such groups are called "e-jihadis," "cyber-terrorists," and "dot-extremists."

Despite what the news coverage might suggest, cyber-terrorism is not the primary online activity in the Muslim communities of the developing world. Most people use the internet to watch movies and sports events, to play video games, to keep in touch with family and friends, to chat and flirt, and to shop. These other domains of social activity can become small political acts and specific expressions of political culture, especially under state-run censorship. Unlike in the advanced democracies, political engagement online in many of these countries is not about voting online, reviewing legislative proposals, and discussing public policy options. It is about discussing the personal politics of sexuality and relationships. It is about getting news and information, sometimes about the West, but more often about neighboring Islamic countries. In large part, these other realms of social activity online are *made* political because of the active censorship in the more authoritarian Islamic regimes. Thus, the topic of "Muslim politics online" is not simply about news consumption or political discussion over the internet—the areas of concern to many mainstream political communication researchers—but about the multiple spheres of social life that are interesting for their cultural politics. Thus, in this book I will often use the term "political culture" to refer not just to the most obvious political content, news, and information, but more broadly to the range of social activities that take on political importance in societies where ruling elites work hard to manage cultural interaction. Cyber-terrorism is not even the most important of the obviously political aspects of internet use in these communities and countries. In this book, I argue that a much more significant, but much less understood phenomena is the development of relatively mainstream, civic discourse over Muslim media systems.

Research on the impact of new information technologies in the developing world is becoming ever more sophisticated, though it is encumbered in three ways: a focus on metrics, indicators, and digital artifacts over theories and explanations; more exuberance about potential social transformation rather than understanding observed changes; and the urge to periodize digital-divide scholarship. This first stage of research often involves trying to map trends in culturally disaggregated ways. Developing indicators can be a sensible first step in social science research: deciding who or what to measure, and how, will have a long-term impact on the data that later scholars have to work with. Yet debates over the methods of measurement, on their own, rarely generate new theories about the causes and consequences of the digital divide. During the research for this book, it was fascinating to see how many scholars rely on a few data sources, chiefly the International Telecommunications Union, the World Bank, and the World Resources Institute. Indeed, these organizations often just duplicate each other's poor quality data. Many researchers rely heavily on this data for their comparative or single-country case studies, rather than collecting original observations or combining data in interesting ways. The same data tables appear over and over again. This dependency has shaped our understanding of the digital divide, by tightly binding the concept of the digital divide to levels of internet and mobile phone use per capita. As argued in this book, there are much better ways of measuring and conceptualizing the digital divide, the conditions of information infrastructure, and outcomes in political institutions or processes. Wherever possible, the tables in this book assemble data from original scholarly sources that are categorical and comparable, rather than only reproducing abstracted indicators. There is another scholarly approach that involves critically reading Islamic digital artifacts, such as websites, videos and emails, for meaning. But it can also be useful to assess the impact of meaning, evaluate how meaning is used in the service of power, and generalize beyond the critic's interpretation to the experience of internet users in multiple Muslim communities.

Second, much of the early academic work has been concerned with stating the potential path from technology diffusion to social transformation. Authors define an archetype of e-government, e-democracy, or e-commerce, and review the potential opportunities or challenges to authoritarian rule and economic wealth. Invariably, authors find more potential challenges than opportunities, because the archetype itself is based on standards and expectations defined by the advanced democracies and economies in the West.

Third, even though the research into ICT diffusion in the developing world is a relatively new field, some scholars have been overeager to periodize the literature. The most common way of doing this is to organize the literature on the digital divide into early, middle, and late periods, across which assumptions have changed. At first, researchers thought the digital divide was about inequality in the distribution of hardware and software; then, researchers thought it was about inequality in the distribution skill sets; and later, researchers thought the digital divide was about the distribution of hardware, software, skills, and the strength of key cultural institutions needed for ICT diffusion. In fact, looking over a wide swath of literature for this book, it is hard to find anyone who ever really thought that the digital divide was just about hardware and software distribution. Quite the contrary, all researchers go to great pains to say that their theoretical contribution goes beyond the digital-divide-is-about-hardware-access rubric. Scholarly literature should only be periodized once in a while because doing so rarely advances our understanding in original ways; it can be a tedious task for the author, and it can result in a tedious text for the reader.

Scholarly endeavors aside, the internet has certainly had a role in shaping Western perceptions of Islam. Based on news coverage alone, readers in the West might think the internet is mostly for helping Islamic terrorists organize, the object of strategic interest in conflict between Muslim groups, and a useful means of censorship by Muslim governments. Propaganda from Islamic fundamentalists has gone online, and the internet is used to circulate videos of beheadings by violent extremists. For example, in 2004, the savage beheading of Nick Berg was recorded and distributed online, providing international news coverage for the terrorists' activities. Digital communications infrastructure is a key asset that parties involved in conflict will fight over. Lebanon's Hezbollah has developed a private network of fiber-optic cables, which it considers a crucial part of its security infrastructure, and attempts by the Lebanese prime minister to disassemble the communications grid caused the worst gunfights in Beirut since the end of that country's civil war. News stories also highlight government censorship in Muslim countries. In December 2007, police in Tehran warned 170 cybercafés that they ran the risk of being closed down. Subsequently the police closed 24 cafés and arrested 23 people for "immoral behavior." Eleven arrested were women, with two charged with publishing false information, disturbing public opinion, and publicity against the Islamic Republic. In May 2009, the Iranian government banned local access to Facebook, presumably because of the fear that opposition leaders were using the social networking site to organize voter turnout in elections. Yet the internet in Islamic countries is more than just a conduit for fundamentalist propaganda, an infrastructure that warring Islamic factions fight over, or a tool for state censorship.

Melvin Kranzberg wrote that "technology is neither good nor bad, nor is it neutral" (1985, 50). Both democratic activists and authoritarian dictators use digital technologies for both good and evil. At the same time, we know such technologies are designed with specific applications in mind and have an impact on the structure and content of political communication. Thus, there must be a way of assessing the overall impact of new technologies across many countries—digital technologies are not neutral. Elsewhere I have argued for a moderate analytical frame, between the technological determinist perspective (purporting that communications tools cause social changes) and the organizational determinist perspective (purporting that society causes technological changes) (Howard 2006). I believe it is more useful to take a position of "soft determinism" in which technology designers and policy makers make decisions that provide capacities for and impose constraints on users. And every once in a while, social groups have the opportunity for collective action that allows for a reshaping or undoing of these design capacities and constraints. The argument that technologies are simply good or bad is rarely convincing, but it would be a mistake to argue that across the diverse Islamic cultures of the developing world, technologies are neutral.

Figures 0.1 and 0.2 chart the rising levels of media use among Muslim households in the countries included in this study. The mass media that dominated systems of political communication in Muslim communities were often controlled by the state or cultural elites. These broadcast media were most often used for approved content that small groups of people produced for the large groups of people who consumed culture. The new digital media, including the mobile phones and the internet, are used both for cultural consumption and personal communication, are not as easily managed by states and cultural elites, and are tools that provide people with the opportunity to produce and consume cultural content. I argue that these systems of political communication are different enough that it is crucial to study the Muslim experience with information technology and democratization in a focused way, and that the comparative method is the best approach to understanding the diverse and shared experiences across Muslim communities. Additionally, I argue that the political internet is an important object of inquiry, and many

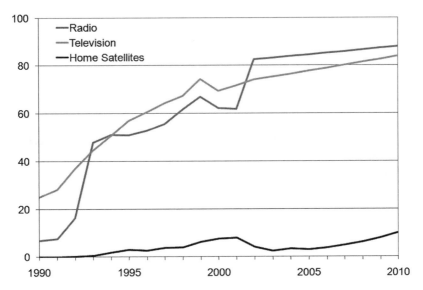

Figure 0.1 Mass Media for Communication and Culture, 1990–2010

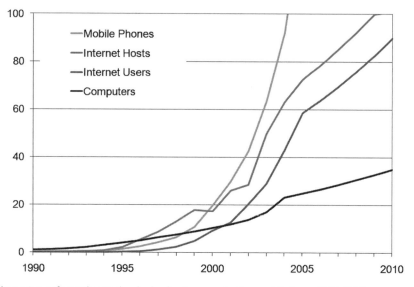

Figure 0.2 Information Technologies for Communication and Culture, 1990–2010

Sources: Based on author's calculations from multiple sources: percentage of population Muslim (CIA 2010); number of households, internet users, mobile phones, households equipped with televisions, households equipped with radios (ITU 2006); internet hosts (Internet Software Consortium 2010).

Notes: Mobile phones, computers, internet users, and home satellites are calculated per 100 Muslim households around the world. Both radio and television are calculated as the percentage of Muslim households equipped with a radio or television. Internet hosts are calculated per 10,000 Muslim households.

of the existing approaches to such inquiry have been biased by the tendency to be more interested in Islamic fundamentalism than civil society.

The number of countries with complete data varies from indicator to indicator. Averages are always computed from the countries with available data, and since 2000 the majority of countries analyzed in this study report this data.[1] The number of Muslim households in each country was computed by taking the estimated percentage of the national population practicing Islam and the estimate of the number of households in each country. In particular countries, Muslim households may be larger or smaller than the national average, but the assumption for this figure is that the national proportion of Muslim populations is similar to that of Muslim households. The household is a sensible unit of analysis for this data because many of these media are resources shared among kin. In wealthy economies it makes sense to collect information on "personal computers" because many people have access to at least one computer, often for personal use, and these computers are replaced every few years. But in many developing countries, mobile phones and computers are shared resources, available for use by several family members and not discarded or replaced as quickly.

To distinguish those technologies that allow for decentralized cultural production, Figure 0.1 includes mass media technologies such as, home satellite systems, radio, and television. Figure 0.2 includes several measures of ICT diffusion, including mobile phones, computers, internet hosts, and internet users. Radio and television diffusion is measured as the percent of households with at least one of these media. Personal computers, home satellite feeds, mobile phones, and internet users are measured as the number of these items per 100 households.

Overall, these graphs reveal how rapidly new media technologies have diffused in comparison with more traditional media. Even though the units of each trend are different, measures for mobile phones, internet users, and hosts per Muslim household over the last 10 years have very steep slopes. Measures for the proportion of Muslim households equipped with a radio or television are high, though the slope for these trend lines is not as steep over the full 15-year period for which there is data. There is a radio or television in 80 percent of households; at least one person in 60 percent of Muslim households has used the internet, though this person is not always a regular user. There is at least one mobile phone in almost every household.

This graph also reveals that the television and radio are important means of cultural consumption for most households around the developing world. While satellites are prevalent in every urban skyline, the diffusion rate of home satellites has been low and stable for several years. Like computers, these resources are sometimes collective resources, tapped to serve multiple households. Thus it is likely that the proportion of households with unregistered satellite access is higher than reported here.

Yet these graphs also suggest that new media—technologies that allow users significant control in cultural production—have steep diffusion curves and increasingly rival the reach of television and radio media. In 2000 there were approximately 20 mobile phones per 100 households, and today there are 144 mobile phones per 100 households. Although this data cannot be strictly interpreted to mean that 20 percent of households in the year 2000 had a mobile phone, it is safe to say that today, there is a mobile phone user in almost every household, and that many Muslim households have several mobile phone users.

It is interesting that computers and internet users had a similar diffusion curve until about 2001, at which point the number of internet users per 100 Muslim households began to outstrip the number of computers per 100 Muslim households. How can there be more internet users than computer users per household? There are likely two explanations for this trend. First, as mentioned above, computers are more often than not a collective resource, so a national estimate of user population must include people who have access through a friend or family member's computer. Second, internet access points such as cybercafés and libraries are an important means of connectivity in Muslim countries, so this number must also include the number of people who use the internet outside the household.

WHY STUDY THE MUSLIM EXPERIENCE WITH INFORMATION TECHNOLOGY AND DEMOCRATIZATION?

There are 75 countries with significant Muslim communities: 48 countries where Muslims are in the majority and at least 50 percent of the population is Muslim; 27 countries where Muslims are an important minority and at least 10 percent of the population is Muslim. Despite the obvious diversity of these countries, three attributes make all 75 countries a useful comparison set: most of these countries have been slow to democratize, compared to the rest of the developing world; most of these countries have more rapid rates of technology diffusion than the rest of the world; social elites in most of these countries use technologies to censor political culture and manage information flows in ways not often found in the rest of the developing world. For readers only interested in the hypothesis that technology diffusion can cause democratic outcomes, these 75 countries represent a good conservative sampling of cases to study.

The goal of this book is to analyze the ways in which new information technologies have contributed to democratic entrenchment or transition in countries with large Muslim communities. Consequently, the comparative method recommends coverage of countries where technology diffusion may have made some countries more authoritarian, along with countries where technology diffusion has been rapid but without clear democratic outcomes. By analyzing the range of experiences across the countries with significant Muslim communities, some of the necessary or sufficient conditions for contemporary democratization can come to light. Since there is a dearth of comparative data on the diversity of political life in many of these countries, the tables and graphs are oriented around relevant subgroups of countries: those that have experienced democratic transitions, those that have experienced democratic entrenchment, those that have remained authoritarian, and those in a liminal state of crisis, war, or collapse. Moreover, there are several good reasons for treating these particular countries as a valuable analytical set.

First, there are several modular political phenomena across nations with significant Muslim populations: political action based in significant part on the emulation of successful examples from others. Such imitation occurs through policy emulation and coordination among many Muslim countries, especially concerning telecommunications standards, technology-led economic development, and internet censorship. For several decades, the interior ministers of Arab countries have held an annual conference to discuss successful ways of securing their regimes, and in recent years their agenda has extended to the best ways of handling media and internet censorship. But such imitation also occurs among communities of social elites and the leadership of democratization movements. As will be demonstrated in the chapters ahead, ruling elites learn about and imitate the successful strategies of their autocratic neighbors. At the same time, successful democratization strategies in particular countries are transported into the collective action strategies of movements in other countries. Through regionalized processes of elite learning and defection, Muslim countries seem to democratize in similar ways, not necessarily following the recipes for democratization that have been followed in other regions and other time periods. Across many Muslim countries, democratization movements appear to be learning to use information technologies from each other, linking up to share experiences, and transporting successful organizational strategies. Yet modular political phenomena are not just found among social movements: state bureaucracies learn censorship strategies from each other; political parties in Muslim countries learn how to use ICTs from affinity parties in other countries; and journalists learn new online research and publishing strategies from each other.

Second, many Muslim countries have shared technology diffusion patterns and similar systems of political communication, which are together distinct from those in other developing countries. Holding economic wealth constant, Muslim countries have among the highest rates of technology adoption in the developing world. Moreover, many Muslim governments have responded to the new information technologies in consistent ways: censorship strategies have been developed with similar objectives of cultural control; internet service providers are held legally responsible for the content that flows over their networks; government agencies work aggressively to support (Islamic) cultural content online. This combination of policy responses is unique to the countries that are home to large Muslim communities.

Since the diversity of experience in Islamic countries is as striking as the similarities, we are faced with the problem of creating appropriate categories to distinguish types of Muslim countries. What are sensible categories for types of Islamic countries? Obviously, every country has some distinct attributes, but rather than always presenting data on all countries in which a significant portion of the population is Muslim, is there a more parsimonious way of comparing and contrasting attributes and trends? Individual countries can be treated as case studies, but it is useful to look for patterns and trends that exceed a single country's experience with a multitude of digital technologies and the many attributes of democratization.

To illustrate this diversity, there are categories in which Muslim countries could be organized into geopolitical regions and institutional groupings. In Central Asia, there are several post-communist regimes governing large, linguistically diverse Muslim populations, where religious expression has simply been illegal for 80 years and dictators maintain strong control over the development of political institutions and natural gas wealth. In contrast, much of Muslim North Africa speaks Arabic as a primary or secondary language. While this region is also home to countries with ruling elites, some of these countries can be described as emerging democracies, with higher levels of income and diasporia communities across southern Europe. The Gulf States include several strong constitutional monarchies, regimes bolstered by significant oil revenues, and countries where the primary concerns of political security include a resolution of the Palestinian-Israeli conflict and the suppression of local democratic initiatives. Several of these regimes also see themselves as guardians of holy sites and texts for particular variations of Islam. Iran is an Islamic republic, without an Arabic culture, which sees itself as a political instantiation of a particular variation of Islamic governance. It too has oil resources, but it also has a rapidly growing population a history of rebellious cohorts of youth bent on regime change.

On the Indian subcontinent, Pakistan, India, and Bangladesh are home to very large and very poor Muslim populations. In recent years, democratic practices in Pakistan have appeared fleeting, practices in Bangladesh have stabilized, and practices in India have deepened. Still, these regimes govern populations with significant income inequalities. These states must also manage a unique set of security issues: environmental degradation regularly becomes a threat to population health and stability; the resolution of the Kashmiri conflict is of primary importance to India and Pakistan (two nuclear states); and military elites are active participants in the political life in Bangladesh and Pakistan. Southeast Asia is also home to linguistically diverse Muslim cultures, wealthy and multiracial Malaysia and Singapore, and the populous but poor emerging democracy of Indonesia. In Russia, Islam is the largest minority religion, and politically dispossessed Muslim communities have been able to put religion on the national agenda through violent insurgencies in several regions.

In terms of economic wealth and geopolitical alliances, it would also be possible to divide the Muslim world into Arabic- and non–Arabic-speaking populations, oil-producing and non–oil-producing countries, Arab League and non–Arab League countries, secular and Islamist regimes, or by the Sunni, Shia, or Wahhabist perspectives of ruling elites. In southeastern Europe, Turkey, and the Caucasus, politicians increasingly look to the West for political support and economic opportunities. And every country in the West has communities of all the aforementioned nationals, communities with their own interesting diasporic politics, and different levels of engagement with political life in their adopted countries. Since this study is particularly interested in technology diffusion, the primary task of the introduction is to develop a new, more meaningful way of categorizing patterns of technology diffusion.

Given the diversity of political structures and institutions and the levels of conflict and disagreement between some Muslim countries, there is not much evidence that the "Muslim world" is a meaningful political category. It is a term of generalization, about as useful as the "Christian world" or "the West." In important ways, Western countries are more homogenous than Muslim countries. Almost all are democracies; almost all have the same high standards of living; English is the language of business; the majority of citizens trace their ancestry to other Western countries; and the majority of citizens travel only to other Western countries. It is not a stretch to argue, as some have, that major urban centers in the West—such as London, New York, and Toronto—have more in common with each other than they do with geographically contiguous secondary cities and rural communities. Yet many would also argue that there is enormous variety in the economic, political, and cultural attributes of these countries; those of us who live in the West know something of this diversity. Similarly, I argue that there is enormous diversity in the economic, political, and cultural institutions of Muslim countries; it is crucial that we try to know something of this diversity.

To describe these countries as homologous—shared economic, historical, cultural, and technology diffusion patterns—is not to say that these countries are culturally homogenous. The 75 cases studied here are a set of homologous countries with similar levels of economic development, some shared history, some shared cultural norms, and a shared media ecology. Moreover, these countries share patterns of ICT diffusion, and there are similar patterns of public use and policy response. Many of the countries in this study share a history shaped by the spread of Islam, but that does not make them all the same; as I argue in the chapters ahead, these important cultural differences help explain differences in the diffusion of technical innovations.

However, to use this category critically, it must be deconstructed through the illustration of common trends, examples that illustrate differentiated experience, and subcategories that have meaningful integrity. For example, the comparison of trends in Muslim countries with trends in other developing countries and highly developed countries reinforces this category by defining it relative to other aggregated groups. Similarly, the comparison of trends between types of Muslim countries deconstructs this category by illustrating the diversity of experience within the Muslim world. In practical terms, this critical deconstruction occurs through the presentation of meaningful sub-categories in tabular data, and by privileging evidence and examples from Muslim communities. There is a vast and growing literature on the impact of ICTs in the developing world, but I favor theoretical insights that have been gleaned from lived experience in developing Muslim communities.

In this analysis I will often refer to the Muslim experience and will often deconstruct trends to illustrate the diversity of experience in types of Islamic polities. I conceive the Muslim experience in the developing world as an analytical category that has many meaningful and coherent subcategories. Sometimes this means describing trends across all the countries sampled, or discussing cultural and historical differences. My approach highlights and explains continuities and uniformities, and pays special attention to change and variety. The case evidence in the chapters ahead is organized around four kinds of institutional change: a group of countries that experienced a democratic transition; a group of countries that experienced democratic entrenchment; a group of countries that experienced very little institutional change and remained somewhat or largely authoritarian; a group of crisis states where the circumstances of political, military, or security crisis make them unlikely to reveal much about the recipes for democratization.

Yet accepting a sample frame always means making some strategic exceptions. There are several important countries, such as China, Thailand, and the Philippines, in which a small minority of practicing Muslims have put cultural and religious issues on the national political agenda through political activism, violent insurgency, and the effective use of information technologies. China is not in the set of countries analyzed here. Even though its Uyghurs have a violent separatist movement, this Muslim community is relatively small in size. These cases may share some of the features of other cases in the study, but they are excluded from comparative analysis because of the relatively small size of their Muslim communities.

Along with some special exceptions, some special inclusions need to be made. Russia is in the set of countries analyzed here. Between 15 and 20 percent of Russia's population is Muslim, with Chechnyan insurgents an important part of the country's domestic political problems. Russian political life is strained by interfaith, security, and state-mosque tensions. Several countries are included in the set at different points for different reasons: Djibouti, the Maldives, Suriname, and Western Sahara have just under 500,000 residents but relatively large Muslim communities; Georgia has a politically significant Muslim population, measured at 9.9 percent of the total population. Western Sahara and the West Bank are not often considered states but are often treated as political units in the large social science data sets about technology diffusion. ICTs have an increasingly important role in politics in these countries, and the status of these political units is extremely important in the community of Muslim nations, so these are included as political units.

This study of the Muslim countries of North Africa, the Middle East, Central, South, and East Asia is important for several reasons. Many are middle income countries, occupying a level of development between the poorest countries of Africa and Asia and the wealthiest in North America and Europe. They represent a kind of developmental mid-point. Understanding technology diffusion and politics in these countries may help us understand how poor countries will develop. Yet at the same time, this is a unique cohort of countries. The existing research on democratic transitions in countries with significant Muslim populations suffers from two seemingly contradictory conditions: much of the existing literature either ignores the political diversity among these countries or is too narrowly comparative to make helpful generalizations. Large-scale, quantitative, and cross-sectional studies must often collapse fundamentally different political systems—autocracies, democracies, emerging democracies, and crisis states—into a few categories or narrow indices. Such studies must also diminish the role of cultural diversity among the populations who practice Islam. Area studies that focus on one or two countries get at the rich history of technology diffusion and political development, but rarely offer conclusions that can be useful in understanding some of the seemingly intractable political and security crises in other parts of the world. Finally, Muslim countries have some of the fastest technology adoption rates in the world, high levels of literacy, computer-savvy populations, and informational sophistication. Many governments are carefully balancing state and individual security concerns, and the balance of security in these countries has implications for stability in neighboring countries and the developed world. Indeed, the information policies of Muslim governments have significant implications for information access not only for their own citizens but for the rest of the world.

There are, of course, some peculiar things about technology diffusion in these countries. The countries with the highest levels of internet use, such as Qatar and the United Arab Emirates, are regularly labeled "not free" by international observers. In some Central Asian countries, governments that have received foreign aid have been forced to develop more open information access policies, while governments with significant income from natural resources have been able to retain tight regulatory control over ICTs. Moreover, many Muslim countries are now at a crucial transition point. Economically they are doing well, but since economic wealth is increasingly dependent on information infrastructure, will the economic benefits accruing through open ICT access for citizens outweigh the risks of cultural exposure?

WHY A SET-THEORETIC, COMPARATIVE METHOD?

Islamic scholars and country specialists may feel that treating countries with significant Muslim populations as an analytical set oversimplifies the diversity in political life and technology use. However, the goal of a comparative method is to carefully simplify events and patterns so that we can see the shared attributes of many countries, rather than be overwhelmed by the contingencies and details of each case or damage the way that particular community experiences are represented. The current research on new media ICT and international development tends to be single-country case studies, studies of particular technologies, or cross-case comparisons of several countries selected for their similarities in culture, geography, and stage of economic development (many of these studies are identified in Appendix B). Currently, scholars are posing several questions about the role of ICT in international development, questions that require comparative analysis to answer meaningfully.

Yet efforts to explain democratization are often least convincing when they are reliant on traditional statistical modeling techniques and large aggregated datasets which explain variation in a sample but do not reveal causal recipes. For example, we know that a democratic transition in one Muslim country may have derived from a similar, earlier change in a neighboring country. Social movement leaders consciously emulate prior examples in neighboring countries, and political leaders deliberately formulate responses based in some part on the recent experiences of regional leaders. Destabilization in one country may have a spillover effect on a neighboring country; policy leaders across countries often form international coalitions based on prior experience together and cultural affinities. In the digital arena local events on the other side of the planet are often monitored daily, such that even though not all political phenomena are modular, it may not be useful to strive for a statistical model in which economic wealth, demography, or cultural factors functionally explain contemporary democratic transitions (Beissinger 2007). To get the causal recipes, the approach taken here is cross-national and comparative.

This research is cross-national in four respects. First, I will often treat a country as an *object* of study. The nation-state is the primary unit of analysis for much of the narrative in this manuscript, but also for the organization of tabular data. This will be particularly apparent in Chapter 2, in which I discuss e-governance in states where a majority of the population is Islamic. While it would be useful to have data that were more grounded in social categories for which people find affinity, the nation-state is often the best aggregate for people within a territorial space. Second, I treat the country as the *context* of study. Many of the social movements I discuss are organized and embedded within particular political environments. Third, I develop theory about technology diffusion and democratization by building on existing studies of single countries, or studies that compare a few cases in detail. This allows me to generalize from many of the small set comparisons in a qualitative, comparative manner. Finally, this research is *transnational* in character, in that the linkages between states and substate actors are of key interest, especially in that such linkages provide a source of identity for Muslims within particular countries (Kohn 1987).

There have been a significant number of single-country case studies in which ICTs have been part of the contemporary narrative of both democracy and dictatorship. The comparative perspective taken here will not be limited to the standard cases, or even to the situations that stand out as incidents of technology driven, enhanced, or enabled regime change. Instead the comparative perspective taken here will embrace situations in which information technologies most assuredly had no role in democratic transitions, situations in which information technologies were successfully used by authoritarian elites to become better better bullies, and situations in which information technologies played a role in modest improvements in regime transparency, but not sudden democratic transitions. Thus, the comparative approach is anathema to those who would generalize from singular studies in which information technologies had a central role in a grand democratization project, and those who would generalize by only relying on statistical models of international data on government effectiveness in terms of internet penetration. Methodologically, the comparative approach is a powerful and productive one that confronts theory with data.

Sometimes this approach is called "set-theoretic," in that attention is given to the consistent connections across a set of cases, especially the causally relevant commonalities that are uniformly present in a given set of cases (Ragin 2009). The set of cases at hand is the population of countries with large Muslim communities, and there are 75 of these. There are many plausible paths to democratic transition and entrenchment, and the argument of this book is that in recent years, information technologies have opened up new paths to democratization in some Muslim countries. Indeed, the lack of technology diffusion may have closed off opportunities for democratization in other Muslim countries. Quantitative researchers often turn "democratization" into an indicator for which the Western democracies are the standard. In this set-theoretic approach, I assume that democratization among these countries is best calibrated according to a more grounded standard, set at the high end by countries such as Turkey and Indonesia and at the low end by Libya and Turkmenistan. This calibration does not preclude the theoretical possibility of an Islamic democratic ideal type. But it does assume that healthy, functional Muslim democracies may not look like Western democracies. If there is to be such a thing as a democratic Islam, I assume that it will have distinctive features, and that only some of the 75 countries with large Muslim populations will have all of these features. Many of the countries will have many of the features. Set-theoretic reasoning allows for fine gradations in the degree of membership in the set of Muslim democracies, and it requires evidence about each country's degree of membership in the set of countries that have experienced democratic transition or entrenchment.

Moreover, a set-theoretic explanation of the role of ICTs in contemporary democratization requires that we identify a consistent set of causal relations between technology diffusion and democratic outcomes. The explanation must provide a high proportion of cases with a given set of causes that also display democratic outcomes. To construct this explanation requires fuzzy set logic, which does not explain variation in a sample through reductive correlational statistics. Instead, fuzzy set logic produces general knowledge about the role of information technology in contemporary democratic transitions through the accumulated experience of particular countries where rapid technology diffusion among political actors such as the state, parties, journalists, and civic groups had an observed impact on the domestic balance of power, the opportunity structure for social mobilization, or the "cognitive liberation" of citizenry.

Fuzzy set logic offers general knowledge through the strategy of looking for shared causal conditions across multiple instances of the same outcome—sometimes called "selecting on the dependent variable." For large-N, quantitative, and variable oriented researchers, this strategy is unacceptable because neither the outcome nor the shared causal conditions vary across the cases. However, the strategy of selecting on the dependent variable is useful when researchers are interested in studying necessary conditions, and very useful when constructing a new theoretically defined population such as "Islamic democracy." Perhaps most important, this strategy is most useful when developing theory grounded in the observed, real-world experience of democratization in the Muslim communities of the developing world, rather than developing theory by privileging null, hypothetical, and unobserved cases.

WHY STUDY THE POLITICAL INTERNET?

New ICTs such as the internet have had a very important role in creating new patterns of political communication in advanced democracies (Chadwick and Howard 2009). Do they also have a role in the development of political discourse in the developing nations with significant Muslim communities? Al Gore, who worked hard to promote the development of a national information infrastructure, used the rhetoric of technological determinism to promote a global information infrastructure to the International Telecommunications Union in 1994: "To promote, to protect, and to preserve freedom and democracy, we must make telecommunications development an integral part of every nation's development" (Gore 1994). Looking back, to what degree have new information technologies undermined authoritarianism and promoted democracy? Has the internet had an important role in creating new patterns of political communication in Muslim countries?

In the Western news media, ICTs have been blamed as tools for Islamic fundamentalism. On the other hand, it is easy for regimes to censor news production, and the internet appears to be the best or only way for many citizens to access uncensored news. Online news sources allow Muslims to read about other Muslim communities. Satellite news services have done much to help create a pan-Islamic identity, but since such services require major capital investment, they are only built by governments and wealthy elites. Although internet use is affected by literacy, education, and costs, the ability of citizens to both produce and consume political culture online is a significant change in the pattern of political communication in many Muslim cultures—especially in the emerging democracies and authoritarian regimes.

Broadcast radio and television provide the staples of news and cultural content for citizens. Yet a growing amount of broadcast content is streamed online, reconnecting diasporic communities with political events, security issues, and daily life in home countries. The internet is the way that the West learns about life in Muslim countries, and the way that Muslims in many countries learn about each other and about the West.

Political leaders in Muslim countries face important challenges in both regulating and promoting internet use. The study of political issues around internet use reveals much about larger political issues in modernizing Muslim countries. And even though leaders in these countries are considering the political, economic, and cultural implications of the internet, it may be difficult to predict the full impact of the information revolution.

ORIENTALISM ONLINE

Edward Said's well known accusation is that Western scholars, policy makers, and journalists read the East in a way that actively reproduces tropes, including the homogeneity of Islamic identity and the burden of religious fundamentalism. Interestingly, both the journalistic and scholarly coverage of the role of technology in the development of political Islam has continued this trend.

In the English languages news media, stories about how the internet is used for terrorism outnumber the stories about how the internet is used for civic discourse (Kelley 2002; Rozen 2003). Special terms are fashioned to reveal the clash of modernity with anti-democratic intent: young Muslims with internet access are most likely to be "e-jihadis," organizing "online fatwas," and coordinating "cyber-terrorists." Indeed, scholars and pundits have also been focused on "terror online" (Weimann 2006; Dartnell 2006; Cragin et al. 2007; Giustozzi 2001) and "internet jihad," often missing the importance of the aggressive, systematic and successful campaigns to draw young Muslims into civil society (*Economist* 2007). The internet, I argue here, has a much more important and understudied role in the development of civil Islam. Yet a critical review of the incidence of such attacks, at least against the United States, reveals that few may even qualify as what is commonly understood as cyber-terrorism. If cyber-terror is a politically, religious, or ideologically motivated attack against a national information infrastructure that instills fear through destruction or disruption, then (fortunately) we have only fictional scenarios and sensationalist headlines that set up cyber-terrorism as a prognostic—not diagnostic—analytical frame (Cavelty 2007).[2]

Cyberterrorism is certainly worthy of study but must not be treated without equal attention paid to civic Islam online. At the very least, any sample of terrorist emails, websites, or other digital artifacts is made problematic by the active production of such content by Western security agencies attempting to sow dissent, as well as distrust among militant organizations (Schmitt and Shanker 2008). Moreover, Giustozzi's close study of the Taliban in Afghanistan revealed that many of the ICTs adopted were, in fact, quickly abandoned for lack of electrical power, computer training, and the risks of physical exposure (Giustozzi 2001). While there certainly are individuals using the internet to produce anti-Western rhetoric and to loosely support terrorist activities in the West, the actual connection between these individuals and armed resistance fighters in the Middle East is tenuous.

Along with the news trope of terror online, the "network" concept itself was appropriated by the U.S. administration—and then echoed by the press—for use as a narrowly defined, onerous, and insidious organizational form synonymous with Islamic dissidents (Stohl and Stohl 2007). For these policy makers, networks were treated as information systems for uniplex and ahistorical social relations that were hierarchically organized, top-down command and control structures, with globalized reach connecting homophilous groups. Most important, this orientalized version of network theory stipulated that specifying the boundaries of networks would reveal politically meaningful relations. In contrast, research on network dynamics has demonstrated their multifaceted nature as communication systems. The network form of organization is held together by historically constructed—and limited—relations that allow for dynamic, emergent, adaptive, and flexible associations. Ultimately networks are constructed from other heterogeneous networks that can be described as local s global, or both (Stohl and Stohl 2007). By using the network metaphor in these unusual ways, crucial conduit of modern terrorist networks is the internet, which in the initial reaction to 9/11 was quickly characterized as the fundamental infrastructure of anti-Western, Islamic fundamentalist activity.

Thus, both news coverage about the role of the internet in global politics and a new network metaphor for peculiar organizational forms have helped reproduce orientalist tropes. Bunt's work on the translation of Islamic culture to digital media has done much to illustrate how the internet can support civil dialogues, and the next steps are to demonstrate how much of this is happening, to demonstrate specific political outcomes, and to identify general institutional consequences (Bunt 2000, 2003, 2009). The intellectual object of this book, then, is to disabuse us of these tropes by investigating the multifaceted aspects of contemporary political communication in Islamic media systems and highlighting the impact of the internet on civic life in the developing countries with large Muslim communities.

BOOK OUTLINE

This book is about political communication and democratization in Muslim countries. Some scholars have argued that the internet does not reach enough of a mass audience in the Middle East to warrant comparing its effect to more accessible mass communication media such as radio, television, satellite television, books, and newspapers (Rugh 2004). There are four major reasons why this position is no longer tenable. First, in many Muslim countries internet use has increased rapidly, to the point where it is a widely used information technology, whether access is at home, work, or a public internet access point such as a library or cybercafé. Second, the rubric of "mass communications" is probably no longer suitable, given that ICTs enable both the production and consumption of political culture and given that they distribute personal communications between networks of family and friends. Third, technology access has become a touchstone for modernization in almost all of the countries studied here. Public policy goals are geared toward stimulating IT industries; modernization is equated with telecommunications infrastructure; cybercafés spring up in cities and rural areas alike. Fourth, the arrival of new information technologies is providing opportunities to reinterpret Islamic texts, discuss gender politics, develop collective identities, and articulate shared grievances and aspirations. Chapter 1 offers a conceptual framework and some useful indicators for studying technology diffusion and political institutions.

Chapter 2 addresses two important questions: Which governments are online, and what is the relative capacity of their information infrastructure? There are many aspects to the information society, and this chapter reviews the e-government literature relevant to Muslim countries. It traces the recent history of technology adoption by Muslim governments and presents some unique data, collected by the World Information Access project (wiaproject. erg) and the Project on Information Technology and Political Islam (pitpi. org), which allows for the comparison of wired states. This chapter has two important findings. First, there is a surprising amount of *dependency* in the global information society, with much of the information infrastructure of Muslim countries actually residing in advanced democracies such as the United States, the United Kingdom, and Canada. Second, while information technologies seem to be at the heart of newfound efficiency, transparency, and accountability in emerging democracies, pursuing economic benefits and extending state capacity have forced even the most authoritarian states to make policy trade-offs that create the conditions for transparency and accountability.

Which political parties are online, and what is the capacity of their information infrastructure? Chapter 3 reveals that political parties play different roles in Muslim countries. In some, parties participate in competitive elections; in others, a single political party manages the state apparatus; and in yet others, political parties are hollow and ineffectual. The majority of these political parties support a vibrant secular political discourse online. This chapter traces the recent history of technology adoption by political parties and presents two findings. First, whereas in the past political parties could easily own, control, and incapacitate the news media, today it is much more difficult for them to maintain the same control over digital media. Second, contrary to received wisdom, the internet has not been taken up significantly by minor parties and radical challenger groups. Rather, it is the large, long-standing political organizations that have invested in ICTs in a big way. Chapters 2 and 3 explore the innovative ways that states and political parties use ICTs to offer more said services and opportunities for a political voice to citizens.

Perhaps one of the most important changes over the last decade has been in the business and practice of journalism in countries with large Muslim communities. Chapter 4 reviews the ways in which the internet has changed the organization of the newsrooms and the resources available to journalists. It documents the rise of an important new political actor—citizen-journalists.

Equipped with a cell-phone camera or blog, they have had tangible impacts on the local and global news supply during political and security crises.

Chapter 5 develops grounded theory about the role of information and communication technologies in civil society development. Civic groups are important for democratization because they are, by definition, social organizations independent of the state. Across the Muslim world, civic associations are sprouting up as a result of the new, supportive information infrastructure provided by ICTs. Relatively cheap consumer electronics allow such civic groups to find new members and build affiliations with groups in cities and other countries. Such groups are particularly important in Muslim countries where political parties are illegal, and this chapter reviews the ways in which the internet has had an impact on the political pacts negotiated between social elites and authoritarian regimes, pacts that determine the pace of political change.

In contrast, Chapter 6 explores the more pernicious applications of ICTs, which are used in many Muslim countries not simply for censorship but for actively managing collective identity. The first part of the chapter explores the ways that political culture is now produced and consumed in Muslim countries. A review of the most recent findings about techniques for political censorship and the efforts of activists to overcome these constraints follows. This chapter then demonstrates how political elites have effectively used the new media to construct and manage a transnational Muslim identity for people with significantly different cultural backgrounds. Through digital technologies, social elites attempt more than news censorship and email surveillance. They work to manage particular domains of Islamic political culture and identity formation for youth.

In the concluding chapter, I take a transnational approach to answering a crucial question: What role does the internet have in the democratic transitions of Muslim countries? The previous four chapters review the impact of ICTs on four principal political actors: states, political parties, citizens, and journalists, exploring the causal pathways that particular countries have taken to becoming strong, resilient democracies. This chapter puts it all together using an innovative new statistical approach—fuzzy set logic—to summarize the real-world relationships between technology diffusion and democratic change. Using original data, and using data from established sources in original ways, I demonstrate that technology diffusion has had a crucial *causal* role in improvements in democratic institutions.

I find that technology diffusion has become, in combination with other factors, both a necessary and sufficient cause of democratic transition or entrenchment. For the majority of Muslim countries, the closest thing to civic debate is occurring online. Blogs and online multimedia content, produced both by diasporic communities and by activists within authoritarian states, form the oppositional narratives in countries like Iran, Saudi Arabia, and Pakistan. Neither state bureaucracies nor political parties can monopolize the production of political culture: civic groups and individuals now contribute in significant ways. New ICTs are used for debates over the interpretation of Islamic texts, gender, and security issues. While there is certainly a strong presence of radical Islamic sects and terrorist propaganda online, the number of civic groups and political parties using the internet for democratic discourse and activism is more impressive (and in need of support). Protests and activist movements have led to successful democratic insurgencies, insurgencies that depended on ICTs for the timing and logistics of protest. Sometimes democratic transitions are the outcome, and sometimes the outcome is slight improvement in the behavior of authoritarian states. Clearly the internet and cell phones have not on their own caused a single democratic transition, but it is safe to conclude that today, no democratic transition is possible without information technologies.

A NOTE ON PRESENTATION OF COMPARATIVE EVIDENCE

This argument is made from a qualitative, comparative perspective. In practical terms, this means that much of the data about developing countries has been recalibrated with other developing countries as reference points, rather than using the advanced democracies of the West as reference points. Instead of relying on absolute counts of internet users per capita, or daily newspapers per country, values are indexed across the comparison set. In other words, online news in a country is said to be important not just because it has many online news sites compared to the rest of the world, but because it has a relatively large share of the all the online news sites, and a relatively large share of the internet user base found across the full sample of 75 countries. In this way, the evidence marshaled here is grounded in the most sensible comparison set. Moreover, to standardize the comparison, tables in the chapters ahead use a common set of icons. Many of the icons are intuitive, and serve to help summarize lots of case-specific knowledge in a comparable manner. Other symbols are used for topic-specific comparative attributes that are described in the text accompanying each chapter.

Re-calibrating data in this way is a important epistemological advancement. Rather than comparing the Muslim experience with technology diffusion, democratic politics, or economic productivity to the ideal as represented by Western countries, it is possible to compare the experience among Muslim communities. This means that instead of using a metric of internet use

Table 0.1: Presenting Comparative Data

Table Symbols	Meanings
▲, ▼, ✕	Improving, declining, no change
·, •, ●	Small, medium, large
·, ▪, ■	Low, moderate, high
+, **+**, ✚	Slow, moderate, rapid growth rate
□, ◻, ■; ○, ⊙, ●	Poor, modest, good or other categorical attributes as described in specific tables
✓	Known to have attribute
✗	Known to not have attribute
..	Missing data

relative to the highest values in the West, the metric should be relative to the high and low values of neighboring Muslim countries and communities. Much of this calibration is done through indices based on ratios of ratios (Howard et al. 2009). For example, we already know that economic wealth is the best predictor of how many computers are in a country. So it would be most useful to index the level of computer diffusion across all the countries in the comparison set, holding wealth constant. First, the ratio of a country's economic output to the output of all countries in a given year is calculated. Then the ratio of computers in a country to all the computers in all the countries is calculated. The ratio of these two ratios, after some mathematical adjustments, reveals whether a country has about the proportion of ICTs it should given its productivity. Expression A reveals the level of computer diffusion in a country, given its share of economic output, relative to all the other countries in the study.

Expression A: Ratio of Two Ratios

$$Ratio\ of\ Ratios_T = \frac{\dfrac{PC_{country}}{\sum\limits_{all\ countries} PC}}{\dfrac{GDP_{country}}{\sum\limits_{all\ countries} GDP}}$$

Half the distribution of possible values from this ratio of ratios ranges from 0 to 1 (disproportionately small share of computers in a country, given its GDP) and the other half ranges from 1 to +infinity (disproportionately large share of computers in a country, given its GDP). However, by taking the natural log of the ratio of ratios, the index will become more balanced: from– infinity to 0 becomes less than proportionate share, and from 0 to +infinity becomes more than proportionate share.

Expression B: Technology Diffusion Index

$$TDI_T = ln\left(\frac{\dfrac{PC_{country}}{\displaystyle\sum_{all\ countries} PC}}{\dfrac{GDP_{country}}{\displaystyle\sum_{all\ countries} GDP}} \right)$$

Expression B creates a value for how far above or below a country is from the technology diffusion and economic productivity norm of the countries in the study. Where ever possible, GDP is reported as purchasing power parity. Computing such values for all 75 countries yields an index of how far each country is from this grand mean.

Much of the data used in this study will be recalibrated so that the major points of comparison are set by other Muslim countries. It is particularly useful to do these kinds of calibrations to help weight for economic wealth or population. Per capita income in the United Arab Emirates is 200 times that in Somalia, so these two countries represent the upper and lower bounds of wealth in the set of countries. For more on this calibration, see Philip Howard, Laura Busch, Dawn Nafus, and Ken Anderson, "Sizing up Information Societies—Towards a Better Metric for the Cultures of ICT Adoption," *The Information Society* 25, no. 3 (2009): 208-219. Appendix A and B provide technical notes and a case-specific reference list. For replication data, photos, digital copies of this manuscript, and fs/QCA syntax, please visit www.wiaproject.org and www.pitpi.org.

Chapter 1

Evolution and Revolution, Transition and Entrenchment

Since the early 1990s, 23 Muslim countries have developed more democratic institutions, with fairly run elections, energized and competitive political parties, greater civil liberties, or better legal protections for journalists. Some of these transitions have resulted in more durable political systems, a few have not. In some countries, evolution rather than revolution best describes the hard-fought, incremental improvements in democratic practices. And in a few countries, this evolution has really just meant a change from very authoritarian to somewhat authoritarian governance.

The ways in which people in the Muslim communities of the developing world communicate with family and friends and produce and consume culture have radically changed over the last decade. In 1996, 80 percent of the population in 50 Muslim countries did not have regular access to a telephone. By 2006, this proportion had dropped to 20 percent. The diffusion rates for other information and communication technologies are also high, generally higher than those in non-Muslim developing countries: between 2000 and 2010, the compound annual growth rate of internet users was 32 percent, compared with 24 percent for the rest of the developing world.

Perhaps a more telling figure is that of the "doubling time," a figure used by demographers to refer to the amount of time it takes for a country's population to double. Applied to technology diffusion, a similar measure reveals particularly rapid trends: between 2000 and 2010, the internet population in Albania, Nigeria, and Syria doubled every year. On average, since 2000, the number of internet users in Muslim countries doubled every 8 months. In non-Muslim developing countries, the internet population grew at a somewhat slower pace, and doubled every 16 months.[1] Logically, the doubling time of a country's internet user base will eventually be measured in years, but for a fixed period of study, it is a useful measure of how rapid the diffusion of technologies has been. Simply reporting percentage increases in the internet user base is less meaningful information, since such growth would be measured in tens of thousands of percent.[2]

Scholars are understandably careful in the use of words like "revolution," especially in studies of socio-technical change. But to describe the impact of ICTs in some countries, revolution might not be a misnomer. In some Muslim communities, democratic activism would barely exist without the internet. In many countries, political opposition has long taken the form of governments in exile, or political parties that risk being co-opted or suppressed by ruling elites. In many of these countries, the internet has actually provided the enabling infrastructure for secular, civic, and democratic discourse that formerly had no such infrastructure. In some Muslim countries, the only site of political discourse is online.

In 1998, Suharto's rule over Indonesia was broken by a student movement that successfully used mobile phone infrastructure to organize their protests. During Kyrgyzstan's Tulip Revolution of March 2005, mobile phones were again used to organize activists to join protests at key moments, helping democratic leaders build a social movement with sufficient clout to oust the president. Kuwait's women's suffrage movement was much more successful in 2005 than it had been in 2000, because it was able to use text messaging to call younger protesters out of schools to attend demonstrations. With little more than the online publication of a position paper in 2007, Turkish military leaders let it be known that they would act to protect the secular character of the country if voters elected too many Islamists—what several Turkish commentators called a "coup by website." In 2004, when the Egyptian government cracked down on opposition parties, the banned newspapers of the Labour Party and Muslim Brotherhood reappeared as websites with the additional capacity to help coordinate opposition candidates running for office. On several occasions, when authoritarian regimes shut down opposition websites, political organizations easily move their content to servers in other countries: Tunisia's online news site TUNeZINE.com was able to migrate to internet hosts in France; in Kazakhstan, political parties were able to relaunch from new locations after being banned just before elections in October 2007. Such authoritarian regimes are especially sensitive to investigation by citizen journalists, who use digital technologies to research and expose graft. In 2008, bloggers reconstructed flight paths for the Tunisian president's plane using photos from plane watchers across Europe—at times when the Tunisian leader was known to be in-country. The research revealed that the president's wife had been using the plane for shopping trips, greatly eroding the leader's credibility.

Multiple blogs in Iraq, Iran, and Afghanistan provide alternative sources of news and photos, and often help mainstream media break news stories. Al-Qaeda uses the internet to organize and publicize its attacks, and for some fundamentalist organizations it is only electronic networks that hold them together. In 2005 it was estimated that there were more than 4,500 terrorist websites (Weimann 2006). Yet even at that time there were over 500 major political parties online and over a thousand online newspapers, 200 major libraries, and over two thousand civic groups online. It can be difficult to assay the number of "terrorist websites" actively maintained and read. But it is certain that today, the volume of citizen blogs, online newspapers, and mainstream political content is significantly greater, is more widely read, and is a constituent component and defining feature of civic Islam. As both Giustozzi and Dartnell demonstrate, ICTs are valuable to those who want their propaganda to reach the political leaders of an enemy army (Giustozzi 2001; Dartnell 2006). When ICTs play a role in more democratic transitions, threatened political elites in authoritarian regimes and emerging democracies try to strip social movements of communications tools. Both Iran and Albania, for example, have blocked internet gateways and mobile phone networks during politically tumultuous periods.

THE IMPACT OF INFORMATION TECHNOLOGY ON ISLAMIC POLITICAL CULTURE

It has been difficult to establish a causal link between the diffusion of information technology and the democratization of political cultures. On a case by case basis, scholars acknowledge that information technologies are part of many recent democratic transitions, whether these transitions take the form of sudden surges in social protest and rapid political turnover, or incremental improvements in the effectiveness of democratic institutions and practices. The leaders of social movements have used ICTs such as mobile phones and the internet to mobilize public opinion, organize mass protests, project their demands onto national and international agendas, and challenge authoritarian regimes.

What has been the overall political impact of the internet on the Muslim countries of the developing world? Have information technologies played a part in making Islamic countries a little more democratic? These kinds of questions about the political impact of ICTs are not asked just by political communication scholars in the West; they are being asked by Muslims as well. In 1997, as the Saudi government was considering the introduction of public internet use, several intellectuals argued that the internet was in fact the primary tool of globalization. "Since you have agreed to adopt this civilization's instruments," opined a columnist in *Al-Yawm*, "including its factories, its weapons, and its computers, then you are forced to adopt its ideas and values" (Teitelbaum 2002). In what ways is the internet a Western technology, and how is its design and content being reshaped by Muslim political culture? Does the internet homogenize, Americanize, or democratize political culture?

First and foremost, I argue that the internet has had a crucial role in bringing about contemporary currents of democratic Islam. I also argue that the new media technologies, such as mobile phones and the internet, have radically transformed the means of political communication in Muslim countries. ICTs have mediated an extensive transnational Islamic identity, one that is constituted by *both* the production and the consumption of political culture by Muslims around the world. Thus, I argue that the internet has had a causal role in the formation of contemporary transnational Muslim identity. Spiritual iconography and the shared text of the Koran have always provided the basis for Muslim collective identity. International incidents, such as foreign military intervention (Russian or U.S.) in Afghanistan and the ongoing conflicts between Israel and its neighbors, have also provided a source of shared grievances and a collective sense of persecution. Specialized news services, such as the Interpress wire service, BBC Arab service, and Al Jazeera, have been instrumental in constructing a transnational news audience. But there are forms of social interaction and cultural content that are unique to the internet and that have created the conditions and opportunities for contemporary transnational identity. The formation of transnational Islamic identity began with satellite and specialized cable TV services, but these unidirectional elite-owned infrastructures for political communication did not offer opportunities for user-generated content and the permanent connectivity that mobile phones and the internet now provide.

New media technologies support significant community debates about gender politics, international security, and Koranic interpretation. A number of scholars have argued that for every new information technology, a battle over the presentation and interpretation of Islamic texts ensues. The history of Koranic interpretation is beyond the scope of this book, but it is within the scope of this book to analyze the mediated structure over which such interpretation occurs online. In recent decades, the Muslim diaspora in the West produced a significant amount of politically critical content via mass media such as radio, television, film, and newspapers, but such content was consumed in the diaspora and rarely in-country. Now this critical content does reach the home country as webpages and digital media streams, and some of it is actually produced in-country. I argue that the internet has a causal and supportive role in the formation of democratic discourse in the Muslim communities of the developing world.

Participation in the political economy of information societies has become a policy goal for most governments in the developing world. ICTs have enabled many of these countries to participate in the global information economy in new ways. Some of these economic opportunities come as outsourcing, for example when the Bibliothèque Nationale de France contracted a Moroccan company to digitize government archives. The documents were scanned in France and edited in Rabat. Though this kind of informational outsourcing, the technology sector in many Muslim countries is expanding, with local entrepreneurs and engineers who design their own software and hardware. Craftspeople sell their wares online. A growing number of governments announce tenders for public works projects online, as they do in Algeria and Tunisia. In Senegal, local fishermen use mobile phones and PDAs to improve the distribution, pricing, and marketing of their catches; in Tanzania, mobile phones help fishermen identify endangered species and deliver sustainable harvesting information by SMS; when police payroll systems in Afghanistan began distributing monthly pay through SMS, many officers discovered their real salaries were 30 percent higher than what local bureaucrats had been giving out. Information and communication technologies enable the transfer of significant amounts of remittances back to home countries from the diaspora.

Finally, information technologies themselves have a symbolic role in contemporary political life and a discursive role in the formation of modern political identity for many Muslims—especially the youth. Political parties without websites simply aren't considered modern. Challenger candidates in Iran use Facebook to help their supporters find a shared sense of community, and in Malaysia both challengers and incumbents actively blog around election time. Since 2002, almost every Muslim president and prime minister has developed a national ICT action plan to satisfy international and local business interests—and multilateral lending agencies.

Perhaps more subtle is the way that technology itself increasingly shapes people's political identities. In the West, for example, video games are helping to shape young players' understandings of the world in which they live (Machin and Suleiman 2006; Souri 2007). NovaLogic created "Delta Force" using terrain maps from declassified U.S. Department of Defense imagery and scenarios; it was designed by the same firms that create simulations of military air and ground operations. Video game players become immersed in virtual environments where they conduct military "missions" into Islamic countries. To "contest the view of Arabs and Muslims being portrayed as terrorists in Western games and introduce the Resistance to the young people" (Karouny 2003), the video game "Special Force" was designed. In this video game, a group of Islamic resistance fighters must defeat Israeli commandos to return water diverted from villages in southern Lebanon. Whereas "Delta Force" sourced its imagery and scenarios from the U.S. Department of Defense, "Special Force" sourced its imagery and scenarios from Hezbollah's Central Internet Bureau. These two games share striking similarities: both have overt political messages; both promote violent military solutions to social problems; both are digital artifacts designed to help shape the political identity of youth (Machin and Suleiman 2006).

ICT ACCESS IN THE MUSLIM COMMUNITIES OF THE DEVELOPING WORLD

Currently, there are approximately 1.4 billion Muslims living in the 75 countries where Muslims are known to be a majority (more than 50 percent of the population) or a sizable minority (more than 10 percent). If we assume that internet use rates for a country are consistent across the country's subpopulations, then across these 75 countries, some 141 million Muslims are online.[3] Based on these numbers, about 10 percent of the global Muslim population is online. This is almost certainly an underestimate, since there is evidence that internet access in developing Muslim countries is not only a personal, home, or work-based information service for wealthy elites. A much larger— and difficult to assay—population uses public internet access points such as cybercafés and libraries.[4]

As in many other countries, new information and communication technologies were first available to the social elite across Muslim Europe, North Africa, Central Asia, the Arab peninsula, the Indian subcontinent, and Southeast Asia. Technologies such as mobile phones and the internet were for the wealthy and well educated, business and political leaders who often traveled to the world's urban centers. Not only did internet users in these parts of the world need to be computer literate, they needed to be able to read English and afford the high cost of international dial-up connections. Since 2000, however, the cost of computers and internet use has dropped, mobile phones have become an additional platform for connectivity, and many people have access to information technologies through family and friends. To understand how Muslims go online is both a question of history and modalities. How has information infrastructure in these countries developed? How do people now use this information infrastructure?

Before 1990, only a few hospitals and universities in these countries had some form of internet connection, primarily for distance education and telemedicine. Indeed, the first significant Muslim communities online were émigrés living in the West; based in London, Los Angeles, Toronto, and New York, they had established ethnic broadcast networks and quickly found created community online (Naficy 1995). "They created mailing lists, news groups, and Web sites dealing with topics ranging from Arabic music to searching for cheap tickets to the Middle East, from looking for wives to finding Halal grocers and the nearest mosque or church" (Ghareeb 2000). International development projects sometimes outfitted urban community centers or rural schools with computers and internet connections, but they rarely achieved project goals because of irregular electricity supplies, the high costs of landline connections, bureaucratic blockages, and the fact that most computer donations came in the form of older models unable to run contemporary software. Such early projects often succeeded in generating interest in computer use, getting teachers to communicate using email and to use pedagogical materials from the internet, but they rarely succeeded in improving the computer literacy of students, drawing the community into education or technology policy issues, or increasing the local production of digital content, learning materials, or curricula (Sluma, Brode, and Roberts 2004). Across a range of projects to build youth cyber clubs or put computers in schools during the 1990s, one of the most consistent findings was that internet access did most to improve the organizational capacity of school teachers and education administrators—student learning of computer skills or internet search skills occurred in some of the projects but was difficult to correlate with project funding amounts or design elements (Thioune and Camara 2004).

During the 1990s, state policy makers reacted differently to the perceived opportunities and risks of new ICTs. In many countries, the publicly owned telecommunications provider monopolized the provision of such services. The organization that provided telecommunications services also regulated content and reported directly to the executive branch of government. This provider determined the pace of national ICT development, almost always with direct political supervision. Singapore became a hub of ICT design and manufacture. Other countries simply banned new information technologies: Tanzania initially banned computers; Syria and Saudi Arabia banned internet access. But as the economic value of computer access became evident to the Tanzanian government, and Saudis began using dial-up services in Bahrain and Syrians began using dial-up services in Jordan, even the most recalcitrant bureaucrats began crafting policy regimes for permitting and regulating internet access. Over time, international development agencies learned that their connectivity projects had to include training, build in incentives to attract boys and girls equally, and work out technical solutions that did not burden schools and community centers with old equipment or onerous phone bills (Katahoire, Baguma, and Etta 2004).

Established democracies in the Muslim world responded somewhat more quickly than other regime types, often allowing open competition in the market for consumer electronics, and sometimes allowing competition in the market for telecommunications services. Constitutional monarchies were somewhat slower to organize, and when they did they built in censorship mechanisms. For example, planning for Saudi Arabia's first internet node began in 1997. Both the information infrastructure and the organization for connecting to the internet were guided by the principle that, with proper planning, Saudis could have the benefits of information access, without the risk of cultural corruption from the West. The social risks of internet access could be minimized by building both the information infrastructure and the cultural habits of internet use. Through a combination of public education, advertising, and internet regulation, the state would train Saudi users to not partake in illegitimate uses such as viewing pornography, gambling, sending or receiving coded information, using the network to cause "annoyance, threats, or spreading rumors," and activities that violated the "social, cultural, political, media, economic, and religious values of the Kingdom of Saudi Arabia" (Teitelbaum 2002). Over 200 subcontractors applied to provide internet access within the Kingdom, but they had to share the responsibility of managing internet exposure, and promise to only allow customers to connect via the censoring proxy servers of the King Abdulaziz City for Science and Technology. The state co-opted commercial operators to participate in ideologically safeguarding state power. By building both infrastructure and the culture of use, ruling elites can involve citizens in self censorship, and today Saudis themselves can nominate words and websites they world like blocked by the government firewall.

Autocracies, especially those with significant oil and natural gas revenues, were the slowest governments to develop a national internet service provider (ISP) and internet access policies. Because they were less beholden to multilateral lending agencies such as the European Bank for Reconstruction and Development (EBRD) and the International Monetary Fund (IMF), they were less obliged to meet the policy reform conditions of loans. In petroleum-rich Central Asia, for example, ruling elites have been able to retain firm control of the media and telecommunications infrastructure, because they have not faced the pressure to privatize public assets (Mcglinchey and Johnson 2007).

In many small communities, telecenters provide ICT access to photocopying, telephony, and training in computer hardware, software, internet access, and word processing. Faxing, document design, processing, and printing and email services are often also available. If the connections are speedy, internet users also download movies and software and make voice-over-internet-protocol (VoIP) phone calls. The range of services in multipurpose community telecenters is often greater than in private telecenters or cybercafés. In many developing Islamic countries they are run by NGOs, international aid agencies, and secular or religious madrasahs.

Gomez and colleagues (1999b) identify five types of telecenters. The most basic telecenters are usually located in rural marginalized areas, where there is limited access to basic services in general and where training of potential users is a popular service in addition to internet access. Telecenter franchises are independently owned and managed, or are supervised by a local organization, which offers technical and, on occasion, financial support. Civic telecenters, the most common, are established where a public organization such as a university opens up its facilities, like computers, for use by the public. These telecenter services tend to be an addition to the other day-to-day activities of the organization. Commercial cybercafés are often found in affluent neighborhoods or hotels in major towns and cities. Finally, the multipurpose community center, one of the newer models recently introduced in a number of countries, offers more specialized services such as telemedicine. In the Muslim communities of the developing world, however, where internet use is often a culturally managed practice, many youth have internet access at their madrassa. The secular madrassas offer telecenter services not unlike the civic telecenters, but the more religious madrassas allow for more culturally bounded technology use.

In many rich countries, there is a generational divide between older people who cannot or do not choose to use the latest information technologies and younger generations for whom these technologies provide not only communications options but status markers. In recent years, the gender divide has closed, such that the internet user population in most wealthy countries is a balanced population of men and women. This gender imbalance in public places where technology is available is anecdotally consistent in many Muslim communities. In 2000, women usually made up a fraction of the user population in public internet access points: 30 percent in Mozambique and Uganda, 23 percent in Mali and India, and only 6 percent in Jordan (Etta and Parvyn-Wamahiu 2003; Hafkin and Taggart 2001). Today, the gender gap in such public internet access points is still noticeable, but women have taken to the internet from access points at home or work. In Egypt, some 60 percent of the popular Facebook group "Yeah, We Are Seculars and We Are Proud" are women. Although it is difficult to assay the gender distribution of online groups, it is certain that women are active in many corners of the Islamic internet (Fleishman 2008).

Telecenter use, for the most part, seems to involve more social and cultural activities than economic activities. The most frequently used services are contacting friends and family for email, preparing documents for social events such as weddings and funerals, streaming cultural content from radio and television stations, viewing films that have been digitized for online distribution, and reading online newspapers. Often, professional and economic needs, such as finding agricultural information, tax rules, or banking, are only a secondary reason to use a telecenter. For example, in Uganda, only 10 to 20 percent of telecenter users reported making a commercial transaction. Often telecenters are meeting places, places of shelter and safety, and places for training groups of people (Etta and Parvyn-Wamahiu 2003).[5]

If cultural production and consumption is the primary purpose of tele-centers in the developing Muslim world, economic activity a close, secondary purpose. Project reports in Senegal suggest that telecenter computers are most frequently used for office tasks, to capture or store data by business-people and small groups (e.g., artisans and other micro-enterprises), and for recordkeeping by community associations (Etta and Parvyn-Wamahiu 2003). It is likely that different kinds of telecenters are used for different things: those established by aid agencies and libraries may see more of these professional and business-oriented activities; those commercial and less reg-ulated telecenters may see more entertainment and social activities. Given the various modalities of internet access in Muslim countries and the wide range of activities online, how can we compare technology diffusion and democratization across these very different countries?

INDEXING DEMOCRACY AND ICT DIFFUSION

Poor countries have computer and internet penetration rates that are a fraction of those found in wealthy countries, but among these, some rates of change are high. By 2010, 8 out of every 1,000 people in Mali, 8 out of every 100 people in Georgia, and 8 of every 10 people in the United States had used the internet. However, the proportion of countries with a small fraction of the world's internet users has not changed much over the last 10 years. Since there is a strong link between economic wealth and ICT access, expressing internet use per dollar of GDP, rather than per capita, makes the inequality in the distribution of ICTs between and within countries—the digital divide— much less dramatic (Fink and Kenny 2006). Of course, the digital divide is not simply between countries, but within countries; in rich countries the digital divide by categories of race, gender, and income is slowly closing (Youngs 2002; Hoffman and Novak 1998; Howard, Rainie, and Jones 2001; Margolis and Fisher 2002; Howard and Massanari 2007).

Research suggests that economic performance is the strongest single pre-dictor of a country's technology adoption rate (Nour 2002). Although some researchers determine ICT diffusion through simple counts of computers or mobile phones per capita, a more revealing method is to look at whether a country has more or less ICT than reasonably expected, given its economic performance. Economic wealth is not the only predictor of a country's tech-nology adoption rates and does not explain all of the variation among differ-ent countries. Many of these secondary factors, such as education, language, public policy, and level of corruption, are all components of a country's political culture. This secondary category of explanatory variables is large, and in any particular country these variables will be relevant in different ways. Thus an index of technology diffusion in Muslim countries should offer a way of classifying countries that in some way controls for the impact of economic growth and isolates the impact of political culture. This method must allow distinctions among the diverse political cultures that make the rate of technology adoption in Muslim countries high considering their wealth, about what can be expected given their wealth, or unusually low given their wealth.

To better weight for the impact of economic wealth and isolate the impact of political culture on technology diffusion, it is possible to formulate a weighted index of technology diffusion. This index relates the number of internet users to the GDP of each country in a way that allows us to identify, for example, countries where the number of internet users is more or less than what would be expected. For instance, countries with a lower GDP may have surprising numbers of computer, mobile phone, and internet users, while countries with high levels of GDP may have fewer such users.

Countries with an index score of around zero have about the levels of ICTs expected, given the size of its economy. Consequently, a country with a high ICT diffusion score has a surprisingly high number of computers, given its GDP. A country with a low index score has a lower number of computers than expected, given its GDP. Missing data does not affect the rankings, though countries with several low levels of some ICTs are also those with missing data for other ICTs.

Many Muslim countries in Central Africa and Central Asia have low index values because computers, mobile phones, and internet access have been slow to come to these parts of the world. India has about the number of internet users it should have, given its economic productivity, but it may seem surprising that it has such low index scores in other ICT categories, given the amount of news reporting on that country's booming technology industries. Since this index is a ratio of ratios, however, India's low scores suggests that it actually has fewer computers, mobile phones, secure servers, and internet hosts than would be expected, given its economic productivity. Its index values suggest that, given how large India's economy is—some $3.9 trillion in 2010—it should actually have more ICTs than it currently does. The number of internet users in India is in keeping with its economic productivity, but the proportion of computers, mobile phones, secure servers, and internet hosts is disproportionately small.

Of the six different ICT indicators indexed this way, many countries have a positive value for mobile phones. This gives quantitative evidence for the anecdotal observations that in many of these countries, mobile phones seem to be in every hand. It is easy to claim that there are lots of mobile phones, on a per capita basis, in these countries. This index allows the additional analytical purchase of revealing that some countries have a surprising number of mobile phones, given their economic performance. To assess the impact of ICTs on Islamic political culture, an index of institutionalized democracy is also needed.

DOES INFORMATION INFRASTRUCTURE ENHANCE DEMOCRACY?

Perhaps the most pernicious theoretical problem for scholars of development, communication, and international relations is the question of whether information and communication technologies "cause" societies to become more democratic. In theory, we might also be interested in the possibility that democracy causes technology diffusion. This causal possibility, however, has been examined elsewhere and found to be weak. As explained above, economic wealth has a much more distinct and direct impact on ICT diffusion. It might be that democratic countries are more likely to be wealthy, and therefore also will be rapid technology adopters. Yet when technology adoption is weighted by economic wealth and treated in time series analysis, the effect of being a democratic regime has little statistical significance (Howard and Mazaheri 2009). Indeed, it is specific types of policy reforms that provide the most useful insight into the causes of technology adoption, and these reforms have been enacted by both dictatorships and democracies (van Dijk and Szirmai 2006). So there is little evidence that generally democratic institutions will cause greater levels of technology use in a country. Is it plausible that technology use might cause political institutions to become more democratic? What would evidence of this causal relationship look like?

There are several methodological approaches to answering this question: a quantitative approach using large-N datasets and statistical tools that demonstrate how variation in democratic outcomes are correlated with variables that serve as proxies for theoretically interesting explanatory factors; a qualitative and comparative approach using specific cases and narrative arguments that trace out causal connections in a more direct and nuanced manner. Visualizing real cases as data points that deviate from a grand theoretical trend could mean graphing trend lines for ICT use and democratization. Visualizing real cases as having degrees of membership in a theoretically interesting set—the set of countries where technology diffusion has led to democratization—could mean graphing cases as being fully in, partly in, or fully out of the set.

One approach has been to use qualitative evidence and single case studies about the importance of communications media in democratic transitions (Horwitz 2001). Scholars build carefully formed and nuanced arguments about democratic transitions in a single country, with detail about causal connections and narratives of change over time. Unfortunately, while single case studies help generate theories about the importance of ICTs in democratic transitions, such theories cannot be meaningfully tested on a single case alone. When such detailed causal theories are transported to other countries, invariably some factors lose relevance, and new factors seem important.

Once equipped with some theories about the role of ICTs in a country's transition to democracy, comparative research is the next step to test which theories apply most broadly and under which conditions. Thus, comparative research often works with multiple cases and a reduced set of properties for each particular case (George 2006; McMahan and Chesebro 2003). Studies such as these successfully argue that over time, democratic transitions occur as media systems modernize. Unfortunately, authors using this approach must forfeit strong language about causal connections. As more cases are added, more caveats, nuances, and variations are added. They find strong correlations between attributes of media systems and political cultures, and their knowledge of the cases gives credibility to their claims of causality. Such comparativists work to generalize trends and form transportable theory about how technologies can drive drive the evolution of democratic political practices. Appendix B identifies the useful single case and small set comparative studies of technology use and regime change used in this study.

The third approach to studying the role of technology in democratization has been quantitative, working with many if not all available cases and severely reduced sets of properties for each particular case (Milner 2006; Howard and Mazaheri 2009). This approach seeks parsimonious models of the impact of country case attributes on scales of democratic performance. The models are used to test theories of how communication technologies bring about democratic processes, theories that are usually developed by the qualitative and comparative researchers. Unfortunately, many of the traditional statistical techniques do not lead to conclusions about causal connections. Instead, they lead to models of "explained variation," a different thing altogether. To explain the variation in a range of country experiences, researchers often have to pool data from multiple years, artificially expanding the number of case studies they have so that the assumptions of traditional statistical methods can be met.

To accommodate correlational analysis, researchers often have to make significant sacrifices in the amount of variation a model can explain. Regression analysis takes into account the impact of variables on a given outcome, but the resulting explanation is fitted for only a few real cases. Indeed, qualitative researchers are very good at explaining nuanced, causal pathways; through in-depth case studies, comparativists must privilege some causal pathways shared by multiple countries; quantitative researchers have yet to develop the toolkit for analyzing causal pathways. To an eye trained for seeing correlations, the points of data in Figure 1.1 are important inasmuch as they are some distance from a central tendency. (In this figure, a linear trend line is provided, but a nonlinear trend line could also fit within the distribution of cases.)

Correlational statistical techniques help explain the observed variation from a central tendency. If there is a plausible theoretical relationship between the diffusion of digital information technologies and democratization, a simple correlational approach reveals that 6 percent of the variation in democratization can be explained by technology diffusion. This means that 94 percent of the variation remains unexplained. A host of additional explanatory variables could be added, interactive effects could be tested, and outlier cases could be cut out of the sample. Ultimately, a Nonlinear model would probably make for a better fit. Yet the outlier cases are usually very interesting, and it is rare that this extra work yields more explained variation

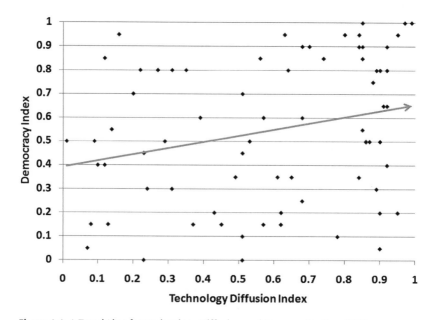

Figure 1.1 A Trend Line for Technology Diffusion and Democratization, 2010

Source: Based on author's calculations with data from Polity IV (2007) and the World Bank (2007).

Notes: The index for technology diffusion was created from World Bank data, transformed as described in the text to be weighted by economic wealth, then turned into a fuzzy set variable and calibrated to distribute cases across the theoretical set of countries where information and communication technologies have diffused. The index for democracy was taken from Polity IV, adjusted for particular countries as described in Appendix A, then turned into a fuzzy set variable and calibrated to distribute cases across the set of countries with significant Muslim communities.

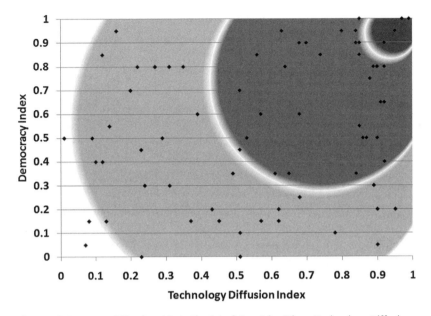

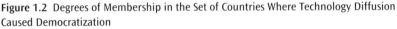

Figure 1.2 Degrees of Membership in the Set of Countries Where Technology Diffusion Caused Democratization

Source: See Figure 1.1.

Notes: See Figure 1.1.

than unexplained variation. Some would argue that any explained variation is better than none at all. But to reveal how ICTs may be an ingredient for democratization—as experienced by Muslim communities around the developing world over the last 15 years—a qualitative and comparative approach is even better.

Figure 1.2 charts the degree of membership for 75 Muslim countries in two theoretically important sets: the set of countries that experienced a democratic transition between 1994 and 2010; and the set of countries that experienced rapid technology diffusion over this period. The points of data are the same as those in the previous figure. Membership in the set of countries that experienced a democratic transition is defined by having at least a 3-point change in the index of democratic institutions offered in the Polity IV dataset.[6] The set is constructed according to the magnitude of the transition so that countries which experienced significant democratic transitions are given high index values, countries that experienced little change are given median values, and countries that receded into dictatorship are given low values. Comparatively, Indonesia experienced the most sweeping transformation of these countries, a democratic transition in 1998–1999 that is graded as an 11-point rise in the Polity IV index, so with full membership in the set of countries experiencing a democratic transition,

Indonesia is valued at 1.0. In contrast, Pakistan experienced a slide into authoritarianism, graded as a 13-point drop, so it is fully out of the set of countries experiencing a democratic transition and is valued at 0.0. In terms of membership in this set, the other countries fall in between these high and low values.

The index of technology diffusion was computed using the expression described in the introduction, for mobile phones, internet users, internet hosts, personal computers, national internet bandwidth, and broadband internet users, and then averaged and transformed into set-theoretic values (a process of calibration that is described in Appendix A). A few countries are full members in the set of countries experiencing rapid technology diffusion in recent years: Bosnia, Morocco, Singapore. Others are out of the set because they have comparatively smaller information infrastructure than would be expected, given the size of the national economy: Iraq, Turkmenistan, and Yemen. At the midpoints are countries such as Eritrea and Kuwait; though they have very different levels of economic development, they have about the level of information infrastructure expected, given the level of economic development they do have.

To introduce this comparative study of the role of information infrastructure in democratic transitions in the Muslim communities of the developing world, Figure 1.2 organizes countries according to their membership in these two theoretically interesting sets. There are many recipes for democracy, and there are clearly some countries for which technology diffusion has been a key ingredient.

Cases appearing at the top right of the figure, in the dark grey circle are those that are fully in the theoretical set of countries where technology diffusion contributed to democratic outcomes. There are only a few of these countries, but in important ways they help define the set. Moving below the threshold of full membership in the set reveals a much larger number of countries that are mostly in the set—though membership values vary. This larger collection of cases, which appear over a grey background, are countries that have high levels of technology diffusion and high levels of democracy. Another threshold, sometimes called the transition point, distinguishes these cases from those that are not members of the set. These cases may have high levels of technology diffusion but low levels of democracy, or vice versa. Either way, these cases are mostly out of the theoretical set, and they appear in the light grey area.. Finally, there are a handful of cases that are definitely out of the set. Countries such as Saudi Arabia and Turkmenistan are definitely not members of the set of countries where technology diffusion has contributed to democratization. Cases at the bottom left of the figure are countries where the absence of technology diffusion probably contributed to a lack of democratization.

Countries with high levels of democratization but low levels of technology diffusion probably democratized for reasons unrelated to the availability of information technologies to state agencies, political parties, journalists, and civil society groups. These cases do not undermine the theoretical relationship between information technology and democratization, because they are not directly relevant. In other words, whereas the democratization recipe for the cases in the top right of the figure includes technology diffusion as an ingredient, the democratization recipe for the cases in the top left of the figure is probably different.

Figure 1.2 also helps us think about how technology diffusion may be a sufficient or necessary cause of democratization. Imagining a diagonal line from the point 0,0 to 1,1 separates the cases into two groups. For countries above the diagonal, information infrastructure may have been a sufficient causal condition for the democratic transition, because all values for the causal condition are less than or equal to their corresponding outcome values. Cases in the upper-left corner of the plot may be there because of other causal conditions, suggesting that information infrastructure may be a sufficient but not necessary condition for democratization. However, this relationship is not consistent across all cases, because those below the imagined diagonal are ones in which information infrastructure is a necessary but not sufficient cause of democratic change. For these countries, the set of countries experiencing a democratic outcome is a subset of those experiencing rapid technology diffusion, meaning that all the values for the outcome are less than or equal to the values for the causal condition.

In conventional correlational explanations, cases in the lower right corner are considered errors that undermine the correlation between the causal condition of information infrastructure and the democratic outcomes. These cases are still substantively valuable, however, because they reveal much about how information infrastructure could be a necessary causal condition that must be combined with other causal conditions. When is information infrastructure a necessary or sufficient causal condition for a democratic transition?

Appendix A presents evidence about technology diffusion and political transformation in a way that allows for easier comparison among countries; 1994 is a sensible start date because internet use in these countries would have been minor before 1994, and many of the political transitions just before 1994 were part of the wave of democratization that followed the collapse of the Soviet Union. It is reasonable to expect that there are no cases of political transformation prior to 1994 in which internet, mobile phone, or other ICT use had much of a role.

The regime type rankings from the Polity IV dataset offer a full spectrum from very authoritarian (scored as –10) to very democratic (scored as +10).

If the range –10 to –6 is considered authoritarian, –5 to –1 somewhat author-itarian, 0 a transitional rank, 1 to 5 somewhat democratic, and 5 to 10 democratic, then it is possible for a country to have a significant shift in sev-eral directions: it can become more authoritarian, more democratic, a little less authoritarian, or a little less democratic. Appendix A presents countries that have undergone such shifts, the period in which the transition occurred, and the point shift over this period. Many countries have improved or regressed only one or two points since 1994, or did not change rank at all; a few experienced more complex changes. Some countries had several transi-tions of more than three points, but only transitions begun after 1994 are included.

The democratic transition regimes include countries that underwent a 3-point transformation in the level of institutionalized democracy, between 1994 and 2010. The regimes that experienced democratic entrenchment had young democratic institutions that became more effective and durable. There are no examples of high ICT diffusion countries that became more authoritarian, and the only countries that became much more authoritarian had average or low levels of information infrastructure. There are many countries that became more democratic and had average or high levels of information infrastructure. There were no examples of democracies that became less democratic, at any level of technology diffusion. Moreover, countries that were authoritarian and became less so tend to be countries with average or below average levels of ICT diffusion. In some cases, the tran-sitions were meaningful but took a long time—as much as a decade in coun-tries such as Georgia and Algeria. In other cases, the transformations were rapid, with significant improvements in democratic policies and practices. Some countries, such as Somalia, probably have relatively high technology diffusion because of the influx of foreign aid workers (Ein-Dor, Goodman, and Wolcott 2000).

For countries such as Bosnia, Georgia, and Indonesia, good ICT infra-structure supported strong democratic movements. For Azerbaijan and the Central African Republic, the lack of technology diffusion has allowed for deepening authoritarianism. For countries such as Benin, Eritrea, and Gambia, technology diffusion has not been particularly rapid, and democra-tization movements in these countries have had little success. Several of the states that did not go through political transitions are in crisis, where both war and institutional collapse make democratization and technology diffu-sion impossible.For explanatory purposes, these cases are irrelevant. Some countries have had very low levels of technology diffusion and became more democratic anyway. Information technologies probably have little to do with political change in Algeria, Comoros, and Liberia. Yet a causal argument cannot be neatly composed from this evidence alone. Ideally, the countries would be clearly distributed into two batches: a group with high levels of ICT diffusion that became more democratic over time; and a group with low levels of ICT diffusion that became more authoritarian or made little democratic progress. Unfortunately, real cases cannot be grouped so easily. Instead, there are many countries with high levels of technology diffusion that had little change in democratic institutions, and many countries with low levels of technology diffusion that had little change in authoritarian institutions. And there is a long list of countries that had only a one- or two-point improvement over time.

The goal of this chapter has been to introduce some of the complexities of studying the impact of new information technologies on political life in countries with large Muslim populations. Indexing countries by level of democratization and level of technology diffusion suggests that there might be a statistical model for explaining the variation of countries from hypothetical trend lines, but a theoretical argument for why democracy enhances technology diffusion or why technology diffusion enhances democracy is still needed. Treating countries by cross-case comparison allows for some theorizing along the way: any connection between information infrastructure and democratization is not just theorized, it is observed. A large-N quantitative approach, with its assumption of well-defined categories and populations and quest for the net effects of independent variables in linear models, is the least appropriate template for this research. Therefore, this argument will use one of the new alternatives available in the social sciences: analysis of relations among the set of countries with large Muslim populations experiencing political transitions and technology diffusion, between 1995 and the present.

Perhaps the best reason to proceed in a qualitative and comparative way is that the categories of "democracy" and "technology diffusion" are themselves aggregates and proxies for other measurable phenomena. Separate assessments could be done for different components that built the democratization index: how regulated or independent are the heads of state; how open and competitive is the process to replace the head of state; how regulated political participation is. Separate assessments could also be done for the different parts of a country's information infrastructure: mobile phones, internet users, internet hosts, personal computers, internet bandwidth, broadband internet subscribers. Researchers have assessed the role of mobile phones in executive turnover in Indonesia and Kyrgyzstan, the importance of websites for civil society groups in Bahrain and Turkey, and the restrictions on internet users in Saudi Arabia and Tunisia. To preserve the nuances of cross-case comparison while seeking generalizable knowledge, the argument in this book proceeds in a comparative manner. Moreover, the book is organized in chapters dedicated to types of political actors, largely because the single country studies and small set comparisons that form much of the knowledge base also make these causal distinctions. How does information infrastructure enhance or support democratic transitions? Answering this question with confidence in generalizable conclusions and being respectful of the diversity of experience among Muslim countries is the goal of this book.

Chapter 2

Lineages of the Digital State

Governments develop their national information infrastructure so as to improve the management capacity of the state and provide economic opportunities for businesses. Through strategic investments in public information infrastructure and policy reforms in the telecommunications sector, many governments hope to expand the consumer market for communications products and services, to encourage entrepreneurs in other sectors to start new businesses, and to make global innovations in science and engineering available in-country. Using ICTs to take advantage of these perceived benefits of globalization is a key priority for governments in countries with large Muslim communities, though at the same time, such governments work hard to prevent internet exposure from affecting public morals. Over the last fifteen years, the internet has become a a tool of governance.

In the 1970s and 1980s, many developing countries feared the impact of new information technologies. Some communist countries, such as Tanzania, simply banned computers; and some dictatorships, such as Libya, required that all computers, telephones, fax machines, and other communications devices be registered with the government. Even in the 1990s, some authoritarian countries, such as Saudi Arabia, were unwilling to allow private internet service providers. Ruling elites in many Muslim countries developed policies for monopolizing information technologies so that the state could better manage citizens and resources. Yet governments allocated significant amounts of money to ICTs to build their own administrative capacity, and they aggressively solicited multilateral lending agencies for computers, satellite systems, and other technology support. At the same time, private businesses and citizens were actively discouraged from importing new information technologies. Among government agencies, the revenue authority and human resources agency were usually the first to benefit from technology spending. They acquired commercial software for automating tax, import or personnel record keeping and sometimes designed software for their own bureaucratic needs. The key parastatals that accounted for significant amounts of state income—the telephone, cement, oil, and power utilities—were the next to acquire mainframes and microcomputers

(Danowitz, Nassef, and Goodman 1995). Increasingly, telecommunications licenses became a source of state revenue, though with international pressures for privatization, much of the rent from public resources such as the wireless spectrum ended up in private hands. Additionally, the new ICT capacity enabled the state to detect graft, measure organizational efficiency, and sometimes to make government records available to journalists and civil society actors. Both technologies and services were imported; there were few initiatives or incentives for local computer vendors, and little encouragement for the local capacity to repair technology, train IT workers, or design customized hardware and software applications.

An increasing amount of research is focused on development communication and the role that ICTs have in improving the capacity of the state to solve social problems and offer public services (Dunleavy 2006; Fountain 2001; West 2005). Evidence suggests that public health services, environmental impact assessments, agricultural research, distance education, and micro-credit loan services became significantly more effective when ICTs were employed (Edejer 2000; Grant 2000; Jimba 2000). Yet there has been significant variation in success between types of e-government projects. Those designed as service portals for citizens in countries where few citizens are online are not as successful as the portals designed in countries with large numbers of internet users; service portals designed for the internal use of government agencies generally have a positive impact (Akther, Onishi, and Kidokoro 2007; Macueve 2008; Waema 2009).

In addition to the specific goal of improving the logistics of development work, researchers often harbor a hope that ICTs will help developing countries leap-frog over some of the difficult political, cultural, and economic problems that developed countries have already overcome. Whereas developed countries have had to make significant infrastructure investments in wired telecommunications, for example, developing countries may be able to avoid this investment by building an infrastructure of wireless communication technologies (Butler 1999; James 2001). In democracies, there is some evidence that effective state services online breed trust and confidence among citizens in their government (Tolbert and Mossberger 2006; Welch, Hinnant, and Moon 2005). ICTs such as mobile phones, listservs, and intranets improve internal communications within and between branches of government, and the use of computers makes many government departments more efficient and better at record keeping.

Perhaps even more than the internet, policy makers in many developing countries associate mobile phone use with economic growth. In Egypt, 59 percent of the small businesses surveyed reported that mobile phone use was linked to increased profits, even when the cost of calls increased. Economic forecasters and industry advocates report that across Africa, countries with an average of 10 more mobile phones per 100 population between 1996 and 2003 had 0.59 percent higher GDP growth than an otherwise identical country. The causal connection is not as simple and unidirectional as this kind of modeling suggests, but such industry research findings get significant play across communities of government economists in the developing world (Vodaphone 2005). In Ethiopia, Ghana, Kenya, Mozambique, Nigeria, Tanzania, and Uganda, surveys of medium-sized enterprises in both the formal and informal sector report high returns on ICT investments (Esselaar et al. 2007). In Kuwait, Saudi Arabia, Turkey, and the United Arab Emirates (UAE), information technologies have supported the rise of Islamic banking products such as the Ijarah (leasing agreements), Murabaha (cost-plus or markup contracts), Musharaka (equity participation arrangements), and Mudharabah (profit-sharing contracts) (D'Orazio 2007).

Assessing the digital state in the Muslim world involves answering three important questions about how Muslim governments work to build the management capacity of state bureaucracy through information infrastructure: What information infrastructures are in place in nation-states with significant Muslim populations, and what is their capacity? What ICT policies have been put in place, and how do such policies contribute to technology diffusion or political transitions? Is it possible to distinguish the impact of information infrastructure investment, e-government services, and telecommunications policy reform on development?

ICT POLICIES IN THE MUSLIM WORLD

Research suggests that holding economic wealth constant, several key policy reforms in the telecommunications sector are among the most important causal conditions for technology adoption. Worldwide, many countries have sought to improve their information infrastructure through policy reform. Muslim countries are no exception. While some scholars argue that new technologies diffuse when there is a good foundation of publicly owned infrastructure and the state maintains supportive technical standards (Mendoza 2005; Howard 2007), others argue that new information technologies spread more quickly when there is limited government involvement in setting standards and investing in infrastructure. Information technologies spread in complex patterns and are shaped not only by engineers' assessments of technical advantage, but also by the needs of users and the design of the underlying infrastructure (Rogers 2003; Hughes 1983; Fischer 1992). Altogether, states have tried a wide range of public policy initiatives to achieve some combination of four outcomes: using ICTs to increase remittances coming into the country; using domestic ICT industries to spur economic development; using ICTs to control cultural life; and using ICTs to improve the effectiveness and efficiency of government bureaucracies.

Most of the research suggests that economic growth and regime type are associated with rapid technology adoption, but there is a debate over what role privatization might have in the adoption of new communication tools. Whereas early research into the digital divide found economic factors to outweigh others (Norris 2001), more recent research illustrates that political and social variables also contribute (Milner 2006; Howard and Mazaheri 2009). Wallsten (2005) found that regulatory regimes, such as agency independence and transparency, explained growth in the number of internet users and internet hosts in 45 countries in 2001. In contrast, for 1997–2001, internet use in 61 countries increased among countries that privatized their telecommunications provider, introduced competition for consumer telecommunications services, were democratic, and were core members of the world system (Guillén and Suarez 2005). Unfortunately, such quantitative modeling lacks parsimony, and the main point of consensus is that a country's degree of modernization explains its degree of internet use. The use of Western technologies, often with policy conditionalities currently imposed on developing countries, has complex political, economic, and cultural implications (Canclini 1996; Arunachalam 1999). Beyond the obvious logistical benefits of observing elections, documenting crimes against humanity, and providing disaster relief, these technologies are often used by challenger groups to project their political grievances onto the international stage (Cleaver 1998; Kalathil and Boas 2003).

For several decades, governments in the developing world, including Muslim countries, have been encouraged to reform their telecommunications sector through four primary reforms. By privatizing the national telecommunications provider, a government would sell its majority stake in the public information infrastructure, changing the mission from national service to investor profits. By legally separating the agency that regulates the telecommunications sector from both the service provider and the executive branch of government, governments would transfer public oversight from politicians to technical experts. Making the legal separation through constitutional changes, however, still allowed political leaders to control the regulatory authority by making political appointments and interfering with standards setting. Thus, many governments have also been pressured to meaningfully depoliticize their telecommunications agency by leaving appointments and decisions to technology experts. Finally, governments have been encouraged to liberalize the markets for consumer electronics and communications services by breaking the monopoly status of the national telecommunications provider and allowing competition between firms. Although other policy interventions are possible, these four are the most commonly chosen and the most often promoted by multilateral lending agencies (Howard 2007). To influence internet use, nation-states can develop comprehensive privacy policies that protect the rights of citizens to use information technologies.

Table 2.1 presents the policy reforms attempted by Muslim countries. There are four common reforms, and on their own or in combination they have had varied effects in different countries. By 2008, 26 countries had privatized the state telecommunications provider, 52 had separated the regulatory authority from the executive branch, only 18 had meaningfully depoliticized the regulatory authority, and 36 had liberalized their commercial communications markets. Of the 75 countries with significant Muslim communities, only 5 had comprehensive privacy policies by 2007. Only 36 countries were openly providing information on the rules and fees for using the public broadcast spectrum, and who was using which frequencies. As might be expected, countries with only a few means of reforming their telecommunications industries in recent decades have ended up with lower levels of technology diffusion, while many of the countries attempting several reform strategies in the late 1990s had average or high levels of technology diffusion. For many countries in the developing world, it is difficult to learn about official government policies online. But it is very revealing that a large number of countries where it can be confirmed that no policy reforms were attempted have had little improvement in the democratic nature of their regimes.[1] These reforms have diverse consequences: mobile phones become widely available in many cities, long-distance calls become cheaper than ever before, and many local entrepreneurs have started new businesses in this sector.

The number of countries pursuing these types of reforms has increased. Policy reform in Muslim countries has outpaced that of other developing countries. By 1990, only five small countries had attempted any telecommunications reforms: Benin, Brunei, Liberia, Mauritius, and Niger. By 2000, more than half of the Muslim countries had reconfigured this sector, and by 2007 fully three-quarters of the countries had tried at least two types of policy reform. The rest of the countries in the developing world have lagged behind. By 2007, only two-thirds of 134 developing, non-Muslim nations had enacted some policy reform. Telecommunications reform is not only outpacing the developing world, but most of these reforms were enacted after 2000.

However, Muslim governments tend to prefer some types of policy reform over others. Three are worth noting. First, Muslim governments have been more inclined to liberalize the local markets for ICT goods and services rather than meaningfully depoliticizing the regulation of the media and communications sector. Across the developing world, 40 percent of countries have liberalized domestic communications markets, but only 20 percent have effectively depoliticized the appointment of regulators. In most countries—even wealthy countries such as the United States—such offices remain political.

Second, Muslim countries are less likely than other developing countries to experiment with privatizing the national telecommunications provider. Whereas 42 percent of 132 other developing countries have privatized the national phone company, only 30 percent of 60 Muslim countries have done so. There are two plausible reasons for this. Privatization is encouraged, if not demanded, by multilateral lending agencies. Many poor countries may only borrow from agencies such as the EBRD and the IMF if they meet specific policy reform conditions; in recent years it is common for these agencies to make the privatization of profitable state assets a loan condition. Muslim states with oil revenues are able to secure loans in private bond markets and are not dependent on multilateral lending agencies. Many of the oil-producing states identified in Table 2.1 have done little to bring transparency to their telecommunications sector. In addition, many Islamic political leaders see the national telecommunications provider as a cultural asset and a culturally strategic resource. Although privatizing the state telecommunications provider does not automatically mean surrendering regulatory oversight, it does mean surrendering control of day-to-day operations.

Third, Muslim countries at all stages of democratization are much more likely than other countries to separate the regulatory authority from the executive branch of government. Whereas 68 percent of Muslim countries have made their telecommunications regulator independent, only 58 percent of other developing countries have implemented this reform. Indeed, this is the most popular policy reform, probably because it is easy for governments to change the formal administrative lines of authority than to end the informal structures of patronage and co-option. Moreover, since many Muslim countries are constitutional monarchies or authoritarian regimes, governments in these countries often have a easier time of cosmetic constitutional changes than energy democracies where such changes are contested.

Interesting patterns in telecommunications reform in the Muslim world emerge with comparative analysis. In recent years, compared to the rest of the developing world, Muslim countries have more aggressively enacted multiple types of policy reform. However, they are less likely to embark on full privatization and more likely to give the media and communications regulator some limited independence. While most wealthy countries have implemented most of these reforms, depoliticizing regulatory authorities remains difficult. In the vast majority of Muslim countries, the regulator of the telecommunications industry has been given some independence from the executive branch. But governments in the Muslim world are much more reluctant to fully privatize the national telecommunications company; only 30 percent of Muslim governments have done this.

Critically, it is not always possible to determine which types of reform have an impact on technology diffusion and democratization. While several high-profile indexing projects, by the International Telecommunications Union and Davos World Economic Forum, reveal simple correlations between indices of economic wealth and policy reform, there is limited evidence that implementing such policy reforms either causes economic growth or explains the variation in economic growth patterns around the world.

Table 2.1 compares the ways in which different countries have sought to develop the conditions of their telecommunications sector. In part, this has been done by making telecommunications markets more transparent and accessible to industry and consumers. It has also meant developing a suite of policies encouraging the use of new information technologies, including explicit privacy policies or open rules about spectrum allocation.

Separating the regulatory authority from direct control by the executive branch has been the most common reform, but many of the countries that initiated multiple reforms also belong in the set of countries that experienced a democratic transition. This reform in particular was a common condition for receiving loans from multilateral lending agencies in the 1990s, so many of these countries committed to this reform before many ICTs were commercially available in their countries. And in an important way, this reform is one of the easiest of the four to enact—a straightforward constitutional change can remove an explicit line of administrative authority without actually removing the behind-the-scenes political authority over the telecommunications industry. While legally making the telecommunications regulator independent is an important step, it is interesting to note that the number of countries who have effectively depoliticized the telecommunications regulator is always less than the number of countries who have made cosmetic legal changes. Very few countries with above average levels of technology diffusion have privatized their national telecommunications provider. In terms of internet policy, only two countries in this group have developed comprehensive privacy policies, and only six countries allow unrestricted internet access. The countries that were most aggressive with telecommunications reform—and did not restrict internet use—were pursuing specific outcomes.

Table 2.1: Conditions—Telecommunications Reform and ICT Policies in the Muslim World, 1960–2008

Country	Privati- zation	Regulatory Separation	Regulatory Depolitici- zation	Market Liberali- zation	Privacy Policy	Spectrum Policy
Transition						
Albania	×	1998	1998	2000	○	✓
Algeria	..	2001	..	..	●	×
Bahrain	×	1996	×	2004	○	×
Bosnia	×	1999	1999	2006	●	✓
Comoros	1997	..	..	..	..	..
Djibouti	..	1998	..	..	..	..
Egypt	..	1998	..	..	○	✓
Georgia	..	2000	×	1994	●	✓
Ghana	1996	1996	1996	1997	○	×
Indonesia	×	1993	×	2003	○	✓
Kenya	2004	1999	1999	1999	○	✓
Kuwait	×	×	×	×	..	×
Kyrgyzstan	..	1997	×	2003	..	×
Lebanon	×	2007	..	×	..	..
Liberia	1962	2006	..	1962	..	×
Macedonia	2000	2005	2005	..	●	
Maldives	×	2003	×	2003	..	..
Mauritania	2001	1999	1999	2001	..	✓
Montenegro	2005	2001	..	×	..	×
Niger	1963	..	..	1963	..	..
Nigeria	1999	1992	1992	2004	✓	..
Senegal	1997	1997	..	2004	..	✓
Sierra Leone	..	..	..	..	..	..
Suriname	×	2004	×	1999	..	×
Tanzania	2001	1994	1994	2005	○	✓
Uganda	1998	1997	1997	1998	●	✓
Entrenchment						
Bangladesh	×	2002	×	1998	○	✓
Benin	1963	..	..	1963	..	
Bulgaria	2004	1998	×	2003	●	✓
Cyprus	..	2001	×	2003	○	✓
Guinea-Bissau	1989	1999	..	..	..	
India	..	1997	1997	1994	●	✓
Israel	×	×	×	×	●	..
Malawi	2006	1998	1998	1999	○	
Malaysia	..	1998	×	1996	○	✓
Mali	..	..	..	2002	○	
Mauritius	1968	1988	1998	1968	●	
Mozambique	..	1992	..	..	○	
Turkey	2005	2000	×	2004	●	✓

Authoritarian

	Privatization	Regulatory separation	Regulatory depoliticization	Market liberalization	Privacy policy	Spectrum
Azerbaijan	✗	✗	✗	..	◉	✗
Brunei	✗	2003	1960	..	..	✗
Cameroon	..	1998	1998	..	..	
CAR	..	..	..	..	..	
Chad	..	1998	..	..	○	
Eritrea	..	1998	..	..	..	
Ethiopia	..	1996	1996	..	◉	
Gambia	..	..	..	..	○	
Guinea	1996	..	..	..	..	
Iran	✗	2003	✗	..	..	
Jordan	2006	1995	1995	2005	◉	✓
Kazakhstan	✗	2003	✗	2004	..	..
Libya	..	..	..	..	..	
Morocco	2001	1997	..	..	◉	
Oman	✗	2002	✗	✗	..	✓
Pakistan	✗	1996	1996	2004	●	✓
Qatar	..	..	..	✗	..	✓
Russia	✗	✗	✗	✗	◉	..
Saudi Arabia	✗	2001	✗	✗	..	✓
Singapore	2001	1992	1992	1997	○	✓
Sudan	1994	1996	..	2004	..	
Syria	✗	✗	✗	✗	..	✗
Tajikistan	✗	✗	✗	..	○	..
Togo	..	1999	..	..	..	
Tunisia	..	1995	..	2002	○	
Turkmenistan	✗	✗	✗	✗	..	..
UAE	✗	2004	..	2004	○	✓
Uzbekistan	✗	1997	✗	✗	○	..
Yemen	✗	✗	✗	✗	..	✓

Crisis

	Privatization	Regulatory separation	Regulatory depoliticization	Market liberalization	Privacy policy	Spectrum
Afghanistan	2002	2003	✗	2003	..	..
Burkina Faso	1998	1999	..	..	..	
Côte d'Ivoire	1997	1995	1997	1996	..	
Iraq	✗	✗	✗	✗	..	..
Somalia	1995	..	..	1995	..	
West Bank & Gaza	..	..	..	..	..	
Western Sahara	..	..	..	..	..	

Sources: Based on author's calculations from multiple sources: Henisz, Zelner, and Guillen 2005; Howard 2007; Banisar 2006; Howard and World Information Access Project 2007; Sandvig 2008.

Notes: Missing data means evidence could not be found for the country. Privatization, regulatory separation, regulatory depoliticization or market liberalization indicated by the year of that reform, or as having not occurred by 2007 (✗). Privacy policy indicated as being non-existent (○), pending (◉), or comprehensive (●) in 2007. Spectrum allocation policy indicated (✓) indicated if the state was making information on spectrum regulations, assignments, and fees publicly available, and indicated (✗) if it was not doing this by 2007. Acronyms provided for the Central African Republic (CAR) and United Arab Emirates (UAE).

GOVERNMENTS ONLINE IN THE MUSLIM WORLD

With the myriad forms of political organization in the Muslim world come different ways of using new information technologies to make governance more efficient, provide more services to citizens, and give government agencies an online interface. In some countries, using ICTs to improve state capacity has resulted in greater organizational transparency, in others it has resulted in improved capacities for censorship and social control. The use of ICTs by state bureaucracies in the Muslim world varies with the forms of governance in place, but it is not simply that more authoritarian states use information technologies for more forms of social control. One of the more consistent outcomes of policy reforms has been in encouraging government agencies to develop digital infrastructures for their own organization and service delivery.

The world's 1.4 billion Muslims live within a range of political systems: democracies, emerging democracies, constitutional monarchies, Islamic republics, dictatorships, and crisis states. Each type has slightly different approaches to the development of ICTs for state capacity and the regulation of public ICT use. Countries with large internet user populations have been more interested in committing resources to new ways of interacting with government. States develop e-democracy tools partly in response to demand, but the process of making these technology investments varies by regime type. These different types of governments have taken different approaches to investing in information infrastructure, using the infrastructure for economic development, and designing e-government services and telecommunications policies.

Table 2.2 compares the informational infrastructure of states in the Muslim world, for five important branches of government. Almost every nation-state has these five major branches of government: a revenue authority to collect taxes and manage state finances; an executive branch to support the head of state; a legislative branch that contributes (sometimes modestly) to the formation and enactment of laws; a foreign affairs department responsible for diplomatic relations with other states and for serving citizens abroad; and a judiciary for interpreting and applying the law. Whether or not these major government agencies have websites indicates how each regime type values information infrastructure. States are grouped by regime type, their type of political transition, and their level of technology diffusion. In addition, the overall averages for states in the Muslim world are compared with the averages for other developing, non-Muslim countries, the averages for wealthy developed countries, and the global average. Comparing evidence about which types of regimes develop websites for which domains of governance reveals much about how political leaders value information infrastructure and its role in building state capacity.

While many government branches have an online information infrastructure, not all these agencies have the capacity to actually manage their own infrastructure—they rely on commercial hosting services in other countries. Tracing the route that Internet Protocol Packets take reveals the location of the nation-state's informational assets.[2] For example, among the 24 emerging democracies in the Muslim World, 20 states have an online portal for their revenue authority, but half of these websites were actually hosted on servers in other countries. Hosting services in the United States, Canada, and Germany actually have the capacity to manage financial information for nation-states that do not have this capacity themselves. Mapping out which government agencies have websites and, subsequently, which government agencies have the capacity to maintain their own information infrastructure reveals the relative weight of priorities for different regimes, nations with different levels of institutionalized democracy, and different levels of technology diffusion. Perhaps the most wired of these states is Singapore, where 9 out of 10 people have had some transactionwith government over the internet, by SMS, an automated phone system or stand-alone information kiosk (Government of Singapore 2006).

This table also offers an evaluation of the kinds of e-government services developed in each country as of 2008 (West 2008). About a dozen countries in this comparison set offer no publications on their government websites, nor offer access to large databases. The vast majority of governments do offer these things, and through the internet or mobile phones, government-citizen transactions can include applying for official documents like passports, registering for unemployment insurance, paying taxes, or applying for government jobs. Thirty of the seventy countries for which there is data offer none of these things. But forty countries do, and it is in these countries that citizen expectations for government responsiveness and transparency are on the rise, and it is here that governments are making efforts to meet these expectations.

Democratic Transitions

In contrast, transition states have much more tentative exercises in representative governance: decisions on difficult public policy questions are not always considered by the wider public or in legislatures; civil society groups may be small, inexperienced, or excluded from the political process; and the ruling elites must sometimes rely on military authority to maintain stability. In Egypt, for example, only the lower levels of government have competitive elections, and significant opposition groups are excluded from the election process. These countries are administered by strongmen who make most of the top administrative appointments and curtail many democratic freedoms in the name of protecting democracy. Several countries that call themselves Islamic republics, such as Pakistan and Mauritania, are such in name only;

Table 2.2: Government Offices Online in the Muslim World, 2008

Country	Revenue	Executive	Legislature	Foreign Affairs	Justice	E-Government Services
Transition						
Albania	●	●	●	○	●	□
Algeria	○	●	○	○	○	□
Bahrain	●	○	○	●	●	■
Bosnia	●	●	●	●	○	□
Comoros	○	○	○	○	○	□
Djibouti	●	●	●	○	○	■
Egypt	○	●	●	○	●	■
Georgia	●	●	●	○	●	□
Ghana	○	○	○	○	○	■
Indonesia	●	●	●	○	●	□
Kenya	○	○	○	○	○	□
Kuwait	●	●	○	●	●	■
Kyrgyzstan	●	●	●	●	●	□
Lebanon	●	●	●	○	○	□
Liberia	○	○	○	○	○	■
Macedonia	●	●	●	●	●	..
Maldives	●	●	○	○	●	□
Mauritania	○	○	○	○	○	□
Montenegro	●	●	●	..	●	□
Niger	○	●	●	○	○	□
Nigeria	○	○	○	○	○	■
Senegal	○	○	○	○	○	□
Sierra Leone	○	○	○	○	○	□
Suriname	○	●	○	○	●	□
Tanzania	●	●	●	○	○	□
Uganda	○	○	●	○	○	□
Entrenchment						
Bangladesh	●	●	○	○	●	□
Benin	●	●	●	●	●	□
Bulgaria	●	●	●	●	●	□
Cyprus	●	●	●	●	●	■
Guinea-Bissau	○	○	○	○	○	□
India	●	●	●	●	●	■
Israel	●	●	●	●	●	□
Malawi	●	○	○	○	○	□
Malaysia	●	●	○	●	●	■
Mali	○	○	○	○	○	□
Mauritius	○	○	○	○	○	■
Mozambique	●	○	●	○	○	□
Turkey	●	●	●	●	●	■

Authoritarian

Azerbaijan	●	●	●	O	●	□
Brunei	●	●	●	●	●	■
Cameroon	●	O	O	O	O	□
CAR	O	O	O	O	O	□
Chad	O	O	O	O	O	□
Eritrea	○	○	○	○	○	□
Ethiopia	●	○	O	O	O	□
Gambia	O	O	O	●	O	◪
Guinea	●	●	O	○	●	□
Iran	O	●	O	●	O	◪
Jordan	●	●	●	●	●	■
Kazakhstan	●	●	●	●	●	■
Libya	○	●	O	O	○	□
Morocco	O	●	●	O	●	◪
Oman	●	●	●	O	●	◪
Pakistan	O	O	O	●	O	■
Qatar	O	●	●	●	○	■
Russia	●	●	●	●	●	◪
Saudi Arabia	●	●	●	O	●	■
Singapore	●	●	●	●	●	■
Sudan	O	●	●	O	O	□
Syria	●	●	●	●	○	■
Tajikistan	○	O	O	●	○	□
Togo	○	O	●	O	○	□
Tunisia	O	O	O	O	O	◪
Turkmenistan	○	●	○	○	○	□
UAE	●	●	●	●	..	■
Uzbekistan	●	●	●	O	●	□
Yemen	●	●	●	O	●	□

Crisis

Afghanistan	O	O	O	O	O	◪
Burkina Faso	●	●	●	●	O	□
Iraq	○	O	O	O	○	◪
Ivory Coast	O	O	●	O	O	■
Somalia	○	O	O	○	○	□
West Bank & Gaza	..	..	..	.	..	..
Western Sahara	..	..	..	..	..	..

Sources: Based on author's calculations from multiple sources: Howard and World Information Access Project 2008; West 2008.

Notes: Route tracing conducted in March 2007. A URL was sought for each type of government office, and then if an URL was obtained, the IP address was traced to find a physical location. Government agency websites are indicated as being not found (○), found but not hosted in-country (O), or found and hosted in-country (●). E-Government Services indicated as poor (□), modest (◪), or good (■) in 2007.

they are more accurately described as emerging democracies. Some countries, such as Kyrgyzstan and Georgia, have political cultures with increasingly democratic norms, but remain functionally democratic at the pleasure of their military leaders. When political gridlock is imminent or Islamist interests become too powerful, military leaders have been known to weigh in and adjust the course of national politics.

Transition democracies often have mixed administrative systems that simultaneously constrain political dialogue and yet remain sensitive to public opinion. In recent years, governments in countries such as Morocco and Tanzania have become more transparent. In contrast, countries such as Egypt and Pakistan show signs of moving in the opposite direction. By definition, transition democracies have made important changes to the way politics is conducted, but some aspects of political culture may still reflect older autocratic traditions. Some 32 percent of the global Muslim population, around 459 million people, live in 26 polities that have recently shown signs of democratic transition.[3] Many government agencies in these types of regimes have websites, but overall only 41 percent of government portals from these countries are hosted in-country.

In the rest of the developing world, the first government bureaucracies to benefit from new information technologies are the revenue authorities—these states always invest in technologies that improve their ability to collect and manage financial resources. But among strong and emerging democracies, election administrators are often also the beneficiaries of ICT programs. Modern elections are a technology intensive enterprise, and ICTs in emerging democracies are often used to register voters, collect and count votes, and report results.

In these states, the internet has become a tool for economic development: government agencies encourage small entrepreneurs to develop new technology businesses and telecenters. It is common for these types of states to make investments in public ICT infrastructure, rather than deregulating the telecommunications sector and leaving its development to the vagaries of the market and international investors. Such states also tend to be dependent on foreign aid to subsidize internet access through public access points in libraries and community centers. For emerging democracies, the information infrastructure of the legislative branch is a priority. Overall, 84 percent of the major ministries in emerging nations have a website, but only 34 percent of these agencies can maintain their information infrastructure in-country, the lowest among regime types.

Democratic Entrenchment

At the most democratic end of the spectrum are strong, stable polities where citizens participate in political discussion and run for office, the executive branch is composed of people who are elected, and there are clear constitutional checks on the executive branch. Some 27 percent of the global Muslim population, around 392 million people, live in 13 countries where democratic institutions and practices are increasingly entrenched. In the established democracies of the Muslim world, the majority of voters and political candidates are Muslim, and elections are competitive and regular events. International monitoring agencies usually judge these countries' elections to be free and fair, and changes in political leadership do not involve violence or require military intervention. There are several examples of strong, stable democracies in the Muslim world. Bangladesh, Indonesia, Malaysia, and Turkey have held successful elections with candidates and parties that represent diverse ideological perspectives and different positions on the role of Islam in the state. However, even in established democracies, political leaders must sometimes negotiate—and even share power—with military commanders who feel the need to guard the secular state, Islamic fundamentalists who command mass appeal and seek greater involvement in governance, and student activists who have their own policy perspectives and special political clout among young Muslim populations. Just as in the most advanced democracies, established Muslim democracies have an active civil society, with public debates about the distribution of wealth, the role of religion in the state, the concentration of power, and the impoverishment of minorities. For the most part, civic conversations about these difficult issues takes place through proven political processes, such as elections and referenda, and in accepted political institutions, such as legislatures and courts.

Democracies prioritize their executive and legislative branches for ICT resources, and their revenue authorities are most likely to receive significant investment in domestic information infrastructure. Established democracies also use the internet as a tool of economic development, but compared to other types of regimes, these states are much more tolerant of political expression online and are less concerned about public exposure to Western culture. Digital information infrastructures are paid for by states but developed through private firms, though the states often initiate public-private partnerships to extend connectivity and to encourage household technology use. Turkey and Egypt in particular have had success with these kinds of partnership (Bennett and Howard 2007).

Authoritarian Regimes

In authoritarian regimes, the competition for political positions is restricted by political elites, chief executives are chosen through a regularized process within a small community of power brokers, and there are few constitutional checks on the executive branch. Autocratic regimes sharply restrict or suppress competitive political participation, there are few institutionalized constraints on ruling elites, and often (though not always) these ruling political elites exercise control over cultural and economic activity.

In Central Asia, North Africa, and parts of Southeast Asia, political strongmen run personal fiefdoms that extract wealth from their country's natural resources and labor. Such wealth enriches the dictators and ruling elites and is used to help the state co-opt political leaders or oppress social movements, as needed. In many of these countries, religious practices are simply illegal. Dictators may claim that banning Islamic observance is part of modernization; however, the real objective is ensuring the separation of church and state so that the authority of the state is clearly centralized and embodied in the dictator. In such countries, new media technologies are closely regulated, if not banned or directly owned by ruling families or administered by the state. This effectively prevents other sources of cultural and political authority from any mechanism of disseminating news, information, or other cultural content. Over the last 15 years, 29 regimes that have neither become entrenched democracies nor transitioned toward democracy in some substantive way: under these regimes, 35 percent of the global Muslim population, some 509 million people, live difficult lives.[4]

Among dictatorships, the executive branch is prioritized for ICT resources. Justice and revenue authorities get limited investments, largely because state capacity and transparency in these domains is anathema to the ruling elite. To contrast democratic and authoritarian states, democracies are more likely to invest in internet infrastructure for their bureaucracies but less likely to want to build that technology capacity in-country. Yet in many dictatorships, especially those with significant natural resource wealth, the state has little incentive to build a national information infrastructure, much less one that can improve state capacity to serve citizens. These states employ some means of censoring internet use, but it is more often the paucity of infrastructure and the culture of surveillance that effectively discourages the use of new information technologies. The national ownership of broadcast media and reluctant construction of digital media infrastructure allow dictators to maintain control of the means of political conversation. Whereas the authoritarian ruling elites in Islamic republics and constitutional monarchies use ICTs to manage a broad range of cultural interactions, in many dictatorships ICTs are used to specifically restrict political opposition and organization. The ICT infrastructure that is available is often the only conduit for news about the outside world, the only means of exchanging information with diasporic communities, and the primary tool for political organizing. The markets for consumer electronics tend to be small or nonexistent. Until very recently, most shipments of computer hardware arrived in Central Asia's post-Soviet dictatorships on overland truck routes from Moscow or Tehran.

While countries such as Saudi Arabia and Bahrain have legal traditions similar to those of the Islamic republics, in these countries the aristocrats prevail: ruling families rather than clerics provide the central guidance to the state. As with all monarchies, the ruling families have legitimacy as long as they appear to be working for the best interests of their subjects and protect the Islamic culture that bequests their power. The constitutions of these countries legitimize the centralization of political authority in ruling families, but often also empower legislative bodies and courts that serve the executive branch but prevent complete dictatorship. The power of political appointment and veto authority usually resides with a handful of princes or emirs, and through the state these political leaders often control significant oil and natural gas wealth.

Like the Islamic republics, the constitutional monarchies have been slow to allow internet access for their citizenry. The state bureaucracies themselves use ICTs for propaganda purposes and to endorse interpretations of the Koran that reinforce their hold on power. Saudi Arabia in particular moved quickly to develop online portals for key Islamic texts, spiritual practices, and holy landmarks. Many of the ruling families retain tight control over the apparatus of state, especially through control of media and telecommunications systems. But unlike the clearly authoritarian states, these ruling families do have to work under some constitutional checks and balances.

In terms of regime type, the constitutional monarchies seem to put significant resources into the internet portals for their government ministries. Most branches of government are online, and for the most part these states have built up their own capacity to host their own information infrastructure. Evaluating 45 government agencies—5 branches of government from 9 constitutional monarchies—reveals that 40 are online. Moreover, the vast majority of these are hosted in-country, suggesting that the constitutional monarchies are the regime type with the most comprehensive, national information infrastructures.

Islamic republics are governed by Sharia law, and while several countries are Islamic republics in name, Iran is perhaps the best example of one. Just as France and its former colonies are administered by the legal traditions of the Napoleonic Code, and England and its former colonies are administered by the legal traditions of Common Law, the government of Iran practices interpretations of Sharia law. Republics are usually defined as states that protect and preserve individual liberties and reject governance by an aristocratic class. While the Islamic republics do not give individual liberties a high priority, they have eliminated aristocratic rule in favor of governance through the spiritual wisdom of mullahs.

In these states, new information technologies are heavily regulated and used by the state as a means of spreading propaganda. Internet access is heavily controlled and cultural content heavily censored: foreign news sites are often blocked. Perhaps in response to these restrictions, most of these countries have active blogging communities. Online cultural tools that are beyond regime control and independent of the paltry domestic information infrastructure, such as YouTube and Flikr, are popular. Diasporic communities of Syrians and Persians—living in Los Angeles, New York, Toronto, and London—have long been sources of news content that contradicts government sources and cultural content with more liberal and Western values. Radio and television programs produced overseas have rarely been available in-country, but this is changing with ICTs that allow digital content to cross platforms. Moreover, mobile phones and the internet allow some of this content to actually be produced in-country. These ICTs also allow news and cultural content production from unofficial sources within these countries, resulting in multiple perspectives on contemporary events: political views from ruling elites as expressed through state media; critical responses from dispossessed political voices in the Western diaspora; and underground critiques of both ruling elites and Western diaspora from critical voices in-country.

Crisis States

Most functioning regimes in the Muslim world fall into the three types described so far. There are several countries, however, that are in the midst of chaotic political transitions and turmoil. Some countries are being ravaged by civil war, or have been destabilized by neighboring countries, while others have been consistently unable to form a state bureaucracy. In some cases, governance is temporary and fleeting, or limited to the territory surrounding large cities. Crisis states are labeled such if foreign military powers have disrupted local governance structures, if the country is in a period of interregnum or anarchy with no apparent lawful governance, or if the country has no clear political leader. Social revolutions can bring about the collapse of central political authority and a fundamental transformation in the norms of governance. Sometimes social revolutions change the character of government without actually collapsing the state. But often there are transitional years in which the institutions of governance are particularly fragile, and the state is in crisis. Afghanistan, Iraq, and Somalia are certainly examples of countries in crisis, where the government is not capable of ensuring security for citizens or regular provision of public services. Six percent of the global Muslim population, some 86 million people, live in seven regimes that are best described as crisis states.[5] States in crisis have been largely incapable of extending their management capacity through information infrastructure and have less domestic capacity to maintain such infrastructure for their government offices.

Some 86 million people live in crisis states with nominal and ineffective governments and have experienced revolution, civil war, invasion, or natural disasters. Basic human needs are so wanting that ICT policies are only important inasmuch as they impact the work of aid agencies working on complex humanitarian disasters. Even though such states barely have the capacity to maintain an informational infrastructure, these technologies are vital to nascent political life. The information technologies available are often used by journalists who report events to the international community; by UN aid workers who observe elections, investigate human rights abuses, and conduct peacekeeping activities; and by members of civil society desperate to reconstruct their political institutions. Just as important, new technologies allow diasporic communities to follow crises at home.

Other Levels of Comparison

Across several regime types, wiring up the revenue authority and executive branch of government seems to be a priority, while ministries of justice are the lowest priority. By comparison, crisis states have paltry information infrastructure, constitutional monarchies the best.

There are interesting patterns in the way states in the Muslim world invest in internet infrastructure for their administrative branches. At the same time, there are important points of contrast between the digital state in the Muslim world, other developing states, and the wealthy states. The "developed world" is a term often reserved for the 24 high-income members of the Organisation for Economic Co-operation and Development (OECD). The "developing world" refers to the low- and middle-income countries, along with high-income countries who have unique economic profiles with oil wealth or large economics, but are not members of the OECD.[6] Wealthy countries can maintain a public digital infrastructure, regulate the telecommunications industry with reasonable and consistent policies, and promote high rates of technology diffusion. In comparison with the developed world, of course, the ICT investments of all developing countries seem modest. Almost all OECD member states have almost all of their government agencies online. Non-Muslim developing nations seem to be making different kinds of strategic investments in information infrastructure. Non-Muslim nation-states are more likely to invest in improving the efficiency of revenue authorities, and more likely to develop their own infrastructure for foreign affairs and justice branches of government.

By 2007, all five types of government agencies in all developed countries had e-government services of some kind, and all were hosted in-country. On several occasions, these wealthy countries even had mirror websites in the United States. Not only do wealthy countries have the capacity to maintain their own information infrastructure, but these government agencies attract so much use by citizens that additional hosting services are required.

The priorities that different kinds of Muslim states have for their own informational capacities are reinforced by the ICT policies these states develop to encourage—or discourage—ICT use by their own citizens. Whether government agencies have been equipped with websites to provide information, organize public records, and publicize policy documents is a good proxy for the overall informational capacity of the state. Along with investing in the information infrastructure of government agencies, many political leaders have used telecommunications policy as a way of shaping the development of their information societies. What are the various tools of policy reform in the Muslim world, when are they used, and what have they achieved?

OUTCOMES: REMITTANCES, ICT-LED GROWTH, AND STATE CAPACITY

States in the Muslim world have used telecommunications policy to develop different kinds of information societies. Table 2.3 compares the outcomes from the various policy strategies that governments have pursued. Data on remittances per capita are given for states where using ICTs for remittances has been an important policy objective. For many of the poorest countries, and those with a large diaspora, the state has encouraged ICT use as a way of increasing connections to family and friends who supply remittances. Such remittances can be a significant proportion of a country's income, so states will encourage programs that make it easy to send funds from overseas over communication networks. Keeping these networks open and unrestricted has significantly increased the amount of remittances being wired home each year. Countries with significant oil revenues are less dependent on remittances and have been less active in encouraging their populations to maintain overseas contacts with friends and family. Some states have also sought to develop their local software and hardware industries, with varying levels of success. Data on exports of computer and information services are given for countries where the state has sought to provide some incentives for this economic sector.

State capacity is a measure of the quality of public service provision, the quality of bureaucracy, the competence of public servants, and the independence of the civil service from political pressures. Several international governmental agencies have ways of measuring the ability of governments to effectively deliver public services and make policy, through metrics for the efficiency and impartiality of the civil service and the quality of public infrastructure and the bureaucratic framework. Indeed, the capacity of the state to identify and meet public policy goals requires a civil service that is independent from political pressures and well trained to formulate and implement policy. Today, all of these aspects of state capacity depend on an information infrastructure that allows for competent record keeping and channels of communication between government offices. By combining data from 2000—when many governments began developing national ICT strategies—and today, Table 2.3. offers comparative detail on how effective each national government is currently, and how much improvement there has been over time. In some countries, especially the Islamic republics, constitutional monarchies, and dictatorships, improvements in bureaucratic efficiency also result in more effective management of culture and communication.

CONCLUSION: WIRED STATES

New information technologies are playing a significant role in public sector management, even in the least-developed Muslim countries. There are patterns in the ways that governments in the Muslim world have used technologies such as the internet to extend their own state capacity, as well as the ways that these governments regulate public technology use. The diffusion index developed in the introduction enabled a ranking of countries by ICT diffusion, weighted for economic performance. This index sorted countries into three groups: those with less ICT capacity than expected, given their economic productivity; those with about the ICT capacity expected, given their economic productivity; and those that surpass expectations with a surprising amount of ICT capacity. In this chapter I have made a comparative analysis of the informational infrastructure of all countries with large Muslim communities and reviewed the impact of policy reform on remittances, ICT-led economic growth, and state capacity. I conclude that telecommunications reforms have set the causal conditions for some outcomes. Chief of these—from the point of view of state capacity—are the rise in remittances, improvements in government information infrastructure, and the overall ability of the state bureaucracy to service citizens. Although states often seek economic growth from a home-grown ICT sector, this outcome is less frequent. Countries that have neither invested in e-government services, built their capacity to host their own government websites, nor modernized their telecommunications policies have relatively fewer ICT resources—even if their economies are booming.

Comparing the evolution of e-government in Muslim countries has uncovered the different ways that political elites negotiate the perceived benefits and risks of developing information infrastructures. Burkhart and Older (2003) call this the "dictator's dilemma" of technology-led economic

Table 2.3: Outcomes—Remittances, ICT-led Growth and State Capacity, 2010

Country	Remittances	ICT-led Growth	State Capacity	ICT and IP Policy Effectiveness
		Transition		
Albania	517	1	■, ▲	..
Algeria	162	..	■, ▲	□
Bahrain	..	..	■, ▼	■
Bosnia	504	..	■, ▼	□
Comoros	119	..	□, ▼	..
Djibouti	..	..	□, ▼	..
Egypt	45	23	■, ▼	■
Georgia	328	..	■, ▲	□
Ghana	37	..	■, ▼	□
Indonesia	17	..	■, ×	■
Kenya	..	0	..	□
Kuwait	..	..	■, ×	..
Kyrgyzstan	160	1	■, ×	..
Lebanon	1,496	0	■, ▼	..
Liberia	51	..	□, ▲	..
Macedonia	253	5	■, ▲	□
Maldives	..	..	■, ▼	..
Mauritania	31	..	■, ▼	..
Montenegro	5,319	..	■, ▲	..
Niger	16	0	□, ▲	..
Nigeria	40	..	□, ▲	□
Senegal	53	0	■, ▼	..
Sierra Leone	27	..	□, ▲	..
Suriname	718	..	■, ▼	..
Tanzania	8	0	■, ×	□
Uganda	21	4	■, ▼	□
		Entrenchment		
Bangladesh	54	5	■, ▼	□
Benin	33	..	■, ▼	..
Bulgaria	164	15	■, ▲	□
Cyprus	..	86	■, ▲	□
Guinea-Bissau	..	..	□, ▲	..
India	22	11,366	■, ×	■
Israel	..	3,657	■, ▲	■
Malawi	7	..	■, ×	□
Malaysia	95	216	■, ▲	■
Mali	62	0	■, ▲	□
Mauritius	285	9	■, ▼	□
Mozambique	27	0	■, ▼	□
Turkey	105	..	■, ▲	□

Azerbaijan	230	..	□, ▲	..
Brunei	..	..	■, ▼	..
Cameroon	15	..	□, ▼	..
CAR	17	..	□, ▼	..
Chad	14	..	□, ▼	□
Eritrea	90	0	□, ▼	..
Ethiopia	8	0	◨, ▲	□
Gambia	52	..	◨, ▼	◨
Guinea	29	0	□, ▼	..
Iran	31	..	◨, ▼	..
Jordan	443	..	■, ▼	■
Kazakhstan	327	1	◨, ✕	..
Libya	22	..	□, ▲	..
Morocco	181	..	▲, ▼	■
Oman	..	..	■, ▼	..
Pakistan	38	34	◨, ▼	□
Qatar	..	..	■, ▼	..
Russia	98	175	◨, ▲	□
Saudi Arabia	..	..	■, ▼	..
Singapore	..	334	■, ✕	■
Sudan	20	0	□, ▲	..
Syria	36	50	□, ✕	..
Tajikistan	146	0	□, ▲	..
Togo	25	1	□, ✕	..
Tunisia	152	19	■, ▼	■
Turkmenistan	70	..	□, ✕	..
UAE	..	..	■, ▲	■
Uzbekistan	105	..	◨, ▲	..
Yemen	37	..	□, ▼	..

Afghanistan	78	..	□, ✕	..
Burkina Faso	35	0	◨, ▼	..
Côte d'Ivoire	118	..	□, ▼	..
Iraq	16	2	□, ▼	..
Somalia	87	..	□, ▲	..
West Bank & Gaza	305	..	□, ▼	..
Western Sahara	..	..		..

Sources: Based on author's calculations from multiple sources: International Fund for Agricultural Development 2007; Banisar 2006; UNCTAD 2005; Kaufmann, Kraay, and Mastruzzi 2008.

Notes: Remittances given per capita in 2007. ICT-led growth given as exports of computer and information services in millions of U.S. dollars in 2003. State capacity indicated as poor (□), modest (◨), or good (■) in 2007, and as improving (▲), no change (✕), or in decline (▼) between 2000 and 2010. Law making effectiveness in the area of telecommunications regulation and intellectual property (IP) protection indicated as poor (□), modest (◨), or good (■) in 2007.

growth: building the information infrastructure for government and commerce raises the risk of expectations for access to information and personal freedoms, along with the risk of exposure to the norms and content of other cultures. Political elites operate in every type of state, and the opportunities for and consequences of ICTs use vary. Many of the democracies studied here are wired and promote government services online and also develop telecommunications policies for encouraging political conversation through unrestricted personal and public communication. The technologies themselves are not reserved for specific forms of cultural or Islamic content; indeed, telecommunications policies can be designed to promote diversity. But political elites often treated ICT development in terms of three kinds of trade-offs: some public ICT infrastructure was designed for business but not politics; some countries are wired for personal but not public communications; and some are wired for Islamic but not Western culture.

Wired for Business, but Not Politics

Turkey, Singapore, and Malaysia in particular have realized the economic benefits of having a modern information-rich economy. They have encouraged technology remanufacturing industries and have provided financial incentives to start-up software and hardware businesses. They build economic zones for the high-tech sector, where companies are exempt from customs duties and pay fewer taxes. At the same time, they work actively to contain ICT use within the economic sphere. They develop policies for improving price signals and the transparency of markets; they aggressively discourage the use of ICTs to improve the transparency of the political process, or to support public opinion formation online. They recognize the economic benefits of a modern information infrastructure.

Saudi Arabia, for example, uses ICTs to brand itself online as the center of Islam, the home of Mecca, and the source of Islamic exegesis. It uses ICTs to protect the ruling family's control over both economic resources and politics. Many of the countries that are wired for business but not politics have strong central governments, such as Islamic republics, constitutional monarchies, and dictatorships, and are able to impose and ban technologies and uses. They have government agencies with practice at policing political culture; their citizens are used to living in a political culture with few privacy guarantees and restricted information access. Such governments want the business benefits of a modern information infrastructure, but do their best to prevent communication of political critiques. They may liberalize their consumer markets in limited ways to signal that they are "open for business." They make the legal statement of separating the telecommunications provider and regulator from direct control by the head of state. Yet functional control is rarely surrendered by privatization, and the management of these regulatory agencies is usually retained for political appointees. Political elites in these countries see the state communications infrastructure as a political asset and are recalcitrant about depoliticizing bureaucratic oversight, reluctant to separate the regulator from executive management, and fearful that privatization of the infrastructure might make it harder to regulate cultural content.

To this end, Muslim countries are often eager to develop the informational infrastructure of the executive branch of government. These kinds of states build websites and maintain them in-country. Muslim democracies invest in the informational infrastructure of their legislatures. Revenue authorities in Muslim countries are a secondary priority when it comes to information infrastructure, though in the rest of the developed world, building the capacity of the revenue authority seems to have been as much a priority as building the capacity of the executive branch. Ministries of foreign affairs are also a secondary priority across the Muslim world; interestingly, many of these websites are not hosted in-country. This is in keeping with the idea that most of the users of such infrastructure are in fact overseas, so the websites are more likely to be designed and hosted in countries where journalists, business leaders, members of diaspora communities, and outsiders are eager to learn about a country and diaspora communities to need consular services. Perhaps most revealing is that the informational capacity of justice ministries seems to be the lowest priority among the five types of bureaucracies. Emerging democracies put the most effort into the informational capacity of state legal systems, but creating or maintaining such resources in-country is a relatively low priority for authoritarian and crisis states. Countries that are wired for business will use ICTs to extend the capacity of the state to collect taxes and make regulations available online, but will also use this capacity to monitor and restrict political conversation.

Wired for Personal but Not Private Communication

Political elites in some Muslim countries are committed to encouraging personal but not private communications. To do this, they allow mobile phones and internet use for communicating with family and friends, but will monitor networks and will not enact privacy policies. As we will see in Chapter 4, many of these states crack down on digital expression. For example, the Iranian government may encourage the personal use of information technologies, but discourage the consumption of public content and content from outside the country. Some of these countries have been open to

privatizing the national telephone company, but more often they simply liberalize long-distance telephone markets and domestic competition among
internet and mobile phone service providers. At the same time, they actively
regulate the use of cable news, work hard to restrict access to international
websites, and limit the speed of internet access so that news and other
streaming media are difficult to use.

There is an important relationship between state capacity, regime transparency, and the regulation of the media and telecommunications sector.
Countries that have taken steps to depoliticize and open up the telecommunications sector, developing comprehensive privacy policies and unrestricted
internet use, are likely to be among the group of countries with significant
remittances and an informationally sophisticated state bureaucracy.

Wired for Islamic, but Not Western Culture

States that choose to regulate the internet heavily, by not enacting privacy
policies and by monitoring or restricting internet use, usually do so to prevent
the distribution of critical content from outside the country, and discourage
digital forums for political debate within the country. Among the Islamic
republics and constitutional monarchies, such restrictions are ostensibly to
protect the political leadership, but they are enacted in the name of safeguarding cultural values. Some states enact restrictions but actively develop
an information infrastructure precisely so that volumes of ideological content
can be distributed over multiple media. Some states even work to "brand"
Islamic content online through national libraries that hold sacred texts, websites for sacred sites within territorial boundaries, and the digitization of
archives belonging to particular Islamic sets. Thus, states whose identity and
political order is closely tied to particular interpretations of Islamic tradition
will quite actively use new media to fill out the information infrastructure for
that tradition. Concomitant with using state information infrastructure to
privilege certain Islamic sects is using such infrastructure to exclude cultural
content, news, and other information from Western sources.

In Sum

In adopting and adapting new ICTs, many state bureaucracies have made
policy choices that result in better internal record keeping and accounting,
and more open flows of information between administrative offices and with
the outside world. The management and human resource practices from
wealthy countries have not always been easily adapted for use in developing
countries, sometimes proving to be unstable and unsustainable (Mellahi and
Frynas 2003). But overall, information technologies seem to be at the heart of

newfound efficiency, transparency, and accountability in developing coun-tries with large Muslim communities. Some governments have built their information infrastructure in-country, while others remain dependent on hosting services in other countries. In the pursuit of the economic benefits of either using ICTs to improve their state capacity or building a high-tech sector for their economy, even the most authoritarian states make policy trade-offs that create the conditions for transparency and accountability. In important ways, these decisions are not ones made by ruling elites, but by upper level bureaucrats with training in information management. And ultimately, reforming technology policy has immense implications for other political actors, particularly parties, journalists, and civil society groups.

Chapter 3

Political Parties Online

Mobile phones and the internet have been a boon to political parties in many Muslim countries, most notably in the Arab world. Six Gulf countries ban political parties outright, forcing such groups to use other monikers, and most of the other Gulf countries have serious restrictions on party activities. In advanced democracies, political websites evolved in parallel with commercial design trends and the affordability of browsers and bandwidth (Foot and Schneider 2006; Howard 2006). In advanced democracies, first generation websites of the late 1990s were called "brochure ware" because they merely reproduced content from print sources. It was only during the 2000 U.S. presidential campaign that websites were used as organizational tools with content specifically designed for coordinating volunteers, campaign staff, and candidate schedules. And only by 2004 did political parties develop data-mining tools, turning their party portals into a means of pushing news content and collecting data on voters. Political party websites in Muslim countries also went through stages of evolution.

For many political parties, the early investments in information infra-structure came in claiming a website address that clearly identified the party name and in producing content that made party sponsorship clear. First-generation websites were often built and maintained for extended periods by individuals who—with or without the blessing of party leaders—just began putting political content online. Using free Yahoo or Geocities accounts, these independent webmasters went ahead of party leadership to get content online; for some parties their official online presence was maintained for years by a solitary webmaster, the son or daughter of a party official, using free services or working from overseas. These informal websites represented party organizations online, but rarely were they at a named Uniform Resource Locator (URL) that clearly identified a party name and clear official sponsorship. Websites had this irregular status for for much of the 1990s, until party leaders realized that there was a large enough online audience of journalists and citizens to produce online content more formally.

This first change, renaming the website and claiming a branded URL, was a small administrative change but a significant symbolic step. It signaled new value in the role of the party website. Instead of being run by party youth on free hosting services, it would be professionally maintained on dedicated hosts. The homepage would not just be for party insiders who happened to know the obscure URL. The new domain name would be intuitive and easily findable on search engines. Moreover, staking a claim to a named URL allowed for clear sponsorship, a clear assumption of responsibility for content, and clear identity markers in the iconography of webpage design. Since political parties in many autocratic and crisis states are illegal, or the political situation does not make it conducive for all political parties to maintain a domestic information infrastructure, a significant number of parties in these countries maintain content overseas and where it can be managed by webmasters in diaspora communities. Such political infrastructure is difficult to build under authoritarian regimes, but not impossible. Political organizations in countries such as Bahrain or Tajikistan call themselves unions or social movements, and websites are valuable precisely because they can be difficult for authoritarian regimes to control.

The second stage of formalizing the role of party websites came when party leaders began to increase the organizational role of the website. Instead of being just an online portal for propaganda, parties began to give their websites a central organizational role. Committing substantial resources to website development meant creating original content not produced for other media, developing cross-platform applications, and turning the site into a comprehensive news portal for members. It also meant offering content in multiple languages, and making the site accessible to international visitors— supporters and critics in other countries, foreign journalists, and members of diaspora communities. Reaching the diaspora proved an especially valuable way to raise financial support for group activities. But what created the initial conditions by while political parties in closed regimes could have such an opportunity?

ECONOMIC STRATEGIES WITH POLITICAL CONSEQUENCES

Encouraging the use of information technologies has become a major national development goal in many Muslim countries. Beginning in the 1980s, many developing countries focused on building free-trade economic zones and port facilities to attract international industries. Since 2000, many Muslim governments have focused on building high-tech zones with cyber infrastructures that attract direct foreign investment in the ICT sector. Dubai has its Internet City, Kuala Lumpur has its Cyberjaya, and Baku has its Regional Innovation Zone. Since many Muslim countries are "middle income" countries, they are able to take on development goals beyond the basic health and dietary needs. For these countries, public policy goals include equipping schools and libraries with computers, building e-government services, and subsidizing the cost of ICTs or raising the size of the subsidies given to citizens to underwrite their purchase of household ICTs. To attract high-tech industries and reap the perceived benefits of internet connectivity, many governments developed telecommunications policies that indirectly allowed minor and unregistered parties to claim a small part of cyberspace. Malaysia and Egypt are examples of countries that have worked hard to bring a dot-com boom to their countries and for the most part have kept their promise to not create burdensome regulations on content.

Yet promoting technology use without content regulation is a significant compromise for many ruling elites. The beneficiaries of this compromise include political parties, who see opportunities for political organizing and propagandizing that might not be available in newspapers and state-owned television or radio stations. Email and electoral databases are powerful tools for campaigning, raising funds, and communicating with constituents and the news media. So political parties—legal and banned—are quick to go online. In the developing countries with large Muslim communities, what kinds of political parties are online, what kinds of information infrastructure do they have, and what kinds of content are offered? What explains the distribution of infrastructure and content between political parties, types of parties, and countries?

In newly wired countries, the first internet users are usually university faculty and students, civil servants, and the employees of large foreign-owned firms (Johari 2002). They tend to be social elites and to be well educated—often with higher degrees from schools overseas. In almost all Muslim countries, the first internet users are social elites: people in urban centers and key regional capitals who, by virtue of their socioeconomic status, are engaged with political life. In crisis states and countries with autocratic forms of government, such internet use enabled people to get international news. In emerging and strong democracies, these elites use the internet not only for news: checking online for information about campaigns and elections is not an activity restricted to stable, entrenched democracies. In countries where elections are often rigged, the internet is used to get international news coverage and to confirm local suspicions that elections are rigged. Political party websites, such as those run by Egypt's Muslim Brotherhood, Pakistan's People's Party, and Kazakhstan's Ak Zhol (Right Path) have been able to issue news releases detailing electoral mishaps. They provide information that helps voters make decisions on how to vote and information about specific policies or issues of domestic political interest. Sites with more multimedia content allow complex searching, online debates, and customized news feeds. Political communication is never the only activity online, and rarely the most frequent one. But in Muslim countries where this type of communication over broadcast media has been restricted, the internet provides the enabling infrastructure through which political parties become better organized, raise money from supporters, and draw more people into political conversation.

FROM PROPAGANDA TO LOGISTICS

In those Muslim countries where political parties are permitted, the major or ruling political parties have very close ties to mass media outlets. In some cases the ties are direct—the party owns its own media mouthpiece in news-papers, radio stations, or television channels. In countries like Pakistan and India, the ties are indirect: certain media outlets and journalists are given preferential treatment when it comes to licensing or having access to political leaders. In other cases the ties are broadly ideological; parties do not control media resources or editorial content, but the political and media elites are closely aligned on public policy questions.

In many of the countries included in this comparative study, media out-lets are closely guarded resources belonging to political elites, with formal control vested with the state or the ruling political party. In authoritarian countries, media outlets are assets held by ruling families and are heavily regulated by the state. In emerging democracies, media outlets can be directly owned by or indirectly affiliated with a political party. The internet, however, is less easily controlled by political elites and established political parties. The important distinction here is that while political elites can both own mass communications infrastructure and produce content for dissemi-nation over this infrastructure, such close management of the new information technologies is rare. Autarks, political elites, and established political parties can produce content for the internet, but rarely do they own the infrastructure. They might have administrative control over the interna-tional internet exchange points in major cities, but little influence over the content hosted in other countries. Sometimes censorship software can pre-vent access to this content from within a country, but such software is expen-sive and not always effective. Moreover, challenger groups, political outsiders, and new political parties are able to produce internet content to critique and rival that produced by political elites.

In many advanced democracies, it is common practice for political parties to use new media information technologies, such as the internet, for data mining purposes. Especially in the run up to elections, political parties will purchase large datasets that, supplemented with their own records, allow them to "redline" constituents who are clear supporters in safe districts, constituents who should be targeted by the campaign, and constituents who are committed opponents (Howard 2006). Such practices are increasingly common among political parties in the Muslim world.

For example, as early as 1993, the Yemen General People's Congress developed an Oracle-based voters list from government records to assemble personal information and demographic profiles. By 1996, this dataset was available over secure internet connections; party analysts built a successful campaign strategy for the 1997 elections with it. Close races were targeted; candidates who were sure to lose were abandoned. The data predicted victory in 167 of 301 seats in the House of Representatives. In the event, they won 183 seats, even though fewer than half the registered voters had openly declared for the General People's Congress. After the election, party elites believed that the majority of weak supporters were correctly identified and that the effective use of ICTs by its campaign workers had accounted for 40 percent of the votes it received (Goodman et al., 1998).

ICTs have been used to entrench democratic practices through voter registration, and ICTs have been particularly helpful in registering women voters for the first time and surveying them for their political opinions. For example, in Egypt's poor communities, girls are rarely registered at birth, which prevents them from getting the identity cards needed for receiving inheritances, registering for school, voting and receiving pensions later in life. The Egyptian Center for Women's Rights and the World Bank developed an efficient IT system for providing women in the greater Cairo area with identification cards, giving many women access to public services—and the ability to vote—for the first time.

The logistical benefits of such technologies accrue to political parties during elections, referenda, and in times of military crisis. For the countries transitioning to democracy or those political systems with entrenched democratic practices, new information technologies such as SMS allow for additional ways to monitor elections administration. In terms of statistical odds, among the hundreds of the party candidates for Malaysia's 2009 parliamentary election, the blogging candidates had a better chance of defeating non-bloggers, and challenger candidates who blogged had better chances of defeating incumbent candidates who blogged (Gong 2009). During Montenegro's critical referendum on independence, SMS was the primary reporting tool for 200 elections monitors who reported on an hourly basis on the conduct of voters and elections officials. Such just-in-time reporting has also been used by political party observers to monitor elections in Indonesia in 2005, in the West Bank and Gaza in 2006, and Sierra Leone in 2007 (Schuler 2008). Along with exit polls, this digital infrastructure allows political parties both to activate members and to contribute to monitoring the election itself.

THE GROWTH OF POLITICAL PARTIES ONLINE

Political parties in the Muslim world have been quick to adapt to the new information and communication environment, and today more than 350 political parties from these countries are online. In Saudi Arabia, internet users can donate money to the Green Party. In Indonesia, internet users can sign petitions on the website of the National Awakening Party. Major parties, such as Turkey's Adalet Kalkinma Party, or governing coalitions, such as Malaysia's Barisan Nasional, have complex sites with video feeds, news items of interest, and schedules of leadership visits to small towns. Minor parties in these countries rarely attract many votes, but still use the internet to circulate policy papers and advertise strategic alliances with other parties. Over time, more and more political parties have come online, put more content online, and developed more complex websites. All political parties are able to use the internet to research each other's ideological positions and policy alternatives. But political leaders also use the internet to investigate what state bureaucracies are up to. Indeed, in Turkey, the political parties look to the internet for signs of how military leaders react to any perceived threats to Ataturk's secularism.

Party websites provide basic positions on both domestic and foreign concerns, though as in the West they rarely provide direct opportunities for dialogue with party leaders. The development of such websites often occurs during intense electoral contests. Indeed, the quality and quantity of political information available online for use by journalists, citizens, and foreign observers makes for more intense electoral contests, and contemporary democratization proceeds apace with the production and consumption of political content online. A good way to analyze the growth of political life online in the Muslim world is by looking at political party websites, their increasingly complexity over time, and the diversity of ideological perspectives offered on political issues. For comparative purposes, a political party website is defined as content at a specific domain clearly produced or sponsored by the official party organization.

Political Parties Online in the Muslim World

Websites reveal much about the evolving system of political communication in countries with large Muslim communities. Overall, the proportion of Muslim political parties with websites increased from 18 percent in the year 2000 to 39 percent in 2007. In terms of raw numbers, the growth is also impressive. In 2000, 450 parties were found among 48 Muslim countries; in 2005, 587 parties among 62 countries; and in 2007, 1,153 parties among

71 countries. During this time, the capacity of political parties to host their own websites in-country also grew. In 2005, only 16 percent of Muslim parties could do this; by 2008, 25 percent could. Still, many political parties do not have the information infrastructure to host their own content. Given that a user can view internet content from any where in the network, why does it matter where content is hosted? First, there is an important difference between having a website, and having the capacity to maintain a website. A surprising number of political parties around the world rely on commercial hosting services in the United States to maintain their communications infrastructure. Political parties are dependent on the commercial services of businesses in wealthier countries, though some countries have built sufficient information infrastructure to manage their own websites. In times of crisis it can be useful to have a website hosting service out of country (or at least mirrored) where power supplies are stable and authorities cannot seize equipment. Having parties that are able to maintain their own information infrastructure within the country is a sign that the system of political communication there is relatively advanced. Being dependent on hosting services in other countries can signal a party's poor financial resources, lack of priorities in this arena, or fear of state reprisals. In 2008, 41 percent of the political parties in countries with large Muslim populations actually hosted their websites using commercial services in the United States.

Yet the political internet in the Muslim world has also become more interconnected: in 2005, 19 percent of political parties hosted their websites in other Muslim countries; by 2008, 25 percent did this. Similarly, the language offering on many of these websites has changed, signaling an important transition from a time in which party websites were for social elites or the outside, English-speaking world. In 2005, 37 percent of websites loaded in English when viewed from the United States, and fully 50 percent of party websites were available in English. But by 2008, only 23 percent of websites loaded in English, and the proportion offering English-language content had dropped to 43 percent. Moreover, 33 percent of Muslim party websites had content in two or more languages. Hosting websites in-country or in neighboring Muslim countries, de-emphasizing English, and raising the amount of multilingual content is evidence that over this period of a few years, political parties in the Muslim world found a new audience—supporters in their own countries.

In 2008, 46 percent of all the websites studied belonged to major political parties and large coalitions of groups. Major parties were more likely to be online and have domestic capacity to host their own websites. The rest of the sampled websites belonged to minor parties, suggesting that the internet has been able to serve minor political parties that previously had little or no capacity to reach a distributed audience. All in all, major political parties in the Muslim world are likely to be wired, more so than their equivalents in other developing countries. Whereas 69 percent of major political parties in the Muslim world have a website, only 56 percent of such political parties in the rest of the developed world have a website. But those that do have websites are much less likely to have their own website servers.

Political parties in crisis states and authoritarian regimes are particularly interested in building multilingual websites and websites with English language content. This is interesting because usually the online public in their own country is somewhat small, so this online performative work is for the benefit of the international community—political leaders, journalists, the diaspora, and citizens of other countries. The fact that more websites in these regimes are available in English than are multilingual reveals the extent to which some parties go online for an international audience.

Table 3.1 reveals that in 2000, 39 percent of the world's political parties had websites; in 2008, this had increased to 46 percent. By this time, there were over 4,000 political parties, a quarter of which were in countries with large Muslim communities. The proliferation rate for party websites from Muslim countries is higher than that of other developing countries, and today the number of party websites online in Muslim countries is slightly higher than that of the rest of the developing world. Between 2000 and 2008, the proportion of political parties with websites increased from 33 to 37 percent in non-Muslim countries. In comparison, the proportion of political parties with websites increased from 18 to 39 percent in Muslim countries over the same period. This increase represents a significant growth in political content available online and suggests that in important ways, political life in many Muslim countries is more evolved than in many other developing countries. Most political parties in developed countries have websites, though this appears to have diminished slightly over time. In 2000, 85 percent of the political parties in wealthy countries had websites; in 2008, only 68 percent. This reduction is likely due to the disappearance of many joke parties from the sample and the aggregation of minor parties into coalitions and umbrella groups.

Among the different types of regimes in the Muslim world, by 2008, 31 percent of the political parties in transition regimes have websites; 53 percent of the parties in entrenched democracies have websites. Interestingly, the pace at which political parties in authoritarian regimes have built online portals is greater than that of parties in counties experiencing major political transitions. Of all the political parties in the Muslim constitutional monarchies around the world, only a fifth are online. Perhaps more surprising is that the level of information infrastructure behind political parties in Islamic republics, dictatorships, and crisis states is so high. This may be

Table 3.1: Political Parties Online in the Muslim World, 2000–2008

	Number of Political Parties, and Percent with a Website (Italics)			
	2000	2005	2008	Percent Change 2000–2007
All Muslim Countries	446 *18*	588 *37*	1,154 *39*	*20*
Transition	145 *19*	196 *35*	418 *31*	*13*
Entrenched Democracies	132 *28*	183 *46*	256 *53*	*25*
Authoritarian Regimes	165 *10*	182 *26*	397 *34*	*23*
Crisis States	4 *25*	27 *52*	83 *57*	*32*
Other Developing Countries	570 *33*	803 *42*	1,870 *37*	*4*
Developed Countries	261 *85*	253 *83*	1,043 *68*	*−17*
All Countries	1,277 *39*	1,641 *46*	4,047 *46*	*7*

Sources: Based on author's calculations from multiple sources: Norris 2000; Howard and World Information Access Project 2008, 2007.

Note: The number of countries sampled each year of study increased from 139 in 2000 to 165 in 2005 and 209 in 2008. Lists of political parties were re-created each year and cross-checked from a variety of sources: the previous year's list, Lexus-Nexus news reports, Wikipedia, and regional experts.

because such regimes provide little support for, or even disallow, open political communication through newspapers, television, and radio. The internet may now be the primary media face for many unofficial political parties that are based in diaspora communities, are critical of regimes, or consider themselves governments in exile.

The countries that became more democratic over time did so, in part, because the major and minor political parties took to the internet. Strong institutionalized democratic practices permitted an open information culture that allowed political parties to develop websites. By expanding their information infrastructure and contributing to the amount of political content online, these political parties strengthened democratic practices. Simultaneously, having a website became a priority in countries that did not experience much democratization and those that slid into authoritarianism. Such parties were latecomers to the internet, but once the capacity to host services in other countries was available, even authoritarian regimes or states in crisis could not prevent online political content and discourse. In other words, for many of the countries that experienced no democratic transition or became more authoritarian, it was precisely the lack of open media and accessible information infrastructure that forced parties to develop party representation online.

The Growing Infrastructure for Ideological Diversity

Having compared whether parties are online by regime type, level of technology diffusion, and in contrast with other developing and developed countries, the next step is to examine the information infrastructure of the political sphere in Muslim countries in terms of ideologies. Party competition is a key feature of deliberative democracy, so what kind of ideological diversity can be found online? What are the relative informational capacities of different kinds of parties? Table 3.2 compares the total number of parties, the percent of these online, and the percent that have the capacity to actually host their websites in-country. While cataloguing the number of URLs available and locating their host servers reveals little about how often such websites are used, this is still good evidence of the significant growth of online political party portals in the Muslim world.

The diversity of ideologies online is a key feature of Table 3.2, which is organized by four ideological categories found in most countries in the world: liberal, conservative, socialist, and communist parties. Additionally, many Muslim countries have secular and fundamentalist Islamist parties. Since many political organizations in authoritarian regimes try to function as political parties, it can be difficult to categorize them by ideology. Many of the countries in this study have Green parties, or parties that claim to be free of ideology but are very much personality cults for a country's dictator. Some countries also have Christian fundamentalist parties. In 2000 and 2005, parties that were difficult to classify —and organizations that function as parties in political systems where formal parties are illegal were labeled as "Other." In 2008, the category of "Unknown" was disaggregated. In the year 2000, data were collected on the number of political parties and whether they had websites. In 2005, this information was collected again, along with information about where each party's hosting services were located. In 2008, data on party websites and hosting services were collected. In addition, each party website was downloaded and assessed for its number of links, files, and size.

Proportionally, liberal and other parties are among the most wired, while Islamic parties are the least wired. This is true not only in terms of the numbers of parties online, but is reflected in the complexity of website links, the number of files, and the volume of content. Comparing the fundamentalist and secular political internet in the Muslim world reveals that on the whole, communist, socialist, liberal, conservative, and secular Islamic parties are more digitally connected than fundamentalist Islamic parties.

There is a great deal of ideological diversity among the political parties of the Muslim world, so while this typology of political party ideologies uses the categories familiar to observers of political life in Western

Table 3.2: The Growing Infrastructure for Diverse Ideologies, 2000–2008

	2000		2005			2008				
	All Parties	Parties Online	All Parties	Parties Online, and those Hosted In-Country (Italics)		Parties Online, and those Hosted In-Country (Italics)		Thousands of External Website Links	Thousands of Files	Gigabytes of Data
Liberal	18	26	25	29	*26*	20	*19*	15	21	30
Conservative	4	9	11	14	*14*	12	*14*	16	19	6
Socialist	19	16	16	16	*20*	19	*24*	21	25	18
Communist	0	0	4	7	*0*	8	*10*	4	5	2
Islamic – Fundamentalist	3	9	11	12	*6*	4	*5*	3	3	1
Islamic – Secular	4	7	4	5	*0*	6	*3*	3	4	1
Other	52	33	29	17	*34*	16	*20*	33	16	40
Unknown	..	..	..	..	*..*	15	*6*	5	6	2
Percent	100	100	100	100	*100*	100	*100*	100	100	100
Number	450	81	587	211	*35*	406	*105*	725	587	85
Number of Countries	48		62			71				

Sources: Based on author's calculations from multiple sources: Norris 2000; Howard and World Information Access Project 2008, 2007.

Note: West Bank and Gaza Strip, and Western Sahara excluded from this table. Party ideology types were determined using descriptions used in articles found in Lexus-Nexus and Wikipedia, and in consultations with regional experts. In 2000 and 2005 the category of Other and Unknown parties were combined, and these were disaggregated in 2008.

democracies, unfortunately the category of "Other" aggregates much of this diversity. Most of these other parties are unions or social movements that cannot legally self-identify as parties, but perform similar political functions. Yet they are an important category, because they are among the fastest technology adopters. In 2000, liberal and socialist parties had set up many websites, but a third of these unregistered or difficult-to-label parties had established a web presence. Even when the "Other" category was disaggregated from "Unknown" in the 2008 sample, these other groups had 16 percent of all the URLs, 20 percent of all the domestic hosting capacity, 16 percent of all the files, the largest volume of digital content, and made significant linkages to other government, party, and news sites.

One reason the internet is a supporting infrastructure for democratization is that new political parties are not so easily silenced, whether by the state or larger established parties. When newspapers become too critical, authoritarian governments can respond by raising taxes on ink and paper, or by blocking imports altogether. Television stations that broadcast critical news reports or images of social protest can have their licenses revoked and suffer from deliberate power blackouts. But when party infrastructure and organization is targeted by the state, party leaders can move content out of country and keep the production of news and commentary up. When the *Al Shaab* newspaper, an organ of a the Labour Party of Egypt, was banned, it went online and continued publishing critiques. A newspaper belonging to the Muslim Brotherhood, once shut down, also went online. Along with offering news and commentary, the new website became a means of logistical coordination for candidates running as "independents" in local elections in Egypt.

Table 3.2 reveals the ideological diversity of political parties in many Muslim countries. The relative proportion of Islamic fundamentalist parties is small—not surprising, given how much effort is being put into extinguishing them. But more important is that this evidence suggests there is ideological competition in many countries. In democracies, this competition occurs within respected and institutionalized rules of political play; in emerging democracies, this competition occurs, but the rules of political discourse are still being worked out and there are occasional abuses of democratic norms. But even in the constitutional monarchies, Islamic republics, and dictatorships, political parties are springing up from very diverse ideological backgrounds. They may unite for the purpose of securing power for themselves, or for the purpose of establishing democratic rules for party competition, but the diversity is there. By 2008, the distribution of web resources by party ideology was much more balanced than seven years prior.

OUTCOMES: DEMOCRATIZATION AND THE INFRASTRUCTURE
OF MODERN POLITICAL DISCOURSE

Over the last decade, the Muslim world has developed an enormous, main-stream, political discourse online and this is due in large part to the prolifer-ation of political party websites. The political web sphere, even in countries where formal political parties are banned, is increasingly vibrant and com-petitive. Table 3.3 compares countries on the basis of party information infrastructure and content, organized by level of technology diffusion and type of political transition.

In some countries, having a strong infrastructure of political parties has made a difference in democratic discourse. Parties compete for the attention of journalists and voters, they communicate with observers overseas when elections are questionable, and they look for creative ways of engaging their communities online. Other countries experienced a democratic transition without much improvement in the information infrastructure for political parties or growth of political content online. For example, the countries with the most political content online—Morocco, Turkey, and Macedonia—are not all countries that have had high technology diffusion and a significant democratic transition. Still, a nuanced argument can be made about the connection between democratization and technology diffusion. In these countries the pressure to include Islamists in national political life is very high, and ICTs have allowed the political system to accommodate competing interests and discordant voices in a way that allowed for stability in the democratic institutions they do have. Morocco's political parties are very active online, but internet use is not as widespread as it is in other countries, and so authoritarian control remains strong. Turkey's political parties are very active online, information technologies are prevalent, the country has a democratic history: in recent years elected leaders have faced down chal-lenges from the military and Islamist interests have been moderated. Macedonia has become more democratic, and even though it only has average levels of technology diffusion, having this basic information infra-structure has proven key to building the capacity of independent political voices that constructively contribute to national policy debates.

Table 3.3 compares the ways in which political party infrastructure and content online have contributed to political transitions in Muslim countries. Depending on how many political parties a country has, how many of those came online and when, and how many of those host their websites domesti-cally, countries are judged as having weak, modest, or strong political party information infrastructure. In addition, the countries are assessed for having little, some, lots, or substantial amounts of political content online. The first judgment is based on a comparison of three ratios: the ratio of online parties to all parties in 2000; the ratio of online parties to all parties in 2005; and the ratio of online parties with domestically hosted websites, to online parties and then to all parties in 2008. To evaluate the kinds of political content available across countries, Table 3.3 also compares the total number of giga- bytes of political content found at party websites. Data on the number of links and number of files at each website were also collected, but since these three things are highly correlated, only the volume of data is presented.

Countries where political parties have a strong supporting ICT infrastruc- ture have developed websites that do more than provide policy papers and party manifestos. They offer text (and sometimes recordings) of speeches from party officials, biographical information on leaders and electoral candi- dates, and the voting records of legislators. They have dedicated areas for party members and offer news feeds with particular ideological spin. These websites are the most accessible and detailed sources of party information, unmediated by the news editors, state regulators, or media broadcasters.

India and Tunisia stand out as countries with significant Muslim popula- tions and a significant political sphere online, with a strong political party information infrastructure and good content provided for internet users. But even by 2007, very few of the political parties in countries other than India and Tunisia had the capacity to host their own website within their own country. Among the Muslim countries that had democratized, Bosnia, Lebanon, Montenegro, Russia, and Tanzania stand out as countries with wired political parties. Yet even in the countries with a reasonably good information infrastructure of hosts and a proportional number of internet users given national economic productivity, few parties hosted their own websites in their own countries.

Among the countries with high levels of technology diffusion, Indonesia, Israel, and Turkey had a vibrant online public sphere as early as 2000. By 2005 most of the countries with high levels of ICT diffusion and democratiza- tion had several political parties online. Organized political parties in many Gulf states were still not visible. Two years later, by 2007, only Indonesia's political parties were difficult to trace online, probably because that country's irregular power supplies and internet connections have had a serious impact on its online public sphere. At least half the political parties in every other country were online, and Bosnia, Georgia, Malaysia, and Turkey had significant indigenous capacity to host their own political spheres online.

Many political parties in countries with low levels of technology diffusion still choose to develop complex websites because they are eager to get their ideas out to an online readership. Even though the low diffusion countries have little domestic capacity to host such websites, a few of the major political parties in each country have undertaken the expense of hosting websites. Pakistan became more authoritarian over time, and while many of its political

Table 3.3: Outcomes—Information Infrastructure for Political Parties, 2000–2008

Country	Number of Online Parties / All Political Parties, 2000	Number of Online Parties / All Political Parties, 2005	Number of Online Parties Hosted In-Country / Number of Online Parties / All Political Parties, 2008	Volume of Content, 2008
		Transition		
Albania	1/10	3/12	2/6/17	·
Algeria	3/10	8/13	4/11/17	•
Bahrain[a]	0/0	5/14	2/6/7	•
Bosnia	2/7	2/2	1/15/30	•
Comoros	0/0	0/0	0/1/7	·
Djibouti	0/3	4/8	1/4/9	·
Egypt	1/6	6/6	4/9/9	•
Georgia	0/7	0/11	0/5/16	•
Ghana	0/4	3/3	0/0/9	·
Indonesia	9/21	0/4	1/4/8	•
Kenya	1/11	4/4	0/6/9	·
Kuwait[a]	0/0	0/1	0/0/2	·
Kyrgyzstan	0/0	0/0	0/1/14	•
Lebanon	0/10	7/18	7/20/28	●
Liberia	0/6	3/18	0/0/7	·
Macedonia	0/0	7/9	1/8/24	●
Maldives	0/0	0/0	0/4/5	•
Mauritania	0/3	3/7	0/6/20	·
Montenegro	0/0	0/0	1/10/33	•
Niger	0/5	0/3	1/2/13	·
Nigeria	2/3	2/9	0/7/27	·
Senegal	3/11	2/3	0/8/15	·
Sierra Leone	0/13	2/3	0/3/9	·
Suriname	5/24	5/20	0/2/25	•
Tanzania	1/5	2/23	1/3/6	·
Uganda	0/0	5/9	0/5/8	•
		Entrenchment		
Bangladesh	1/6	4/6	3/6/8	•
Benin	0/9	3/23	0/3/30	•
Bulgaria	1/7	14/23	14/22/23	●
Cyprus	4/5	6/8	1/14/26	•
Guinea-Bissau	0/8	4/5	1/2/16	·
India	10/38	4/5	12/16/21	•
Israel	11/23	17/28	10/13/15	•
Malawi	1/3	1/3	0/0/14	·
Malaysia	0/0	12/21	9/14/37	●
Mali	0/8	1/13	0/2/21	·
Mauritius	2/10	2/12	2/3/10	·

98

Mozambique	0/7	2/17	0/1/16	·
Turkey	7/8	14/19	11/19/23	●

Authoritarian

Azerbaijan	0/6	0/3	0/1/26	·
Brunei	0/0	0/3	2/2/4	·
Cameroon	1/12	2/9	0/2/8	·
CAR	0/11	3/14	0/2/13	·
Chad	0/10	2/16	0/1/8	·
Eritrea	0/0	1/6	0/6/6	·
Ethiopia	1/26	3/24	0/6/10	·
Gambia	0/4	2/6	0/1/7	·
Guinea	0/9	1/7	0/1/8	·
Iran	0/4	0/7	0/6/11	●
Jordan	0/0	0/0	1/2/31	·
Kazakhstan	0/5	0/2	3/3/10	·
Libya[a]	0/0	0/1	0/0/1	·
Morocco	2/15	5/6	0/12/38	●
Oman[a]	0/0	0/0	0/0/1	·
Pakistan	0/0	8/20	2/13/32	●
Qatar[a]	0/0	0/0	0/0/1	·
Russia	10/31	9/13	1/30/34	●
Saudi Arabia[a]	0/0	0/1	0/1/1	·
Singapore	1/5	0/0	5/7/12	·
Sudan	0/0	1/7	0/5/10	·
Syria[a]	0/6	6/13	0/8/41	·
Tajikistan	0/6	1/6	0/1/10	·
Togo	0/2	1/3	0/3/11	·
Tunisia	1/6	1/4	0/3/8	·
Turkmenistan	0/0	0/1	0/1/4	·
UAE[a]	0/0	0/0	0/0/1	·
Uzbekistan	0/5	0/5	0/1/8	·
Yemen	1/4	2/5	1/3/6	·

Crisis

Afghanistan	0/0	7/13	0/9/71	·
Burkina Faso	1/4	0/3	0/2/20	·
Iraq	0/0	0/0	1/14/27	●
Ivory Coast	0/0	3/5	0/4/8	·
Somalia	0/0	2/3	0/1/8	·
West Bank & Gaza	0/0	2/3	0/0/0	·
Western Sahara	..	..	0/0/0	·

Source: Howard and World Information Access Project 2008.

Notes: The volume of content provided by political parties for citizens is indicated as small (·) if less than 0.1 gigabyte, moderate (•) if between 0.1 and 1.0 gigabytes, and large (●) if more than 1.0 gigabytes. Montenegro and Bosnia are credited with the same ratios for party infrastructure, but not for content. (a) Indicates a country where political parties are legally or in practice banned, but operate in exile or as informal "associations."

parties started aggressively using the internet for their activism, few have
built out their domestic infrastructure. In this country, and perhaps in
Azerbaijan, the deliberate choice to host party websites overseas probably
had more to do with fear of reprisals than financial constraints.

It is surprising that so many political parties in authoritarian regimes are
online. This is probably because in these regimes the internet is one of the
only media through which political parties *can* present themselves. Major
parties in emerging democracies also seem to value the internet as a means
of political communication with domestic and foreign supporters and journalists. Among most authoritarian and transition regimes, political parties
are eager to develop an online presence but are unable to do so domestically
Whereas most major parties in emerging democracies have a website, only a
fraction of these can provide their own hosting services; in authoritarian
regimes and low diffusion countries the fraction is even smaller. As in authoritarian regimes, many of the political parties in crisis states are organization-
ally based overseas, and their information infrastructure is actually in
London, New York, and Toronto, where political leaders in exile have better
resources for building a web presence.

Political party websites tend to engage the most politically active people—
and those with easy internet access. Given the rapidly growing population of
internet users and the public sphere online, party websites serve more and
more people with political content. During elections or political crisis, they
draw in a wider population. In part, this means that websites contribute to
the democratic practices within parties. Communications among party members, archives of meeting minutes, membership records, and recordings
speeches all supplement the information available to the party base. Such
infrastructure is key when parties need to mobilize their membership or
organize local meetings.

THE CONSTRUCTION OF MUSLIM POLITICAL OPINION

For the most part, public opinion in countries with large Muslim communities has been a construction of ruling elites and state agencies. By so constraining the media diets of citizens, the ability of journalists to investigate
popular sentiment, and the ability of researchers to survey the public, the
boundaries of what constituted the "public" were fundamentally constrained
and knowledge of "opinion" deliberately kept vague. Today, political parties
are using the internet to construct political opinion in a different way. By
deeply integrating digital tools such as mobile phones and the internet into
their systems of political communication, parties are able to reach and activate much larger numbers of people. In this way, the internet is actively used

to challenge the basic relations of power, because political parties use it to amass publics that were not previously reachable.

In countries where a handful of state agencies own the major media outlets, it is possible to define the public through the selection of topics covered in the news, through the framing of stories, and through the gender and ethnic representation of people who appear as journalists and as subjects in news stories. It is rare, for example, to have immigrant Bengalis canvassed for opinion in the nightly newscasts in the Gulf countries. Increasingly, the internet has become an alternative information source, one which holds content related to those minority voices. But public opinion is not shaped by the internet in the sense that lots of citizens find interesting new public policy options online, but in the sense that these major media outlets have added the internet to their tool kit for measuring—and manipulating—public opinion. Autocrats, by definition, work to constrain the size and diversity of their publics through media systems that distribute limited amounts of information, to carefully defined groups. And it is the political parties, legal or not, that make the best use of the internet for extending the definition of who the public is by expanding their membership and increasing the rate of active contact.

Recent constitutional changes in Kuwait provide a good example of how technological changes in a media system provide opportunities for new definitions of a public. While women gained the right to vote and run for parliament in 2005, it was 2009 by the time female candidates actually secured elected office. When they did, it was in large part because political party organizations behind these candidates were able to use the internet, mobile phones, and fax machines to reach out to women who were effectively new citizens. Many were voting for the first time, and for the most part public opinion prior to 2005 was formally constituted by men. Most political parties, because they actively compete for members and financial resources, were aggressive about drawing in new people. This process of extending the number of people who constitute public opinion can diminish the effective power that comes from having a small, concentrated public defined in many authoritarian regimes as the ruling elite who are connected through familial ties, went to the same schools, and serve in a small number of government offices.

Public opinion in the Muslim world was for the longest time constituted by its political and economic elites. Public opinion flowed top-down, as political leaders expressed the sentiments of their states to other parts of the Muslim world. Such leaders did not ignore public opinion, but instead measured it through traditional techniques of consultation that often involved kin and friends of ruling families. There are multiple ways that people in Muslim countries now receive their news and entertainment, often despite the best efforts of government censors. The polling sciences are increasingly able to measure public opinion, but a fundamentally different unit of analysis and sampling frame can now be used, with public opinion aggregated from respondents regardless of their cultural importance. Public opinion polling in Muslim countries is a relatively new field, and while ICTs alone do not render perfect measures of public attitudes, they provide better methods than the more traditional ways of having political leaders extrapolate public opinion by interviewing the male heads of important households. The political parties actively use mobile phones, especially SMS systems, to activate people as voters or protesters at key moments when the parties need "public opinion" to be more than the expression of interests by ruling elites in capital cities.

Perhaps one of the most interesting trends is the construction of "Arab public opinion" or "Muslim public opinion" by news agencies in the West. As Herbst and Howard have shown, the construction of public opinion is in part a process by which policy makers and politicians, in need of evidence about how different policy options will be received, imagine different ways of grouping the public (Herbst 1998, Howard 2006). These studies cover the construction of public opinion in the United States, but a similar process has occurred in many countries with large Muslim communities. Yet public opinion construction is not just something done by ruling elites or political parties nor is it just Muslim political leaders who have a vested interest in managing their publics. Western news agencies, polling offices, and politicians also construe "Muslim public opinion" for their own uses.

On key issues, this means that public opinion now forms with observable gaps between what ruling elites want and what the politicized, wired citizens want. For example, whereas the Sunni Arab political establishment is concerned about Iran's arc of influence through Iraq, Syria and into Jordan, online polling tools demonstrate that a more representative sample of citizens do not fear Iran's influence in the same way (Kiernan 2007). Mobile phone penetration means that it is now possible to survey populations in ways that allow for more careful sampling, often by random digit dial survey instruments with interviewers calling in from overseas. Such sampling strategies more accurately gauge differences between "public opinion" and that of governing elites, but can also gauge fundamental differences in cultural values within and between Muslim communities around the developing world (Pew Global Attitudes Project 2006).

Beginning in the 1990s, Muslim public opinion was constructed by Western news agencies seeking to describe international opposition to the U.S. sanctions and military action in Iraq. Thus, it is not an opinion with a core ideology that brings it coherence, but it is a public opinion with a core set of shared grievances. Journalists in the West have easy access to these grievances when they are expressed online, which may explain why Western news coverage of internet use in many Muslim communities tends to high-light the voices of Islamic fundamentalism. Similarly, in the West, Muslim public opinion is often portrayed as transnational and unified. More impor-tant, this false unity of Muslim public opinion was presented to Western leaders in the lead up to the second Gulf War.

> The United States saw a clear Iraqi threat and assumed that its private commu-nications with Arab allies would secure their public cooperation despite their public opposition.... The surprisingly strong and vocal opposition to the war plans from even the closest Arab allies of the United States demonstrates the power of this evolving public sphere and its transformative impact. (Lynch 2003, 91)

Perhaps the best evidence of how public opinion is constructed in many Muslim communities can be found in the variability of survey results from "the Arab street." In the statistical sense, public opinion in many countries with large Muslim communities is just now being constructed because the sample frame and frequency distribution for gender and ethnicity is still to be gauged. Who counts as a surveyable citizen in Saudi Arabia, and what are the best mechanisms for reaching that citizen? If random digit dialing mobile phone numbers within a country reaches a portion of the population that is not allowed to vote, is it worth querying their opinion? How should researchers evaluate instrument error or effects if state censors accom-pany interviewers or if self-censorship prevents citizens from answering honestly?

The governments in many countries with large Muslim populations have a history of reporting public opinion survey results without the methodolog-ical details needed to understand how sample methods, questionnaire design, and government sponsorship might have impacted the findings. Moreover, in more authoritarian regimes, public opinion is congruent with the political attitudes of fairly small groups of people within Muslim soci-eties: business leaders and educated elites, the clergy and military, and rad-ical Islamists (Pollack 2008). It used to be that these cultural elites were able to define public opinion. Now there are mechanisms for at least allowing some contrasts and divergence of opinion. The internet and mobile phones, in some modest respects, have freed public opinion from being narrowly constituted as the opinion of a small elite (Zayani 2008).

It remains to be seen, however, how long it will take for pollsters and political parties to develop appropriate means of measuring and represent-ing this expanded public opinion. But by using the internet and mobile phones to expand the public arena and take it out of the easy control of the state, political parties have successfully constructed a public whose approval they must vie for, even in regimes where electoral contests have yet to be meaningful. In almost all of the countries with significant Muslim communities—some Central Asian countries might be the exception—political parties have successfully used the ICTs to change the criteria for membership in the public sphere and expand the population that constitutes public opinion.

CONCLUSION: WIRED POLITICAL PARTIES

The internet does not transform political parties and instantly turn dictatorships into democracies. Writing at the height of the dot-com boom in 2000, pundits proclaimed that internet-based technologies would revolutionize politics in the Muslim world, and scholars offered forceful corrective (Peled 2000). But in the years since, we have observed that the internet does have an impact on political parties, even in regimes that are effectively one-party governments and where elections are usually rigged. Along with other ICTs, the internet does level the playing field among political actors by facilitating ideological and programmatic competition, building the party's capacity to organize resources around policy objectives and contributing perspective and critique to the political discourses dominated by governments and elite-controlled media. Across all regime types, ICTs provide the contemporary infrastructure by which political parties organize, communicate with supporters, and challenge state propaganda. Such activities were always possible with newspapers and broadcast television and radio, but now they have international reach over an infrastructure that governments have a harder time controlling.

Whereas large political parties can own and manage television and radio stations or newspapers, they cannot control the internet or mobile phone networks the same way. Dictatorships have long been able to manage the supply of newsprint and to regulate radio and television through licensing and power cuts. Strategic power cuts are still a means of media control in times of crisis, but it is harder to completely shut down the decentralized mobile and internet networks than it is to disable a television or radio broadcast station.

ICTs are powerful tools for political parties. In regimes that are democratic, ICTs have a role in making parties more competitive. Email, computers, and mobile phones are used to reach out to supporters, raise funds, contact journalists, negotiate political strategies, and muster voters at election time. In regimes that are more authoritarian, ICTs still have a role in organizing like-minded dissidents, though without the pressure to compete with other parties for votes. In these regimes, ICTs have the additional role of keeping dissidents in touch with the international community—foreign journalists, sympathetic members of diaspora communities, and international civil society groups. Such linkages are much easier to maintain using networked, digital, communication technologies, and such linkages are especially important in times of political or military crisis and during democratic transitions.

The data analysis in this chapter revealed several interesting things. First, political parties in the Muslim world have been fast to adopt and adapt to digital media, though the reasons for doing so vary by regime type. On average, political parties in Muslim countries were slow to move online compared to other developing countries, but in recent years they quickly caught up. Even states in crisis or run by dictators, with proportionally fewer internet users and paltry internet infrastructure, have aspiring political parties developing websites. Parties value the internet as a means of reaching their own citizens, though in emerging democracies, autocracies, and crisis states they realize that much of their audience may be outside the country. This is evidence that, even in the Muslim countries that are struggling to become information societies, the leaders of political parties consider being online a priority—part of an effective, modern political communications strategy.

More than other media, new ICTs support both party logistics and party propaganda. Moreover, the vast majority of parties online are providing a relatively mainstream volume of political content for internet users. A tiny fraction is Islamic fundamentalists, while traditional socialist, liberal, and conservative parties are found everywhere. In fact, the online political internet in the Islamic world is strongly secular. Of the 406 political parties found online in these Muslim countries, 80 percent, including those self-identifying as Islamic but secular, believe in a political discourse not governed by Sharia law.[1] Islamic fundamentalists use more obscure parts of the internet to post their vitriol. Muslim politics online is dominated by relatively mainstream content from traditional ideological camps, produced by political parties with ever improving information infrastructure.

Several factors explain the burgeoning political content online among Muslim countries. It is much too difficult for governments to completely cut off party websites, and many minor parties can afford to have websites. For minor parties, access to broadcast media may be prohibitively expensive or simply prohibited. But party websites can be found through search engines and news portals, and the costs of gaining a branded address has diminished significantly, as have the costs of hosting services. The mass media that party elites can control in-country are rarely used by diaspora communities and journalists. Today, the online public sphere of a Muslim country includes these external actors, and many political parties seem to court this audience, inviting external eyes into domestic politics by producing multilingual and English content on their websites.

In recent years, savvy use of the internet, mobile phones, and other ICTs has become a high strategic priority for political parties. In crisis states, autocracies, and emerging democracies, websites are the primary organizational means for reaching the international public; domestic users may have a lower priority than foreign journalists, citizens, and governments. Increasingly, political parties in Muslim countries are developing content that is multilingual, not necessarily available in English, and sited on servers that are either in-country or in neighboring Muslim countries. In democracies, websites are an increasingly important organizational means for interfacing with the domestic public. Being without a website is taken as a sign of not being a modern party with high-tech development priorities.

Contemporary democratization, by definition, means developing a public sphere online. Most of the time, people use ICTs for forms of social interaction that are not very political, though Chapter 6 argues that censorship regimes can politicize even the most banal uses of information and communication technologies. During elections, or in times of military and political crisis, these technologies help citizens make effective electoral decisions, quickly pass information to family and friends, and monitor events. For the emerging democracies, ICTs help voters evaluate candidates for office and cast more informed ballots. Technologies such as mobile phones and the internet also provide more diverse sources of political information, expanding the range of available content to include domestic and foreign news, government and party propaganda, and raw unmediated documentation for those who want the full text or audio of speeches, party manifestos, and policy papers.

In Sum

The informational capacity of political parties has greatly increased in recent years. The ability to organize party activities, present a public face online, and tactically use ICT at sensitive moments in electoral campaigning is increasingly important for competitive parties. In some cases, this means that countries that are essentially single-party governments with more capacity for ideological control. Dominant parties used to be able to both own the infrastructure and control the production of political culture. Such parties have a much more difficult time owning ICT infrastructure and controlling the production of political culture online. The result has been a proliferation of minor and moderate parties.

Democratization now proceeds hand in hand with technology diffusion. Representative democracies are strengthened by political parties that can use digital technologies for content and organizational affordances. In doing so, they advance their own interests, and the outcome is new forms of political engagement, greater diversity in ideological voices, and improved organizational capacity for political actors independent of the state. Overall, technology diffusion often results in improved competition among political parties and enriched democratic practices.

Chapter 4

New Media and Journalism Online

In Muslim countries where the state has traditionally dominated media, journalists have started using the internet to bring international stories to national audiences, to give national stories a global reach, and to publish content that could not appear locally. By improving the capacity of journalists to research and publish, the internet has become a crucial democratic information infrastructure.

Independent journalists play a critical role in every healthy democracy. In many different kinds of Muslim countries, new media technologies are transforming the way news is both produced and consumed. Journalists use the internet to do research and to publish their content outside the reach of government censors. Professional associations of journalists, such as the al Urdun al Jadid Research Center in Jordan, run online training sessions to teach journalists about how to use the country's new access to information law. Citizens use the internet to learn about public affairs outside their country, and some even become amateur journalists by providing photos, videos, and text describing political and security crises as they live through them. In many Muslim countries, the internet is used for news during times of particular social crisis, when citizens need to verify national news stories with international reports, or when domestic journalists are so constrained that independent journalism—and certainly oppositional editorializing—is only conducted online by writers living in other countries.

THE CHANGING WORK AND FORMS OF JOURNALISM

Unfortunately, journalists in many Muslim countries rarely have much independence and often face persecution or perverse incentives for doing their work. Journalists should be accountable and responsive to their readers, while also generating content that challenges citizens—and political leaders—to think in new ways about the responsibilities of governance. Given these essential roles, many journalists in the Muslim world adapted to the internet quickly, using it as a research resource that allowed for fact checking, sharing stories with colleagues in other countries, and publicizing stories that would not make it into the domestic broadcast or print news cycle. Journalists have also been known to use the internet to crib content, recycling stories from international sources for local consumption (Hamdy 2009). And as in news organizations around the world, some journalists echo the analytical frame of their sources by uncritically using keywords and photos in stories. For example, Indonesian journalists turned directly to Laskar Jihad's website for news and information about the Maluku conflict in that country. These print media used the website's images and discourse in their own news coverage, thus lending credence to the fundamentalist group's framing of the conflict (Lim 2005, 23).

As in many countries, news organizations are adapting to the new political economy of digital news. Large news organizations in the Muslim world find that they must provide some free content and are struggling to find stable revenue sources. Yet contemporary newsrooms can also be small, agile, and distributed organizations. Even traditional television newsrooms, many of which developed professional practices suited for maintaining the ideological control of ruling elites, have evolved new practices because of the capacities and constraints of the internet. Whereas news organizations in the Arab world were once described as "stagnant, centralized, monolithic, and apathetic to audience views," the launch of multimedia commercial news organizations has helped raise standards of professional and pluralistic approaches to news production (Ayish 2002). In part, these changes have come because the internet has supported widespread conversation among journalists about professional ethics. As in the West, ethics codes in southern Europe, North Africa, the Middle East, and Muslim Asia, embodied by professional codes of conduct and taught in journalism schools, hold that truth and objectivity should be central values of journalism. One difference may be that Islamic journalism is normatively geared toward protecting the private sphere over the public sphere (Hafez 2002). Much online debate has broken out over the degree to which and the ways in which journalists must respect or tolerate political, national, religious, or cultural boundaries to their work. Moreover, for the journalists who do not accept professional socialization about what these boundaries should be, the internet is a means of internationally distributing content that could not be shared domestically.

Digital technologies are being used not only to change the work of journalists, but the meaning and form of journalism. Contemporary journalism takes advantages of digital platforms, delivering news as a continually updated service. Moreover, the structure and content of news changes with readership. Popular stories get referred to more readers and achieve more prominence in search engine results; stories are based on remixing of data from multiple sources, including individual readers. Stories themselves are subject to network effects, whereby the information infrastructure shapes patterns of dissemination along friendship and family ties. Sometimes this is called "Journalism 2.0," "participatory journalism," or "citizen journalism," terms which refer to the fundamentally interactive presentation of content and a dynamic relationship between the producers and consumers of news. Internet users generate content and comment on what they find online: increasingly, Muslim internet users expect this of their online news sources (Abdul-Mageed 2008). Email, instant messaging, and really simple syndication (RSS) feeds and social networking sites such as YouTube, Flickr, and Myspace are not just means of distributing stories, but are themselves tools upon which journalists increasingly depend. Blogs have also become sources of news, largely because they are free.

CHANGING NEWS DIETS: CRISIS, FALSE, AND DIASPORIC NEWS

Television is the most dominant source of news, and holding socioeconomic status and demographic factors constant, attention to television news coverage is a significant driver of (anti-U.S.) public opinion, particularly in the Middle East (Nisbet 2004). As in most countries, the internet is primarily used for entertainment purposes. Still, the internet is an increasingly important part of the news diet of many Muslims, especially for wealthy elites, government policy makers, civic leaders, and students.

Al Jazeera is probably the most widely read single online news source in the Muslim world. Content is frequently updated and is thematically consistent across English and Arabic versions (Abdul-Mageed 2008). Yet, compared to Western media, there are definite differences in the frames used. Websites for the *New York Times* and the *Guardian* consistently framed the Iraq war as a project in rebuilding the country. In contrast, Al Jazeera and *Al Ahram*—the newspaper of record for the Egyptian government—framed the Iraq war in terms of conflict and strife using negative tones and terms (Dimitrova and Connolly-Ahern 2007). Online news sources still exhibit cultural biases: news sources from the United States and "Coalition of the Willing" produced positive content, human interest stories, and media self-coverage; news sources in Egypt, Malaysia, Pakistan, Turkey, and the UAE framed the war in terms of responsibility (Dimitrova et al. 2005). For many Muslims, online news sites are not just an alternative to state-run or state-censored sources, but are an alternative to Western news sources. Regular Muslim readers find Al Jazeera online more respectful of religion, culture, and tradition than the CNN and BBC websites (Barkho 2006).

As such, the internet is a particularly important part of the news diet in three ways: during times of political or military crisis; as a tool for confirming or disabusing false news reports from government agencies; as a way of getting news from the diaspora to a home country, or from a home country to the diaspora. It is true that large majorities of the population do not have internet access. However, in times of political crisis, social elites often do have access to information technologies that can channel news and perspectives from multiple domestic and international sources, and for better or worse it is these social elites who often constitute civil society and are key actors in domestic political affairs. In many Muslim countries, especially the more authoritarian ones, the internet has become the primary source of news in times of political crisis. During times of political and military crisis, news supplies can be especially constrained, whether by infrastructure failure or tightened government oversight.

In many countries, online news consumption peaks during times of political or military crisis, environmental catastrophe, or complex humanitarian disaster, and countries with large Muslim communities are no exception. Sometimes these crises are very real—affecting the lives and livelihood of citizens. Even when only a small proportion of the public was online in Pakistan, internet use spiked during the nuclear tests in the spring of 1998 and the political coup in October 1999 (Wolcott and Goodman 2000). This phenomenon is not unique to the Muslim world—internet use in the United States, Spain, and the United Kingdom also peaked during terrorist attacks on their national soil. But going online during crises is a much more politically risky tactic in regimes where news production is regulated by ruling elites. Many countries have a censorial political culture (see Chapter 6), which can mean that journalists face explicit extra-organizational censorship, put up with internal organizational surveillance or find themselves censoring their own work. In times of crisis, journalists are often drafted into service of national propaganda while undermining such propaganda by publishing with transnational media outlets (Amin 2002). The events of September 11, 2001, were reported very quickly, and not just within the online news sphere of Islamic countries—prominent news sites in China had photos and commentary online 10 minutes after the first plane hit the World Trade Center tower (Xu 2007).

Thus, while large majorities of the population do not have internet access themselves, in times of political crisis, new information technologies such as the internet remain an informational lifeline. Whereas part and parcel of political crisis often meant disruption in the flow of information over mass media such as radio, television or newspapers, or the corrupted use of mass media for propaganda purposes, new ICTs are more likely to keep information channels open in times of crisis. Moreover, since it is usually the social elites who have internet access, it is actually the media diet of social elites that is diversifying the most quickly. Sometimes these crises are falsely constructed by national news agencies, and the consumption of internet news peaks because citizens are checking other international news sources to verify what they have heard or read locally. For example, the use of the internet for news in Azerbaijan peaks when the national newspaper publishes stories that the United States is bombing Tehran.

CHANGING NEWS PRODUCTION: BLOGGERS, LITTLE BROTHERS, AND CITIZEN JOURNALISTS

Muslim bloggers and citizen journalists are an increasingly important part of the system of political communication in many countries. As blogger Alaa Abd El Fattah observes, "with the pervasiveness of mobile phone cameras, it is rare to hear of a human rights violation, a political event or a major incident that isn't accompanied with a mobile phone video published on YouTube" (Fattah 2008). Not only do bloggers write their own essays on news and current events, but they generate story ideas and even break news that eventually gets picked up by professional journalists. Moreover, blogger activities are the subject of international news stories. Unfortunately, one sign of the growing importance of bloggers in political communication is the increasing frequency of their arrests. These non-professional pundits, often called "citizen journalists," had been jailed for posting content online deemed offensive by cultural elites. Thirty seven of these had occurred in Muslim countries, and most of these within Egypt. Table 4.1 identifies the major arrests as reported in major English-language news media, with details on the type of activity and the type of punishment.

Bloggers often expose corruption or human rights violations. Sina Motalebi, one of the first bloggers arrested in a Muslim country explicitly for blogging, embarrassed Iranian officials in 2003. But other kinds of opinions about or evaluations of political figures, even if there is no accusation of corruption, can also earn time in jail. Since 2005, seven bloggers have been arrested for violating cultural norms, and another eleven have been arrested for debating public policy options such as constitutional amendments or foreign policy online. While blogs are often used for posting personal opinion, they are also used to coordinate and report on social protest, and doing these things can attract the attention of national security officials. Even blogging about the arrest of other bloggers has been known to result in jail time. Authoritarian regimes, such as Iran and Egypt, are particularly vigilant about surveilling bloggers during times of elections—or pseudo-elections. That the reasons for arrests are difficult to document is itself evidence of how the state is beginning to monitor this domain—casually and clumsily.

Table 4.1: Blogger Arrests in the Muslim World, 2003–2010

Year	Country	Blogger Name, Given Reason for Arrest and / or Jail Time
2003	Iran	Sina Motalebi, exposing corruption or human rights violations (arrested for being a security threat – 23 days).
2004	Iran	Omid Sheikhan, posting comments about political figures (arrested for satirical comments about Iran's leaders – 18 months).
2005	Egypt	Abdolkarim Nabil Seliman (Kareem Amer), posting comments about political figures and "criticizing President Hosni Mubarak and the state's religious institutions" (arrested because of a security complaint filed by Islamic fundamentalists – 4 years).
	Iran	Arash Cigarchi, posting comments about public policy (arrested for espionage, "aiding and abating hostile governments and opposition groups," endangering national security and insulting Iran's leaders – 3 years). Mojtaba Saminejad, posting comments about public policy (arrested for criticizing the arrests of fellow bloggers – 34 months).
	Singapore	Benjamin Koh Song Huat, violating cultural norms (arrested for making inflammatory comments about Malays and Muslims on the Internet – 3 years). Gan Huai Shi, violating cultural norms (arrested for posting racial remarks – sentence pending). Nicholas Lim Yew, violating cultural norms (arrested for making inflammatory comments about Malays and Muslims on the Internet – 3 years).
	Tunisia	Mohammed Abbou, posting comments about public policy (arrested for criticizing Tunisian government – 2 years).
2006	Egypt	Abdolkarim Nabil Seliman (Kareem Amer), violating cultural norms (arrested for criticizing Islam – 4 years). Alaa Abd El-Fatah, using blog to organize or cover social protest (arrested for participating in a non-violent sit-in – 15 days). Rami Siyam (Ayyoub), posting comments about public policy (arrested for criticizing Egyptian government – 5 days)
	Iran	Ahmad Reza Shiri, using blog to organize or cover social protest (arrested for calling for a boycott of legislative elections – 3 years). Arash Sigarchi, posting comments about public policy (arrested for criticizing the arrests of fellow bloggers – 18 months).
	Syria	Ali Sayed al-Shihabi, No reason given (5 months).

(continued)

Table 4.1: Continued

Year	Country	Blogger Name, Given Reason for Arrest and / or Jail Time
2007	Egypt	Abd El-Rahman Faras, posting comments about political figures (arrested for posting personal details about officers of the State security – pending). Abdul-Moneim Mahmud, violating cultural norms (arrested for criticizing Islam – 2 month). Ahmed Mohsen, violating cultural norms (arrested as part of crackdown on illegal "Muslim Brotherhood" – pending). Hossam El-Hendy, using blog to organize or cover social protest (arrested for covering a university protest – 1 day). Malek, using blog to organize or cover social protest (arrested for taking part in a protest against the controversial constitutional amendments which were approved by Egypt's parliament – 1 day). Mina, using blog to organize or cover social protest (arrested for taking part in a protest against the controversial constitutional amendments which were approved by Egypt's parliament – 1 day). Mohammad Gamar, using blog to organize or cover social protest (arrested for taking part in a protest against the controversial constitutional amendments which were approved by Egypt's parliament – 1 day). Omar El Sharkawy, No reason given – 1 week).
	India	Lakshmana Kailash, violating cultural norms (arrested for posting insulting images of revered historical figure – 3 weeks).
	Iran	Kianush Sanjari, using blog to organize or cover social protest (arrested for posting protests on his blog – 3 months). Reza Valizadeh, posted about political figures (arrested for revealing Iranian president's overpriced dogs – 18 months).
	Kuwait	Bashar Al-Sayegh, posting comments about political figures (for a comment on Bashar's forum regarding the Amir – pending).
	Malaysia	Nat Tan, exposing corruption or human rights violations (arrested for publishing his comment on his blog – 4 days).
	Pakistan	Urooj Zia, posting comments about public policy (arrested for protesting against the government – 4 hours).
	Saudi Arabia	Fouad al-Farhan, posting comments about public policy (arrested for criticizing corruption and calling for political reform – 4 months).
	Syria	Tarek Baiasi, posting comments about public policy (arrested for insulting security services – 2 years).
	Tunisia	Slim Boukhdir, exposing corruption or human rights violations (arrested for aggression against a public employee and affront to public decency – 1 year).

114

2008	Azerbaijan	Adnan Hajizade and Emin Milli, posting comments about political figures (arrested for video parodies hooliganism – 2 years).
	Egypt	Mohamed Adel, posting comments about public policy (criticized the government and expressed support for the Islamist Palestinian group Hamas – Pending). Per Bjorklund, using blog to organize or cover social protest (seen taking pictures/video during protest – Pending). James Karl Buck, using blog to organize or cover social protest (detained after photographing a labor rally near a textile mill – Pending). Ahmed Maher Ibrahim, posting comments about public policy (used Facebook to call general strike on Hosni Mubarak's 80th birthday, detained, stripped, beaten – 12 hours). Hala El-Masry, violating cultural norms (posted about the persecution of the Coptic minority in Egypt – Pending). Mahamed El Sharkawi, posting comments about public policy (distributing leaflets urging Cairo residents to go on strike against food price hikes, arrested by moral decency police unit – Pending). Philip Rizk, offline and online activism (participated in a six-mile walk in support of the Palestinians in Gaza – Pending). Diaa Eddin Gad, posting comments about public policy (participated in a "in a peaceful demonstration in Cairo organized by the Wafd Party – arrested and held for four days).
	Iran	Hossein Derakhshan, posting comments about public policy (offered the first views of ordinary life in Israel to Iranians, arrested for spying for Israel – could face the death penalty).
	Malaysia	Syed Azidi Syed Aziz, offline and online activism (flew the flag upside down and arrested for inciting the public – Pending). Raja Petra Kamarudin, violating cultural norms (posted an article that "insulted Islam" – Pending). Aduka Taruna, posting comments about political figures (posted an allegedly insulting comment on his blog following the demise of the late sultan, arrested for "misusing the media" – Pending).
	Morocco	Mohammed Erraji, posting comments about political figures (convicted after writing an article saying that the King's charitable habits were encouraging a culture of dependency, jailed for disrespecting the monarchy – 2 years). Fouad Mortada, posting comments about political figures (created a false profile on the Facebook website using the identity of the King's brother – 3 years).
	Saudi Arabia	Fouah al-Farhan, posting comments about public policy (discussing social issues and accusing the government of falsehoods, arrested for "specific violations of nonsecurity laws" – Pending). Roshdi Algadir, violating cultural norms (posting a poem, detained, beaten – 3 hours).
	Syria	Osama Edward Mousa, posting comments about public policy (arrested for criticizing the Syrian government – Pending).

(*continued*)

Table 4.1: Continued

Year	Country	Blogger Name, Given Reason for Arrest and / or Jail Time
	Turkey	Amir Farshad Ebrahimi, posting comments about public policy (arrested at request of Iranian authorities, detained in Turkey for two days).
2009	Nigeria	Jonathan Elundu, posting comments about public policy (arrested for "sponsoring a guerilla news agency" – Pending).
	Iran	24 reporters and bloggers are still in jail after June's disputed election, including: Muhammad Ali Abtahi, a former vice president and blogger, and Muhammad Atrianfar, a former deputy interior minister, for offline and online activism, including gathering and acting against national security; propaganda against the Islamic Republic, disturbing public order by joining illegal gatherings on June 15 2009; Shiva Nazar Ahari, blogger and member of the Reporters of Human Rights Committee; Karim Arghandeh, blogger and reporter for pro-reform newspapers Salam, Vaghieh and Afaghieh; Mostafa Ghavnlo Ghajar, contributor to newspapers, radio and blogger; Somaieh Tohidlou, detained blogger and sociologist – Pending.
	Syria	Kareem Arabji, posting about public policy (arrested by security forces for broadcasting false or exaggerated news which would affect the morale of the country – Pending.)
	Tunisia	Fatma Arabicca, posting about public policy (arrested for being a cartoonist – Pending).
	Morocco	Bashir Hazem, using blog to organize or cover social protest (posting a press release about clash between students and security forces and spreading news about protest – 4 months).
	Malaysia	Six people arrested for posting comments on political figures (posting offensive comments on the Internet insulting Perak ruler Sultan Azlan Shah – Pending).

Source: Howard and WIA Project 2008 with additional updates.

Even countries that have experienced some moves in the direction of democratic openness will assign security services to harassing bloggers. In part, this is because bloggers have been known to break news stories, provide fresh photos, and maintain diverse ideological positions or the voices of women and minorities who are not represented by established political interests. In Kuwait, much of the momentum behind the women's suffrage movement was maintained online (Al-Roomi 2007). Bloggers report on organized protest in Egypt, mob violence against women, and the heavy hand of response from state security. As the table suggests, bloggers can be just as eligible as journalists and political opposition leaders for fines and imprisonment.

In important ways, digital technologies allow citizens to surveille the activities of state. During Kenya's tense elections in December 2007, amateur journalists who were passionate about life in their rural communities but unable to access traditional media used mobile phone cameras to upload video interviews from the countryside. During Israel's attack on Gaza in December 2008, Al Jazeera developed an application for collecting incident reports from the ground, using SMS and Twitter (Al Jazeera 2009; Ramey 2007). As Anderson and Eikelman conclude, online Arab newspapers "collectively constitute a new community of communication that is transnational, open to more participants, and interactive in a way that traditional broadcasting has not been" (1999).

For example, analysis of articles published during the second Iraq war on *Al Arabiya*'s site and reader responses to those articles reveal that that Arabs not only challenged the views of the *Al Arabiya* site about the war, but they also offered their own versions of events (Al-Saggaf 2006). Moreover, in their responses, readers also posted news about the events covered that they obtained from other satellite television stations, such as Al Jazeera, or from websites in which news was reported by people who witnessed or were involved in the events themselves (Al-Saggaf 2006). Turkey, Iran, and Egypt have vibrant blogospheres.[1]

Both news websites produced by professional journalists and blogs produced by citizens have an increasingly important role in domestic political life. In Kyrgystan, the "samizdat" or unofficial blogs provided a significant amount of political news and information not available through mainstream media. These online sources were essential in articulating opposition to authoritarian rule and provided a crucial infrastructure for coordinating the Tulip Revolution (Kulikova and Permuter 2007). In these ways, blogs have had a role in democratic transitions, by supplying the information needed by elites in deciding whether to back an autocrat or defect in favor of a pluralistic or democratic pact. Internet access is often limited to wealthy social elites, but these elites have a key role in either accepting or rejecting authoritarian rule.

Access to the perspectives and information produced by international news media and cultural diasporas is increasingly important. Diasporic communities increasingly produce their own news, news that is both for their community and in part addressed to the homeland. And increasingly, the new ICTs have allowed news sources within these countries to address more than a local or regional audience, but to project their news (and perspectives) internationally. This overseas reach has had the effect of helping to maintain flows of information within and between diasporic groups, but also has had the effect of putting slightly more and slightly different news coverage into the news diet of non-Muslims.

THE CHALLENGES OF JOURNALISM ACROSS THE MUSLIM WORLD

Researchers comparing journalistic practices around the Muslim world find multiple challenges facing professional journalists. First and perhaps most obvious, some countries do not have the tradition of free speech that enables citizens and journalists to use information technologies for news and political research. The allocation of broadcast licenses should be open, fair, and apolitical, but such processes rarely are (see Table 2.2 on openness of spectrum allocation). Ideally, a country's libel laws should be clear but not onerous, government offices should be good at keeping records, and journalists should have unrestricted access to these records.

Second, some countries do not have a professionalized cohort of journalists, editors, and news managers. In some countries, journalists are barely able to use information technologies for their investigative reporting: sometimes their informational literacy is low and they lack search skills; sometimes they simply do not have access to the physical resources of computers and steady connections that are needed for research online. There is evidence that such skills come with practice, and there are a host of journalist training programs that attend to information skills. Computer training courses serve to professionalize cohorts of aspiring journalists, a process that includes exposure to the norms of practice in other countries and an introduction to the forums for debating journalistic practice itself. A professional community of journalists develops the norms, rules, and patterns of behavior that encourage ethical practices. Moreover, it allows for some diversity and specialization in the topics reported on, and even allows members to organize for decent levels of pay (which diminishes the temptations of corruption).

Some countries do not have news managers with the experience necessary for motivating and editing journalists, negotiating for independence from political elites in times of crisis, and managing the business well enough to provide newsrooms with ICT resources. Whether print, newspaper, radio, television, or online, such newsrooms require experienced management to work well, and countries with only a few independent newsrooms have few opportunities for professionalization. Such management skills include savvy with the multimedia aspects of the news business, but also the ability to produce research on a news market, to tailor the news to audience needs, and to produce reliable broadcast or circulation data. Often, being a well-managed business, with revenues that are not dependent on government subsidy, allows for editorial independence.

Third, some countries do not have multiple, competing news organizations that work to represent the diversity of interests within a country and critique the public policy options offered by political leaders. Having access to radio and television broadcasts, print newspapers, and the internet makes for a more diverse news diet. In the most autocratic of Muslim countries, it is actually domestic news that is in limited supply: in Iran, Persian-language content is censored more than English-language content; in Central Asia, people report having easier access to news in English or Russian than content in regional languages on regional affairs. In general, having a plurality of news sources is especially important for access to international news and debate over Koranic interpretation. Among non-Arabic speaking countries, such a plurality is important for news content relevant to minority language groups.

Fourth, online journalism is subject to many of the constraints and pressures that can beleaguer the production of news in print or for broadcast. Sensational stories are given the most type, broadcast time, or screen space. Research on Al Jazeera's site has consistently revealed that military and political violence, politics, and foreign relations are priorities for its editors, and these stories in turn receive the most comment from online readership. Branded news organizations like to maintain control of their website content. So while blogs and specialized news portals may allow for more web 2.0 content, sites such as Al Jazeera's only allow readers to contribute textual responses (Abdul-Mageed 2008).

Finally, many of these countries do not have supporting institutions for a modern, wired newsroom. Such institutional reinforcements include legal protections for reporters, trade associations to represent the interests of private media owners, and professional associations to represent the interests of journalists, or civic groups that produce public policy options to compete with those of political elites or the states. It also helps to have institutions of higher learning to train journalists and open market access to the machinery of news production (newspaper suppliers, printers, power suppliers, and radio and television transmitters). Clear tax and ownership reporting rules make it easier to track the activities of media owners, so that consumers can judge the objectivity of news and assess media concentration.

However, new ICTs are having a significant impact on the institutional arrangements that can constrain or support effective journalism in Muslim countries. Research by the BBC into journalistic practices in nine Muslim countries in Africa demonstrated that even though the vast majority of the population did not have a news diet that included the internet, the internet was a key research tool for modern journalists. Policy and regulatory research was becoming easier. Members of national media unions used the internet to communicate and organize when physical meetings were logistically or politically impossible. The internet allowed journalists to stay abreast of global media developments and to issue alerts about media freedom violations. In times of crisis, news teams that were forced to operate with no permanent offices used the internet to write and submit to deadline (African Media Development Initiative 2006). Radio broadcasters that lose power or have their analog transmission equipment destroyed have been known to continue broadcasting online in the interim. Thus, for even radio stations, television broadcasters, and print newspapers, journalists and editorial staff increasingly depend on the digital information infrastructure of mobile phones and internet connectivity. Put another way, it is this digital infrastructure that significantly improves the organizational capacity and efficiency of offline news outlets. Indeed, one of the important lessons learned from this cross-national study is that improving the informational sophistication and digital literacy of journalists resulted in better content through enhanced research skills, the involvement of female, rural, and marginal voices in the authorship and production of local news, and the improved organizational efficiency of newsrooms (African Media Development Initiative 2006). Global news agencies, such as AP, AFP, Reuters, and IPS still provide many of the photographs used by non-English news organizations such as the Arabic-language newspaper *Al-Hayat*, but regional journalists definitely employ their own frames within the body of news articles (Fahmy 2005).

DIVERSITY IN MEDIA OWNERSHIP: BIG, SMALL, AND NEW MEDIA

Ultimately, media ownership imparts control, and for most Muslim countries in recent decades, the mass media has been owned by the state. Even today, across the 15 largest Muslim media systems, ownership patterns vary in interesting ways. In many Western countries, there is less and less diversity in the ownership of media assets because these assets are being concentrated among fewer and fewer corporate actors. In some Muslim countries,

Table 4.2: Media Concentration in 15 Largest Muslim Media Markets, 2010

Country	Cell phone Provider	ISPs	Newspapers	Radio Stations	Television Stations	State Media Market Share
Afghanistan	●		·	•	●	▪
Algeria	·	•	·	·	·	■
Bangladesh	·		●		•	▪
Egypt	●		•		•	▪
Indonesia	·	●	•	•	•	▪
India	●	•	●	•	•	▪
Iran	·	•	·	·	·	■
Iraq	·	·	●	•	•	·
Morocco	·	•	•	•	·	▪
Nigeria	●	●	●	●	●	■
Pakistan		●	•	•	•	·
Saudi Arabia	•	·	·		·	■
Sudan	●	·	•	•	•	▪
Turkey	●	●	●		●	·
Uzbekistan	·		·	•	•	■

Sources: Howard and WIA Project 2008.

Notes: Concentration indicated as media assets held by a small (·), medium (•), or large (●) number of actors. State dominance in media markets through direct ownership or indirect organizational control indicated as low (·), moderate (▪), or high (■).

media assets are also concentrated, but among state actors such as ministries of communications, government secretariats, or publicly traded companies in which state agencies still hold controlling shares. In other Muslim countries, there is modest competition among the state and private owners of television stations, radio stations, mobile phone service providers, newspapers, and internet service providers.

Table 4.2 compares the degree of media concentration in the 15 largest media markets in the Muslim world. In the past, media concentration has referred to the lack of ownership diversity among media assets such as newspapers, radio stations, and television broadcasters. However, contemporary media concentration must also be evaluated in terms of digital infrastructure such as internet and mobile phone service providers. Over the last decade, these critical information infrastructures have proven to be a key means of both organizing political insurgencies and maintaining ideological control. In this chart, state dominance of the media is assessed using data on the ownership of the top five daily newspapers and top five television stations. These 10 media organizations were evaluated for both the percentage control by state actors and the degree of market share that state agencies command with their media outlets (Djankov et al. 2003). This original data was collected in 1999, and the 15 largest media markets were reassessed in 2008 (World Information Access Project 2008).

Comparatively, Indonesia, Nigeria, Pakistan, and Turkey have a large number of competing internet service providers. Overall, Nigeria and Turkey have the most media diversity, while media assets in Algeria, Iran, Morocco, and Saudi Arabia remain concentrated. Yet among these latter countries, Morocco's media industry is comparatively less dominated by state agencies. In advanced democracies of the OECD, media assets are often concentrated by a few private firms, while in these 15 large media markets the problem of concentration concerns the state: in Uzebekistan, Saudi Arabia, Nigeria, Iran, and Algeria, state agencies dominate the production of news. This contrast is important because media systems that seem to have a large number of newspapers, television stations, and internet service providers may still be dominated by state ownership, an influence that can significantly shape public opinion. Thus, while Nigeria has large numbers of different organizations producing media content and running information infrastructure and Iran has few of these organizations, state dominance of the media system is comparable. Similarly, Pakistan and Iraq have fewer distinct media and infrastructure operators, but the state does not play such a strong supervisory role. Of the fifteen largest media markets, only Turkey has a system of political communication that might be considered best equipped to support independent, competitive news journalism—it has a diverse number of media and infrastructure organizations, few of which are managed by state agencies.

Media in many developing countries are owned and operated by the state, but in the Muslim world the state newspaper and radio and television broadcasters are additionally tasked with safeguarding Islamic culture and legitimizing elite control. In the constitutional monarchies and strong autocracies, media are given the straightforward responsibility for maintaining the ideological basis for elite rule, but even in the most secular of democracies, journalists and editors have run afoul of content guidelines designed to "maintain stability." In times of crisis, enforcement of such guidelines can depend on the degree of outrage and insult felt by a country's most devout Muslim communities. Through these mass communications media, write Eickelman and Anderson, "establishments articulate their visions for education, worship, social services, politic and entertainment. Emanating from a center, they provide an authorized, top-down pattern of communication so that competing voices are more likely to emerge through the alternative small media" (1999, 9). Mobile phones and the internet, on the other hand, do not support such centralized sourcing of political communication. Indeed, the opposite may be now be true: ICTs support a system of political communication in which multiple visions of social order are forced to compete in ways that do not always support the replication of cultural norms. Whereas mass media such as radio and television are the traditional provenance of the state, the internet and mobile phone support more individuated processes of identity formation.

One way to weight the importance of online news is in comparison with print media, and to distinguish between the online news sources that are set up in-country and those that are hosted overseas. Table 4.3 brings some comparative perspective to the qualities of online news production in countries with large Muslim populations and illustrates the different degrees to which state dominance of a national media system has driven journalism online. As in previous tables, countries are organized in three groups: those which experienced a democratic transition over the last decade; those which experienced democratic entrenchment over the last decade; and those which collapsed, are in interregnum due to war, experienced little institutional change, or have remained authoritarian over time. Many of these countries have vibrant print media industries, with many daily, weekly, and monthly newspapers and magazines. The best comparable data, however, is counts of daily newspapers. While imperfect, this serves as a proxy for the overall size of the print media industry across countries and is taken from UNESCO and additional sources (UNESCO 2007; African Media Development Initiative 2006). Online news sites are defined as content at a specific domain clearly produced or sponsored by a professional news organization in 2008. These sites can include major national print newspapers with websites, and the websites of news organizations that only produce content online.[2]

The online news websites are sometimes the portals of the large daily newspapers, but sometimes they are independent news sources without offline publications or broadcast systems. In countries as diverse as Somalia, Sierra Leone, and Tajikistan, the online production is more robust than print media. A high ratio of online news sites to daily newspapers does not strictly mean that the online news industry has greater market share than print media. Indeed, many of the countries in this study have very vibrant weekly news magazines, and some news websites are only irregularly updated. However, in countries where there are many more online news sites than daily newpapers, it is safe to say that the internet plays a relatively important role in providing the most diverse, fresh news content.

The online news supplies may be more important for countries that are suffering under authoritarianism or experiencing a democratic transition

Table 4.3: State Media Ownership and Online Journalism, 2007–2010

Country	State Media Market Share	Number of Online News Sites / Daily Newspapers	Number of Online News Sites Hosted In-Country / Number of Online News Sites	Importance of Online News Sphere
		Transition		
Albania	..	9/18	1/9	▪
Algeria	■	29/16	0/29	■
Bahrain	•	12/6	1/12	▪
Bosnia	..	20/..	..	■
Comoros	..	3/2	0/3	·
Djibouti	..	4/..	..	▪
Egypt	•	37/0	4/37	■
Georgia	•	13/15	..	■
Ghana	•	10/11	0/10	▪
Indonesia	·	29/790	17/29	■
Kenya	..	31/..	..	■
Kuwait	•	16/8	1/16	▪
Kyrgyzstan	•	5/2	..	▪
Lebanon	..	56/14	6/56	■
Liberia	..	9/3	0/9	·▪
Macedonia	..	13/	0/13	▪
Maldives	..	12/3	0/12	▪
Mauritania	..	3/3	0/3	·
Montenegro	..	20/..	..	■
Niger	■	2/1	..	·
Nigeria	·	31/45	0/31	■
Senegal	•	7/10	0/7	·
Sierra Leone	..	9/0	0/9	▪
Suriname	..	4/3	0/4	·
Tanzania	·	9/12	2/9	▪
Uganda	•	7/6	0/7	·
		Entrenchment		
Bangladesh	•	57/20	0/57	■
Benin	•	3/27	0/3	·
Bulgaria	•	33/59	29/33	■
Cyprus	·	21/8	2/21	▪
Guinea-Bissau	..	0/0	0/0	·
India	•	208/1681	37/208	■
Israel	·	50/..	33/50	■
Malawi	•	2/2	1/2	·
Malaysia	·	24/33	22/24	▪
Mali	•	1/9	1/1	·
Mauritius	..	8/8	0/8	▪

Mozambique	..	3/14	0/3	·
Turkey	·	74/565	52/74	■

Authoritarian

Azerbaijan	·	17/23	1/17	▪
Brunei	..	2/2	0/2	·
Cameroon	■	11/10	0/11	▪
CAR	..	1/0	0/1	·
Chad	■	4/0	0/4	·
Eritrea	..	2/0	0/2	·
Ethiopia	■	3/3	0/3	·
Gambia	..	1/2	..	·
Guinea	..	2/2	0/2	·
Iran	■	36/130	7/36	■
Jordan	▪	10/5	1/10	▪
Kazakhstan	■	21/0	14/21	▪
Libya	..	10/4	0/10	▪
Morocco	▪	32/23	4/32	■
Oman	..	9/5	0/9	▪
Pakistan	▪	143/197	7/143	■
Qatar	..	8/5	0/8	▪
Russia	▪	170/229	136/170	■
Saudi Arabia	■	26/11	8/26	■
Singapore	▪	18/11	13/18	▪
Sudan	▪	12/20	1/12	▪
Syria	■	14/4	4/14	▪
Tajikistan	..	2/0	0/2	·
Togo	■	4/1	0/4	·
Tunisia	▪	6/8	2/6	·
Turkmenistan	■	3/2	0/3	·
UAE	..	14/9	4/14	▪
Uzbekistan	■	5/4	3/5	·
Yemen	..	19/5	0/19	▪

Crisis

Afghanistan	▪	8/19	0/8	▪
Burkina Faso	..	1/5	..	·
Iraq	·	40/0	0/40	■
Ivory Coast	▪	0/20	0/0	·
Somalia	..	12/6	0/12	▪
West Bank & Gaza	..	40/..	..	■
Western Sahara	..	2/..	..	·

Sources: Based on author's calculations from multiple sources: UNESCO 2007; World Information Access Project 2008; African Media Development Initiative 2006; Djankov et al. 2003; Howard and WIA Project 2008.

Notes: State dominance in media markets through direct ownership or indirect organizational control indicated as low (·), moderate (▪), or high (■). Relative importance of online news industry indicated as low (·), medium (▪), or high (■).

than those that are already strong democracies with relatively free presses. Most of the countries with large online news spheres are in these two groups. Moreover, countries experiencing transition or authoritarianism are more likely to have news websites that are hosted overseas—half the countries in these two categories have little or no domestic capacity to host news websites. This is probably both a practical and strategic choice. The entrenched democracies tend to have more balanced ratios of news sites to dailies, and more of these news sites tend to be hosted in-country.

Journalists in the Gulf report that if the country in which they work will not tolerate their activities, the internet allows for online publication where leading civic flouters go for news anyway (Al-Obaidi 2003). Table 4.3 presents trace route data for the websites of major news organizations, data collected in the same way as that presented for political parties and government agencies in previous chapters. Of the 3,001 online news sites analyzed, 1,468 were based in Muslim countries. Of these, hosting information could be found on 1,313 news websites: 31 percent of online news sites were hosted in the Muslim world though not necessarily in the same news market they served; 54 percent of online news sites were actually hosted in the United States.

This table is also interesting because it reveals how state dominance of the media can drive up demand for online news in many countries. First, in many of the countries where the state dominates the media, the ratio of online news sites to daily newspapers is relatively high. Moreover, many of these same countries have relatively few online news sites hosted in-country: they tend to be hosted overseas. Indeed, state dominance of the national news industry often drives journalism online. Facing strict controls in the newspaper or broadcast industries, journalists will form their own online news agencies, or will contribute content to such sources while formally remaining employees of state agencies. The dominance of state-owned big media drives journalists to develop small and new media alternatives, and drives citizens to seek this kind of content—especially in times of political transition.

The importance of online news is a qualitative comparative judgment based on several important metrics: the relative size of the internet-using population; the number of online news sites compared to print media; and the number of online news sites hosted in-country. These multiple, nuanced measures are crucial because online news can be important for different reasons. Comparatively speaking, new media journalism is valuable in Algeria, Egypt, Iran, Morocco, Russia, and Saudi Arabia because it is the primary forum for independent and critical journalism, generated both by professional and citizen journalists. In these countries, online news is produced by loose organizations of journalists, sometimes writing from outside the country, producing content that has no "hard copy" or broadcast equivalent, and content that may not even be hosted on servers located in-country. New media journalism is important in Indonesia in that many news outlets have found the freedom to build a multimedia news infrastructure: content may appear in digital and analog formats, hosted on a domestic information infrastructure by a formally incorporated news organization with a dedicated full-time staff. This country has a rapidly growing, politically active, internet user base. In Iraq, Lebanon, Nigeria and Pakistan, online journalism is crucial for supplying its literate, far-flung diasporas with news about home, and for providing news and information during the frequent security crises in these countries. Bangladesh, India, Israel, and Turkey have vibrant civil societies, and the online news industry provides fresh interactive content for communities at home and abroad.

DIVERSITY IN NEWS CONTENT: HARD NEWS, SOFT NEWS, IDENTITY NEWS

Research in other authoritarian regimes has demonstrated the way in which online public opinion plays an important role in transforming local events into nationally prominent issues. Internet users in a country have actually helped frame local events. Professional journalists will adapt stories framed by bloggers; in countries dominated by state-owned news agencies, these professionals will reinterpret events in favor of authoritarian rulers and soften a blogger's critique. Moreover, mainstream media coverage of political and security issues does not set the frames used in online discourse, though state-owned media outlets are often successful in reframing news for mass audiences (Zhou and Moy 2008). Evidence from Argentina suggests that the frequency and volume of news produced in the modern wired newsroom dissolves the distinctions between hard and soft news (Boczkowski 2009). Either thesis—that online publics help frame news and that modern newsrooms produce different kinds of content—has yet to be tested across the diverse news agencies of Muslim communities. Yet anecdotal evidence from Iran, Egypt, and Saudi Arabia supports the conclusions that internet users can turn local news issues into national concerns, influence the frame used by national media, and resist attempts by the government or state-owned media to reframe and reinterpret evens—at least in online forums. And evidence from studies of journalism across several countries suggests that the internet has allowed news agencies serving large Muslim communities to produce what might be best called "identity news."

Indeed, one of the primary impacts of the internet on journalism and news diets in many Muslim countries is the production of news valued for its ability to define and reinforce Muslim, sectarian, or nationalist identity.

There are three types of identity news that are on the rise in the Muslim community media diets: first, international items that come over digital news feeds that are selected for rebroadcast or reprinting specifically because they are stories that involve Islam or life in other Muslim countries; second, news items that come over digital news feeds that are selected because they involve life in a country's diasporic community; third, news items that are generated by individual citizens, using personal digital media, that form an additional pool of domestic news content from which national editors and journalists increasingly draw. Topically, items about the plight of Palestinians, the treatment of prisoners being held in Guantanamo, and U.S. relations with Iran top the list. At the same time that these news services offer more information and a diversity of opinions to Muslim viewers, news cultures in these countries are themselves changing, becoming more and more reliant on Western news norms of speed, newness, crisis sensationalism, and commodity news (Ghareeb 2000).

The overtly jihadist media sources—organizations that explicitly try to relay text, audio, and video from fundamentalist groups—usually give priority to the conflict zones in Iraq, Afghanistan, and Somalia (Kimmage 2008). Groups such as Ansar al-Sunnah, the Global Islamic Media Front, and the Al-Fajr Media Institute both produce and distribute content, by recording the speeches of terrorist leaders and producing short videos from conflict zones. Such groups do not qualify as news media for the vast majority of Muslim audiences, but exclusion from the major news media systems around the world drives them to distribute what content they can across the network of like-minded affinity groups. Indeed, for the global jihadist movement, these organizations function as both producers and distributors of news, which is a capacity they have mostly because of digital communications infrastructures (Kimmage 2008).

Since editors and journalists can now choose from a great variety of topics and incidents, summarized by international news wires, they will often select items specifically related to Islam. Even in countries where the majority of the country is non-active Muslim, or the state is proudly secular, the news items that are pulled off the international news wires tend to be items on life in other Muslim countries. Since diasporas are also increasingly able to generate news stories, this category of identity news does not just include news and information from other Muslim countries, but also items involving diasporas in other countries.

The information infrastructure of the internet is often owned and operated by private firms. Despite this, the internet itself is the infrastructure for a culture of freely exchanged information. Even though a particular autocratic state may not have the tradition of free speech or strong legal institutions for promoting such conduct, new media technologies are serving as the conduit for cultural content that promotes such values. For this reason, people in many developing Muslim countries admit that they trust the internet as a news source more than print, television, and radio mass media.[3] If true, this means that Iranians perceive the medium of the internet to be the conduit of trustworthy information—not just foreign news sources—because other conduits of international news content such as satellite channels and foreign-based radio stations are not as trustworthy.

Digital information infrastructure has supported the spread of identity news across much of the Muslim world, with the notable exception of Central Asia. The lack of domestic free speech practices can have different consequences for the peoples' news diets in different parts of the world. When respondents in Kazakhstan, Kyrgyzstan, Tajikistan, and Uzbekistan were surveyed about their news consumption, the majority agreed that they had comprehensive access to information about national politics. But the same proportion of people reported not having comprehensive access to information about regional or global politics (CAICT Project 2006). In contrast, Azeris rely on the internet to check international news stories that are presented in the nationally controlled media. When the *Baku* daily newspaper reported that the United States was about to bomb Iran, students used the internet to confirm that this was a false lead. For some in these countries, the internet is used to supplement what people know to be missing or suspect in their news diets: in Central Asia, this means relying on the internet for supplementary news on international affairs; in the Islamic republics, this means relying on the internet for supplementary news on domestic affairs.

THE EVOLVING POLITICAL ECONOMY OF NEW MEDIA JOURNALISM

The internet has significantly broadened political discourse across borders. Not only do citizens in the Muslim world receive more authoritative news online, but the internet has become a crucial research tool for community journalists. Yet the political economy of online news production in Muslim countries is complex. Activists often report that the internet and mobile phones are the medium of choice for the youth in their movement, but industry insiders report that the consumers of their online content are rarely youth. Just as in many advanced democracies, even though young people are more avid technology users, it is the older cohort between age 26 and 40 that looks for online news. Youth use blogs and chat rooms, while middle-aged professionals who feel that they are not getting what they want from the highly censored traditional media use the internet for news and political information (Gan 2002).

How the political economy of online journalism in the Muslim world will evolve is uncertain. Since so much internet infrastructure is international and independent of any particular government, there are few ways that autocratic governments can regulate content that is hosted overseas. As argued in Chapter 1, many states are actively promoting telecommunications growth, and this has meant both increasingly diverse commercial media offerings, many of which have online media components (Abdulla 2007). Over the last 10 years, the political economy of news has changed significantly because of digital technologies: from a situation where Muslims were mostly consumers of news and culture, to a situation where they produce news as well, have an influence on how news is framed, and have more sources to choose from.

Yet on the whole, neither the rising number of commercial television, radio, print, and online news organizations nor the restricting of government-operated media systems has been sufficient to bring about broader political pluralism (Ayish 2002). The countries that have experienced either a political transition or democratic entrenchment have had increasingly competitive media systems, partnered with increasingly competitive party elections and more active civil society groups. In this sense, the evolution of journalism online is one aspect of contemporary democratization, one that must be coupled or matched by other forms of political change. Many of the countries with a small print news media industry have not experienced a democratic transition, and in these countries the online news sphere is particularly important. Indeed, many of the news organizations publishing online have no offline media product. In contrast, many of the news organizations in transition and entrenched democracies have several news media products, with articles appearing in multiple formats, with some original content only appearing online and in interactive formats. Many of the countries with state-owned media dominating the news industry are among those with large online news outlets.

In the context of many Muslim countries, small media refers to the plethora of occasional newspapers that are produced. Some countries have incredibly active small newspaper industries, and these newspapers tend to have single owners and small circulations. The notion of small media actually comes from the Mohammadis' study of the role of tapes in the Iranian revolution, but it still is a useful concept today, perhaps better used in reference to the small online sources of political news and information (Sreberny-Mohammadi and Mohammadi 1994).

Blogs and mobile phones have become something of an antidote to media concentration in the Muslim world. One advantage of being small or new media is being agile enough to avoid heavy state regulation. Online journalists often do not have to apply for publication licenses. For example, Malaysia's malaysiakini.com has claimed that its independent contribution to democratic debate in that country is possible because the onerous printing and publication rules do not affect them. In recent years, the government has cracked down on dissent by revoking a newspaper's right to print or making the cost of obtaining newsprint prohibitive. Such restrictions have little impact on the website. Heavy state ownership has caused many journalists to publish their work online. A growing number of Muslims—not just digirati—use the internet to diversify their news diet.

The primary impact of ICTs in many Islamic countries has been to extend the depth and breadth of news coverage available. And there is evidence that people in these countries are availing themselves of this diversity of news sources. ICTs have provided new research tools for journalists and have given many citizens the ability to produce their own news and publish their own narratives. In many advanced democracies, journalists are struggling to maintain their independence, media oligopolies are entrenching their power, and news organizations are experimenting with new business models in digital formats. In many developing Muslim countries, journalists are using new ICTs as an opportunity to experiment with producing news in formats that are not so easily managed by political elites. Political elites have been slow to develop ways of regulating news content online, and they have haphazardly applied the censorship and security laws that protected them in the mass media age but are clumsy means of ideological control in the new media age. These new ICTs have had an important role in identity formation for many Muslims, allowing insight and editorial commentary into community problems and prospects.

Chapter 5

Civil Society and Systems of Political Communication

Democracy—and democratization—can no longer be effectively studied without some attention paid to the role of digital information technologies. Not only does the character of this infrastructure have an impact on the opportunity structures for political change and the range of possible outcomes, but the technologies themselves support new forums for political discussion and are themselves politicized media. Even the process of designing information infrastructure can be politicized, such as occasions when designers build video games to represent conflict in Lebanon from their perspectives, or when internet service providers are contracted to build an information infrastructure with easy choke points (Machin and Suleiman 2006). The internet has become a necessary infrastructure for the development of civil society in the experience of Muslim communities around the developing world. First, it is has become an invaluable logistical tool for organization and communication for civil society groups. Second, the internet has become an important incubator for social movements both radical and secular. It is an information infrastructure independent of the state, and civil society groups are by definition social organizations independent of the state so civic political authors are quick to take advantage of the affordances of digital media. Third, the internet has altered the dynamics of political communication systems in many countries, such that the internet itself is the site of political contestation between the state and civil society, and between secularism and Islamism.

In recent years, the news has been replete with stories about how information and communication technologies have been used to coordinate social protest, whether in democracies, emerging democracies, or autocracies. Traditional broadcast and radio are no longer the uniquely pervasive forms of media they once were, especially in modernizing capital cities of the developing world. This has had immense implications for relations between the state and civil society, as well as the meaning of contemporary citizenship.

The virtual communities that have taken root are almost always independent of state control, though they can be monitored and manipulated by the state. Certainly not all of these virtual communities are about politics or even Islam, but their existence is a political phenomenon, particularly in countries where state and social elites have worked hard to police offline communities. Thus, even the bulletin boards and chat rooms dedicated to shopping for brand name watches are sites that practice free speech and where the defense of free speech is a topic of conversation. The internet allows opposition movements that are based outside of a country to reach in and become part of the system of political communication within even the most authoritarian regimes. Banning political parties simply means that formal political opposition is organized online, from outside the country. It also means that civil society leaders turn to the other organizational forms permitted by network technologies.

Different kinds of information technology have long supported discourse and activism in the Muslim communities of the developing world and have often played a role in the political development of secular Islamic states. President Jamal 'Abd al-Nasir skillfully used the radio to help him strengthen his popular base in Egypt, with emotional appeals that fueled nationalist pride in the 1960s. Iranian revolutionaries used cassette tapes to spread their political messages among networks of students, as have radical Saudi Islamists and Yemeni poets (Sreberny-Mohammadi and Mohammadi 1994; Fandy 1999; Miller 2007; Sardar 1993). Email was a crucial communications tool for the opposition organizers in Indonesia who brought down the Suharto government. When the PKK leader Abdullah Ocalan was kidnapped and brought to Turkey to stand trial, email and fax communications allowed Kurdish organizers to plan dramatic demonstrations at embassies and civic centers in 22 different cities across Europe within hours of the kidnapping, and a London-based Kurdish television station helped get supporters into the streets.

Today, there are several countries in which the only examples of meaningful and open discussion about political life are found online. As Warf and Vincent (2007) document, marginalized political minorities have created online communities that allow debate and discussion simply not found offline, such as the Gay and Lesbian Arabic Society (http://www.glas.org). Egypt's Coptic Christians use the internet to publicize their persecution at the hands of Muslim fundamentalists, and in Libya, opposition groups provide websites that effectively function as news portals (Arabic Network for Human Rights Information 2004). In London, the Muslim Brotherhood has sponsored websites critical of the Jordanian and Egyptian governments since 1998 (McLaughlin 2003). In countries where political parties are closely regulated or banned, civil society groups are the surrogate organizations through which some reflection on government activities can occur. Palestinians, at home and in exile, use the internet to overcome political isolation so much that the traditional tactics of activists have altered in significant ways (Aouragh 2008). In Saudi Arabia, the Committee for the Defense of Legitimate Rights and Movement for Islamic Reform in Arabia uses their websites to document corruption, criticize the royal family, debate the utility of Sharia law, and link to content on international websites such as CNN, the New York Times, and Amnesty International (Warf and Vincent 2007). Of course, many of the digital sites for discourse are not directly focused on public policy, but are political in the sense that they enable citizens to discuss topics that would be too sensitive to discuss in other forums.

Civil society is often defined as the self-generating and self-supporting community of people who share a normative order and volunteer to organize political, economic, or cultural activities that are independent from the state (Diamond 1994). Civil society groups are a crucial part of all democracies, concerned with public affairs yet autonomous from the state bureaucracies so that government policy itself—and government corruption—are within their purview. Civil society is constituted by a plurality of groups representing diverse perspectives and promoting those perspectives through communications media and cultural institutions. Moreover, a key tenet of the shared normative order is that no one group can claim to represent the whole of society, and that society is best served by a multitude of groups that contribute in different ways to the dissemination and exchange of information about public policy options and national development goals (Diamond 1994).

Digital technologies are also an infrastructure used by hate groups and have been used both to report human rights abuses to the international community and to coordinate the groups perpetrating human rights abuses (Goldstein and Rotich 2008; Barzilai-Nahon and Barzilai 2005). Muslim extremists use the internet for organizational communication, fund-raising, developing ideological platforms, sending propaganda to members and the outside world, and maintaining a sense of community. Email, VoIP, documentation, and spreadsheet software allow terrorists to keep track of assets and strategy. Video clips of bombings, beheadings, and messages from leadership allow for documentation. Fund-raising occurs through online banking services, many of which are informal, involve exchanges of value other than currency, and appear as donations or remittances. Analyses of terrorist websites often distinguish between the kinds of propaganda meant for insiders and that meant for outsiders. The propaganda meant for group members usually includes ideological or religious slogans and iconography, dates in the political or military history of the group, battle narratives and lists of "martyrs," and structures of leadership and accountability. For outsiders, propaganda is designed to criticize Western media coverage of events usually with links to news sources such as CNN and the BBC, offering reinterpretations of military and political events. The internet even helps support a sense of community, through automated mailing lists that distribute announcements, online discussion forums such as chat rooms, message boards, text/instant messaging, and links to the web ring of affinity groups with like-minded objectives (Chen et al. 2008; Weimann 2006).

Yet it is a mistake to treat the jihadist internet as the most vibrant online Muslim community, or even the most politically significant. There certainly are blogs and websites advocating extremist politics, but the internet has a crucial role as the infrastructure for civil society in countries with large Muslim communities. Chapter 3 demonstrated that the web of political party life online is enormous and energetic. Terrorist organizations are not the only non-state, organized political actor in Muslim communities of the developing world. Civil society groups also use the internet to boost their organizational capacity, offer public policy options, and develop political conversations. Indeed, online civic life appears particularly vibrant under two conditions: when the state is so authoritarian as to ban formal political parties that would normally provide some collective opportunity for engaging with politics and public policy; or when political parties are legal but co-opted or operating in a single-party governance system that harms the credibility of all political parties, rendering them ineffectual organizations incapable of advancing a political agenda for their membership.

The tool kit of contemporary civic engagement involves a variety of internet-based software applications. Study of social interaction on the Turkish site Itiraf.com reveals how much the personal gratification coming from discourse online can serve as a bonding agent for civil society (Ogan and Cagiltay 2006). In Egypt, Facebook has become an important tool for civic organizing. In April 2008, a small planned strike for better wages at a state-owned textile factory in Mahalla, Egypt, became a nationwide strike through a young woman's Facebook networking strategy. That year there were some estimated 160,000 bloggers, and 12 million Egyptians were online regularly, using content-sharing and networking services like YouTube, Flikr, Facebook, and Twitter (McGrath 2009). By 2009, there were some 800,000 Egyptian Facebook members, and it was the third most popular website in that country, after Google and Yahoo. Moreover, the movement that began in an effort to pull off a local factory strike transformed into the 70,000-member "April 6 Youth Movement," made up of young and educated Egyptians, most of whom had not been involved with politics before joining the group (Shapiro 2009). The group has led successful offline campaigns to release journalists from jail, helped organize street protests against Mubarak's diplomatic relations with Israel during Israel's December 2008 air strikes against Gaza, and conducts active online discussions about government corruption.

ISLAMIC CIVIL SOCIETY ONLINE

In many Muslim communities around the developing world, the internet is now the primary means through which young people develop their political identities and articulate their political opinions. This is especially true in the urban centers of middle-income Muslim countries, such as Tehran, Kuala Lumpur, and Istanbul. Here cybercafés abound, multiple information technologies provide connectivity, and bandwidth is plentiful at home and work. In the less developed nations with large Muslim communities, the youthful demographic of internet users is found in both rural and urban settings. And even in the most authoritarian regimes, where "civil society" itself is best described as a small group of well-educated families living in the capital city, the internet provides an information gateway to political news and information about the outside world, connection to the political content produced by a country's diasporas, and some anonymity for talking about politics in ways not easy offline. The internet is used to strengthen existing political groups, to allow people to bridge communities and form new ties, and to create new online communities in which young Muslims discuss—and question—social norms. In some countries, technology policy itself is a domain that attracts new, dedicated civil society organizations. In the Ivory Coast, development practitioners have observed that "five times more NGOs came into being since 1988 than in the entire period of 1916–1988, and many of these NGOs have been drawn to the issues of internet access" (Brunet, Tiemtoré, and Vettraino-Soulard 2004, 42). In countries where there are political battles for more internet exchange points in urban areas or for undersea trunk cables to improve bandwidth, engineers are drawn into public policy debates. In this way, the process of setting engineering standards draws civic groups into technical issues: engineers are politically motivated actors in that they have policy preferences on how best to apply abstract informational rights in specific infrastructure designs, not in the sense that they are using their craft to fight political battles.

Civil society groups have had an important role in developing the information infrastructure of many Muslim countries. Before state agencies developed programs for providing public internet access, it was usually civil society groups that wired up libraries, schools, and community centers with internet access points. These domestic groups, along with international funders such as the Open Society Institute, Aga Khan Foundation, and the State Department's IREX program, pushed state regulators to work out the terms of service delivery. Often these groups had significant input into the engineering and telecommunications standards that states need to set before an ISP can even begin to offer service. Telecommunications officials did not always understand the technologies they were adding to the national information infrastructure, and in this ad hoc policy environment, domestic civil society groups often had a surprising amount of input. In some countries, civil society organizations with financial resources and a technology evangelist on staff could secure internet connections before many businesses. Occasionally, civil society organizations themselves became ISPs, providing inexpensive internet connectivity to members and creating a new revenue source for themselves.

If civil society refers to the non-state forms of organization that help overcome collective action problems, and if new ICTs improve the organizational capacity of civil society, how should we measure these things? There are several ways of comparing the size of civil societies online across Muslim countries, and several proxies for measuring the relative importance of the internet for civil society organization. A simple measure of the proportion of the total population with internet access makes it possible to identify which countries have comparatively small, medium, or large online civil societies.

In many Islamic countries, the political opposition had an online presence before those in power. In part this was because many leaders of political opposition reside in London, New York, Toronto, and Los Angeles, where it was easier to maintain listservs and set up websites on *.net, *.com or *.org domain names. Using their home country's top level domain name often meant negotiating with political elites at home for permissions. For example, Saudi opposition groups such as the Committee for the Defense of Legitimate Rights and the Movement for Islamic Reform in Arabia managed websites from their offices in London several years before the Kingdom itself began considering offering internet access to its citizens.

Not everyone who has internet access will be active members of civic forums, members of nonprofit charities, or participants in social movements. But comparatively speaking, it is safe to say that Liberia, with 0.03 percent of its population online, has a much smaller online civil society than Nigeria (3 percent) or the United Arab Emirates (30 percent). We can assume that internet population is roughly congruent with the size of online civil society. In a given country, the poorest of the poor rarely have internet access, but they are rarely part of a nation's active civil society. Similarly, a country's social elites are often first to get internet access, so in countries where the internet user base is very small, it is safe to assume that these users are wealthy families, students and teachers, lawyers, employees of modern businesses, government officials, and intellectuals. While it is difficult to precisely measure the size of civil society online, this measure is sufficient to

Table 5.1: Civil Society Online, 2008

Country	Size and Growth of Civil Society Online	Libraries Online
	Transition	
Albania	•✚	■
Algeria	•✚	■
Bahrain	●+	☐
Bosnia	●✚	☐
Comoros	•✚	..
Djibouti	·+	☐
Egypt	•+	■
Georgia	•+	■
Ghana	·✚	☐
Indonesia	●+	■
Kenya	•+	■
Kuwait	●+	☐
Kyrgyzstan	•+	☐
Lebanon	●+	☐
Liberia	·+	☐
Macedonia	●✚	☐
Maldives	•+	☐
Mauritania	·+	..
Montenegro	●	■
Niger	·+	■
Nigeria	•✚	☐
Pakistan	•✚	☐
Senegal	•✚	☐
Sierra Leone	·+	☐
Suriname	•+	☐
Tanzania	·+	☐
Uganda	·✚	■
	Entrenchment	
Bangladesh	·+	☐
Benin	•✚	☐
Bulgaria	●+	■
Cyprus	●+	☐
Guinea-Bissau	•+	☐
India	•+	■
Israel	●+	■
Malawi	·+	☐
Malaysia	●+	■
Mali	·+	☐
Mauritius	●+	■
Mozambique	·+	☐
Turkey	●+	☐

Authoritarian

Azerbaijan	•✚	☐
Brunei	●+	◻
Cameroon	·+	◻
CAR	·+	☐
Chad	·✚	..
Eritrea	•✚	☐
Ethiopia	·✚	☐
Gambia	•+	■
Guinea	·+	◻
Iran	●✚	☐
Jordan	●+	◻
Kazakhstan	•+	◻
Libya	·✚	■
Morocco	●✚	◻
Oman	●+	◻
Pakistan	·✚	◻
Qatar	●+	■
Russia	●+	◻
Saudi Arabia	●+	◻
Singapore	●+	■
Sudan	•+	◻
Syria	·✚	◻
Tajikistan	·+	☐
Togo	•+	☐
Tunisia	●+	◻
Turkmenistan	·+	☐
UAE	●+	■
Uzbekistan	•✚	◻
Yemen	•✚	◻

Crisis

Afghanistan	·✚	◻
Burkina Faso	·+	◻
Ivory Coast	·+	☐
Iraq	·✚	◻
Somalia	·+	■
West Bank & Gaza	•+	..
Western Sahara		..

Source: Based on author's calculations from multiple sources: WIA, 2008; World Bank, 2008.

Notes: Size of online population calculated as proportion of national population online in 2007, and indicated as comparatively small (·), medium (•), or large (●). Growth of online population calculated as the annual rate of growth in internet population from the year 2000 to 2007, and indicated as comparatively slow (+), moderate (+), or rapid (✚) growth. Definitions in text. The online library infrastructure of the five largest government, private or other public libraries evaluated as poor (☐) if none or 1 library was online, modest (◻) if 2–4 libraries were online, or good (■) if all five libraries were online.

139

make a qualitative, comparative judgment of whether online civil society is small, medium, or large.[1]

Moreover, growth in the internet user base reveals much about how quickly civil society has grown online. I define the "digital transition" as the point at which a country goes from a condition in which very few active citizens are online to one in which most active citizens have internet access. This is a social transformation from high rates of growth in the internet-using population to low rates of growth. The dynamics of this transition are such that in the initial years of internet or mobile phone use, rates of diffusion are not only high but accelerating. Eventually, the rate of acceleration in technology diffusion declines, such that the bulk of the population is online and the rate of growth dwindles. For example, Singapore currently has a slow growth rate in its internet user base, but the vast majority of its citizens are online. Singapore has completed an important marker of growth in its online civil society: its online population is growing in absolute numbers, but the rate of change in its growth rate is negative. In contrast, Pakistan has yet to go that a digital transition. For its size, only a small proportion of the people in Pakistan are online, but the growth rate is relatively high.[2]

Table 5.1 compares important features of online civil society across 75 countries. The comparative size of online civil society is measured by taking the proportion of the national population with internet access in 2007.

As discussed earlier, the challenges of comparing and interpreting international statistics on internet use by Muslim communities are multiple. First, such data is often reported as a number of internet subscribers, even though there can be many users for each subscription. In 2000, for example, across the Arab world there were on average 3.8 users for each subscription: from a low of 2.5 users per subscriber in the UAE, Qatar, Bahrain, Kuwait, and Oman to 5.0 in Tunisia, Libya, Syria, and the Sudan to as many as 8.0 in Egypt (Franda 2001, 42). To report growth in these kinds of numbers often means measuring change in thousands of percent. Here, I again offer that doubling time, a useful measure in demography, reveals something of the speed of growth in civil society online and its stage in development.

What explains such rapid growth in civic life online in so many parts of the Muslim world? The most straightforward explanation of why civil society online grows rapidly online is the falling cost of internet access. Countries where internet access has become less costly have seen greater use and a greater number of civic groups taking to the internet. Some groups are long-standing contributors to civic discourse; many are new and exist because the internet has facilitated the interaction and organization of like-minded citizens. Table 5.2 demonstrates how much this has changed for the average urban dweller in the major cities. In 2000, the average person living in Karachi would have spent three-quarters of his daily income on an hour of

Table 5.2: Cost of Internet Access in 12 Large Cities, 2000 and 2010

| | Percent of Average Daily Income Spent on an Hour of Internet Access in Major Urban Areas | |
	2000	2010
Cairo	26	4
Delhi	59	8
Dhaka	62	7
Istanbul	..	4
Jakarta	28	6
Karachi	75	7
Kolkata	59	5
Lagos	..	15
Moscow	137	6
Mumbai	89	8
Saint Petersburg	38	3
Tehran	47	8
Average	62	7

Source: WIA 2008 with updates for 2010.

Note: See source for listing of primary and secondary cities for each country.

internet access at a cybercafé, but by 2010 he would spend less than a tenth of that daily income.

While the costs of internet access may explain much about its diffusion as an instrument of political communication, there are some complex trends. The cost of internet access is only partly a function of demand. The cost of going online at commercial internet access points is also shaped by real estate prices. Between 2000 and 2010, the cost of internet access for the residents of primary and secondary cities in India, Indonesia, Nigeria, and Pakistan fell to under a dollar an hour at a commercial internet access point. These service costs, obviously, have had a significant impact on whether or not average citizens could make regular use of the internet.

The wealthier Muslim countries are able to make their own infrastructure investments, and in interesting ways the countries that do not depend on World Bank loans do not face the same policy pressures to develop open and public internet access. This was observed in Central Asia, where the few countries with significant oil revenues were less obliged to international lending agencies to take out loans conditional on telecommunications reform (McGlinchey and Johnson 2007). Countries in Central Asia that did take out such conditional loans have been expected to enact telecommunications policy reform. In the Middle East and North Africa, over the last decade,

World Bank lending for telecommunications to borrowers has also grown significantly with similar outcomes. Between 1992 and 2001, approximately 15 percent of all lending was for telecommunications—some 94 million U.S. dollars[3]—though the vast majority of that sum was borrowed in the last few years for which data is available (World Bank 2001). This amount probably underestimates the amount of money borrowed for telecommunications development given that other categories of lending, such as public sector management, urban development, finance and multisector expenditures would have included ICT investments. Yet the spread of information technologies among Islamic countries has not been driven by economic or technological factors alone, but by civil society.

DEBATE AND DISCOURSE ONLINE

It is through ICTs such as chat boards, blogs, and YouTube videos, that private matters are often brought into public conversation. And in many Islamic cultures, the private matters that are given attention in digital forums are deeply political: honor killings, womens' suffrage, values in education. The internet has three roles in supporting civil society in the Muslim world. First, it has an ideational function. It is the means of introducing diverse new values, ideas, and interests into new social settings. Images—with more or less ideological meanings—are available to many people who would not otherwise see them. Ideas are tested and questioned. The internet has liberated civil society from media production systems run almost exclusively by the state. Thus, its second function is organizational, as the infrastructure for social organization and collective action independent of the state. Finally, it has a symbolic function, as the sign of modernity in civic life and civil discourse.

The first Muslim voices online were diasporas in major global cities. Before 1990, there were only a few research institutions across North Africa, the Middle East, and Southeast Asia with internet access. The connections were primarily for telemedicine and access to academic journals, and they were irregular and limited by the costs and infrastructural problems of international dial-up services. As more and more Muslims in London, New York, and Toronto came online, they created lifestyle content about music and culture, contributed to listservs about political life in the communities they lived in or the communities they had left, and shared information about the challenges of continuing cultural practices in their adopted countries. Indeed, what makes civil society online so unique for the 75 countries in this study is that religion has such a significant role in civic identity. Topically, religion dominates the content of civic debate online, with Koranic interpretation, the role of women in society, and relations with other religions the hot topics of debate

(El-Kashef 2009; Bunt 2009). Online debate about the divine origins of the Koran pits public intellectuals against grand ayatollahs (Tabaar 2008). Defending religious precepts is also the regulatory cause of telecommunications policy makers particularly in the Middle East:

> Two features are characteristic of the Arabic corner of the Internet as it presents itself today. First, religion has a greater weight than anywhere else in the world, and secondly, Arab users are particularly eager to engage in discussion—not least of politics, religion, and sex (Hofheinz 2006, 91).

Despite the boom in civic discourse online, there is a tendency for news coverage to frame the Islamic internet as one dominated by and empowering of terrorists.[4] Indeed, this frame is supported by a security establishment that uses the rhetoric of poorly understood vulnerabilities in our modern, technology-dependent social world (Cavelty 2007). Terrorist groups use computers, the internet, and cryptography for organizational purposes, but terrorists have yet to consistently use cyberspace as an effective weapon or target. Instead, security experts identify information infrastructure as potential targets that can be attacked physically or through communication networks by fundamentalists in other countries. This reinforces the threat image of Islam, with the political implication that defense against cyberattack must be coordinated by a national security policy, even though private industry owns and operates the vast majority of critical information infrastructure in the West (Cavelty 2007).

The capacity for debate has grown significantly in the vast majority of Muslim communities around the developing world, and it is this capacity for debate that remains the most fundamental challenge to radicalism. Historically, the capacity for debate over Islamic texts has expanded whenever new information technologies have been introduced (Miller 2007; Sardar 1993). More recently, Al Jazeera has helped satisfy a hunger for debate in the Arab world by covering Arab issues in depth and hosting debates from a diversity of perspectives: from feminists and traditionalists, Arab nationalists and non-Arab separatists, mullahs and secular parliamentarians, apostate scholars and authoritarian apologists (Ghareeb 2000). The diversity of perspectives and public policy options discussed on these programs is impressive compared to the narrow range of perspectives represented in many Western news media. Hofheinz makes a powerful argument about how digital media have become broad means and media for socialization among young Egyptians:

> The socialization that they experience online, through surfing and choosing as well as through participating in public debate, familiarizes users more than is the case in close-knit traditional communities with the concept that people have different opinions, that one's own views are not necessarily self-evident

to all, that one has to find arguments to justify one's beliefs, rationalize them, and accept (if grudgingly) that one will not be able to convince everybody. (Hofheinz 2006, 94)

While the news media in the West has been quick to cover the ways in which Islamic fundamentalists use the internet for organizing and recruiting new members, there are many more groups using the internet for their own civic goals. These websites easily compete with both state websites, political party websites and the websites of radical Islamists for the attention of users. They attract young Muslim internet users through their own pool of commentators, and by acting as information portals to civic life. For example, www. islamonline.net was set up by Egyptian Islamist intellectuals and operates as a news portal. Yet it is also a place where Muslims from around the world seek advice on spiritual matters and find competing interpretations of Islamic jurisprudence as scholars from around the globe weigh in with responses.

Civic and Scholarly Research Infrastructure

For students and the general public, libraries have a key civic function. Libraries archive the documents of state such as legislation, tax records, and policy rulings. In authoritarian countries, where such documentation may exist but may not be archived for public access, libraries still provide a portal to the outside world through newspapers and journal subscriptions, and the book collections that budgets allow. Internet access has vastly improved the quality and quantity of informational resources available in public and national libraries. While there are still significant disparities in library infrastructures, they allow scholars, journalists, and independent thinkers to research.

While civic groups in many Muslim countries have taken advantage of new information technologies for extending their organizational capacity and contributing to political discourse, the cultures of research and inquiry have also benefited from internet access.[5] Table 5.1 compares the relative capacity of libraries online, summarizing information on the five largest libraries found online for each country: the national library, two most important university libraries, and two most important other public libraries. If none or only one of these libraries was found online, the country is assessed as having a relatively poor online library infrastructure. If two or three libraries were found online in 2005, it is assessed as having modest capacity, and if four or five libraries were found online, it is assessed as having a good capacity online. Library information infrastructure supports a country's aspiring business entrepreneurs and its civil society groups. A country's national library typically houses information on legislation, historical archives, patents, and sometimes court and tax records. University libraries store information on research and are often a gateway to international information services. But not all library portals are created equal. Public libraries serve a broader clientele, often by providing internet terminals and access to electronic databases. But not every country's library infrastructure is up to the challenging task of being an information gateway for citizens. Not all national, university, and public libraries have the capacity to maintain a website, and not all provide website access in the range of languages that their citizens read, write, and speak.

Cyberactivism and Hactivism

In countries such as Turkey, Indonesia, and Georgia, reformist movements have not just challenged Islamic fundamentalists with rhetoric online, but have successfully converted online rhetorical battles into public policy changes and real legislative and electoral victories. At the intersection of political activism and internet use is "hacktivism": the use of hacker skills for political aims. Most commonly, hacktivism strategy has been to mount denial of service attacks against the ISPs that collaborate in national censorship programs. Having strong filtering programs often means that states must maintain a few servers for a lot of traffic, making easy targets for hacktivists.[6] Cyberactivism is distinct from informational warfare and cyberterrorism in that it is not state sponsored, tends to be conducted by individuals or groups who are affiliated with a social movement, but are most interested in promoting information access. In other words, the cyberactivist ideology tends not to be fueled by the perception of historical injustices, but by the ideology that information should be free.[7]

Cyberactivism is the act of using the internet to advance a political cause that is difficult to advance offline. Of course, political discourse online is not always tame. The goal of such activism is often to create intellectually and emotionally compelling digital artifacts that tell stories of injustice, interpret history, and advocate for particular political outcomes. This kind of activism is well practiced by extreme Islamists, who distribute videos of beheadings or prayers from prominent spiritual leaders (Darnell 2006). And the internet is both the object and subject of contestation: citizens and civic groups promote their points of view online, but also use information infrastructure as a tool for resisting state control and battling with opposing points of view. Virtual actors, increasingly, cause very real-world political outcomes.

When such activities involve are supported by the state and involve international targets, they are often called "cyberwar" or "cyberterrorism." Just as social movements can operate with or without state support, Muslim hackers have taken on many of the high-profile political and security issues of the day. One of the first cyber conflicts occurred in 1998 when Pakistani intelligence personnel hacked an Indian army website about the status of Kashmir. This escalated into more than two years of denial of service attacks and website defacements. In Pakistan, the Hakerz Club, Gforce Pakistan, and M0s have defaced hundreds of websites worldwide with pro-Kashmiri, anti-Indian content (Wolcott and Goodman 2000). There have been dozens of exchanges between Israeli and Arab tech-savvy hactivists. But long-running issues as the status of the West Bank and Gaza or Kashmir are not the only ones inspiring online activism. After Kurdish leader Ocalan was arrested, the Kalamata group hacked the Greek ministry of foreign affairs for its role in his arrest (Wolcott and Goodman 2000). There are frequent Turkish internet hack attacks against Kurdish government and media websites (Watson 2007).

Not all such attacks are launched by government agents—they also come from technology-savvy activists. Moreover, these politically motivated attacks do not just involve a few hacktivists, they can involve thousands of young people who use multiple information platforms and are distributed around several countries. This is especially true for issue areas that have gone unresolved for generations: political conflict online often erupts between groups of Israeli and Palestinian supporters, or between supporters of Pakistan, India, and an independent Kashmir.

Because of the authoritarian nature of many Muslim governments, insurgent groups invariably must develop informational infrastructures in the West.[8] Khurdish, Cypriot, and Kashmiri separatists maintain multiple online portals. In countries where even defining and organizing around an ethnic or subnational identity is a crime, using the internet to show cultural leadership, offer alternative histories, and plea for international assistance becomes an act of cyberactivism. There are other countries where the democratic opposition has come to depend on internet access and mobile phone technologies for organizational and logistical support, and for the discursive space for members to debate public policy options and political strategy. In Iran, Saudi Arabia, and the countries of Central Asia, the internet has provided a means and a media for political resistance. Regime censorship, as will be discussed in Chapter 6, also politicizes internet use, turning even the consumption of Western culture into a political act. Where political parties are absent, there is little shelter for meaningful political conversation other than what is provided online.[9]

Throughout the Muslim world, the internet has become both the site and means of opposition. It is not simply that civic activism, popular protest, and political opposition can be found online, but that the internet is the means by which such social movements have formed. Only a few social movements in the Muslim world have come into existence because of the internet. But contemporary social movements would have less cohesion and impact without ICTs. Surprisingly, there are similarities between the way that secular and non-secular states have treated the internet, especially when it comes to permitting civic activism and protest.

The State Response to Civil Society Online

Many of the more conservative Muslim regimes promote internet access for limited modernization: communication that serves business and perhaps educational goals, but does not allow the globalization of morals. In this way, governments in many Islamic countries hope to use new information technologies for economic ends without risking the ideological hegemony of the ruling elite, irrespective of the whether the ruling elite is secular or claims its authority through Islam. Just as new information technologies are tools of state oppression, so too are they tools for resistance.

It is not only the constitutional monarchies and Islamic republics that have ruling elites who work hard to manage political culture by shaping or constraining political discourse over the internet. Whereas the House of Saud justifies its regulation of civil society in the name of Islam, ruling elites in Turkey act out of loyalty to the principles of Atatürk. For example, the Turkish Ministry of Internal Affairs has frequently stated that it will shut down cybercafés allowing internet users to view pornography or Kurdish nationalist content. In some small towns, civic leaders have tried to take additional measures such as banning cybercafés from being set up within 200 meters of mosques or schools. Perhaps surprising to internet users in other parts of the world, internet users in Turkey often accept the state's role in controlling, regulating, and inspecting internet cafés as a public good (Yesil 2003).

New moves into censorship are often triggered by international security crises. Elections—especially rigged ones—are also occasions where the internet is used by citizens for political discussion and by the state for monitoring citizens. Censorship and cultural management is more fully explored in the next chapter. But this kind of censorship can take the form of software settings on ISPs and IXPs, but it can also take the form of hacking and denial of service attacks. For example, during elections in Kyrgyzstan in 2005, the "Shadow Team" of hackers launched denial of service attacks on Kyrgyz opposition groups from within the Ukraine, likely with the backing of the Kyrgyz government. Other types of attacks interrupted internet access through two major Kyrgyz ISPs, Elcat and AsiaInfo.[10]

For the most part, civic groups in Muslim countries use the internet in much the same way that such groups do in the West. They raise funds, and increasingly the internet is an important part of many civic groups' public relations and media strategies. But more than propaganda, they try to use the internet in sophisticated ways, such as activating their publics during elections or controlling their publics during times of crisis. Blogs are perhaps the most obvious example of the ways in which the internet is empowering citizens and allowing nongovernmental organizations to discuss and mobilize in ways not previously possible. Blogs, which are online diaries posted by individuals, can function as news sites (as discussed in Chapter 4) and as sites for discussion and the elaboration of political culture more broadly. Indeed, blog content about political culture, when particularly insightful, timely, and well written, has been turned into books.[11]

More than cyberactivism or hactivism, blogging is the best example of a set of software, hardware, and discursive practices that challenges linguistic and cultural authority. In Islamic republics, this challenge may be most serious and most worrying for those who hold power. Thus one of the unique things about political opposition in the Muslim world is that it is very much a person-to-person opposition. Bloggers, streaming content, listservs, and personalized news services are the means by which contemporary political ideas spread. Certainly some political ideas spread through newspapers, television, and film, but the most controversial, most challenging ideas spread over the internet. Thus several Muslim states have begun cracking down on bloggers, as documented in the previous chapter. When the internet itself is the site of political protest, cyberactivism and hacktivism tend to occur against fundamentalisms of either secular or Islamic forms. Today, information technologies are such an important part of civic organizing that political elites seeking to manipulate election results must also attempt to disable cell phone networks and internet connections. During the 2009 presidential campaigns in Iran, the regime attempted to black Facebook access. When rioting broke out in Tehran, signaling a lack of public trust in the outcomes, the regime quickly disabled cell phone networks. As one reporter noted: "The text messaging that is the nervous system of the opposition was shut down, along with universities, web sites and newspapers the government regarded as hostile" (Worth and Fathi 2009). Protests online and offline are most common during elections, which are sensitive times for many regimes.

Civil Society, Learning Online

It is through communication technologies that civil society learns, and within many Muslim communities the internet is a tool with which to respond to Islamic fundamentalism.[12] A number of scholars have argued that since 1989, democratic transitions have been modular and evolutionary, rather than singular and revolutionary. Social movements increasingly learn from each other, and successful collective action in one country may lead to the emulation of collective action strategies in other countries (Beissinger 2007; Tarrow 1998, 2005). For example, a series of democratic revolutions in post-Soviet countries not only have similar features, but democratic challengers learned from the strategies of social movement leaders in other countries: the events and tactics of the 2000 Bulldozer Revolution in Serbia influenced activists leading the 2003 Rose Revolution in Georgia, and experience from both movements in turn influenced the leaders of the 2005 Tulip Revolution in Kirgizstan.

Not only can regime change happen in small steps, but institutional innovations can diffuse across a neighborhood of states as a kind of contagion effect. These are sometimes referred to as modular political phenomena, in which the features of a particular case of democratic transition or entrenchment look similar to those of previous cases in large part because civil society leaders—and state actors—have learned from previous events in neighboring countries:

> Modular phenomena are made possible by the sense of interconnectedness across cases produced by common institutional characteristics, histories, cultural affinities, or modes of domination, allowing agents to make analogies across cases and to read relevance into developments in other contexts. These shared characteristics produce the monitoring activity across cases by agents in different contexts who see themselves in analogous structural positions. Ironically, these very same policies, institutional arrangements, and modes of domination which in one temporal context are utilized to uphold order become, under the influence of modular change, lightning rods for accelerated challenges to order across multiple cases. (Beissinger 2007)

Such modular phenomena appear in large part because of new information and communication technologies that undermine the ability of ruling elites to manage what civil society learns about political culture in other countries.

The classic understanding of social mobilization is that it depends on the appearance of collective identities, shared motivations and grievances, and ultimately a change in the opportunity structure for collective action (Gurr 2000). Over the last decade, ICTs have had consistent roles in the narrative for social mobilization:

- Coordinating and publicizing massive mobilizations and non-violent resistance tactics against pseudo-democratic regimes after stolen elections;
- Allowing foreign governments and diaspora communities to support local democratic movements through information, electronic financial transfers, off-shore logistics, and moral encouragement;
- Organizing radical student movements to use unconventional protest tactics at sensitive moments for regimes, particularly during (rigged)

elections, elite power struggles, or diplomatic visits, to undermine the
appearance of regime popularity;
* Uniting opposition movements through social networking applications,
  shared media portals for creating and distributing digital content, and
  online forums for debating political strategy and public policy options;
* Attracting international news media attention and diplomatic pressure
  through digital content such as photos taken "on the ground" by
  citizens, leaking videos and documents to foreign journalists and
  diplomats regarding issues such as human rights abuses, environmental disasters, electoral fraud, and political corruption.

Among the regimes that have seen very little political transition, or have
become more authoritarian over time, civil society has learned to use ICTs
mostly to attract international media attention by sharing digital content
that undermines local authority and strengthens civic ties to diasporas. In
these countries, there is no safe physical space inner as central plazas, school
auditoriums, or public commons, for civil disobedience. By contrast, in
regimes where the possibility of civil disobedience is there, information
technologies are the fundamental infrastructure for protesting stolen elections, rallying foreign support, radicalizing student movements, and uniting
opposition groups. In entrenched democracies, such technologies are a
fundamental infrastructure for the kinds of protest that can deepen
democratic practices: tracking political corruption, writing opinion pieces
with wide readership, and proposing public policy options.

DIGITIZING ISLAM; ISLAMIZING THE DIGITAL

It is both a gross oversimplification and misclassification to argue that the
internet is mostly a technological tool for tempting Islamic civil society toward
fundamentalism. It is more accurate—and more useful for policy purposes—
to describe new information technologies such as the internet as a tool for
debate in the Muslim communities. And it is not simply that civil society in
Muslim countries is using a Western technology to replicate Western discursive practices on topics valued in the West. The internet and mobile phones
are being culturally adapted to local needs. In Indonesia and Malaysia, SMS
texting has led to new literary forms such as the Lebaran SMS Pantun; the Al
Quran Seluler service streams Koranic voices to mobile phones; and Mobile
Syariah Banking allows Muslims to conform to local lending practices
(Barendregt 2008). The Islamic laws governing commercial transactions are
formalized and complex, which some argue makes them ideal problem sets
for computer modeling. Entrepreneurial Muslim businesses are looking to

information technologies as a way of not threatening traditional lifestyles, but invigorating them (Winn 2002). Cultural norms are not just instantiated in software, but in hardware as well: a Dubai-based telecommunications firm offers the Ilkone i800 handset to stream Koranic verse, search religious documents, and indicate the direction of Mecca for *kiblah*.

Even within Europe, the internet is not just a network supporting political communication between and within Muslim communities, but a network supporting Islamic legal traditions. These traditions, while not codified in the laws of most countries in the West, can be adhered to by Muslim families living in the West. English-language websites such as www.efatwa.com, muftisays.com, and askimam.com offer advice, and both mullahs and muftis lead discussions in many other forums and chat rooms in a vast range of languages. The "FatwaBase" is a downloadable archive of scholarly opinion on Koranic interpretation. The internet is the means by which mullahs and muftis can be consulted on sub-legal problems. Islam may not be the legitimate source of law in a country, but where digital technologies make it possible to consult with alternative sources of legal authority, they alter social practices and the process of decision making in Muslim communities and families (Sisler 2007; Anderson 2003; Wax 1999). Research suggests, however, that these sites are not used by people who want to learn about the traditions of institutionalized Islam, but by people who seek guidance on personal, everyday challenges (Ho, Lee, and Hameed 2008).

There are several ways in which Western values about acceptable online civic behavior have not transported well. First, while the technology has been transferred, the cultural practice of tolerating hacktivism and online anonymity as a means of civil disobedience has not really transferred (Rogers 2000). Second, there are relatively few examples of online political parody: joke websites are taken very seriously. Indeed, it was through the internet that news of Danish cartoons about the Prophet Mohammed rapidly disseminated around the Muslim world. The ability to include humor as part of the process of deliberative dialogue and public policy critique is probably a sign of Western democratic practices. The Islamic variant of democracy may not share the same sense of humor as that of other advanced democracies. In this way, the Islamic internet reproduces several consistent norms about how Islamic political culture should function.

The internet, mobile phones, and SMS have served to reduce the distance between small Muslim communities in the West and homeland audiences far away (Bonde 2007). There is a lot of Western content online, and concomitantly digital technologies supplement the infrastructure of Islamic organizations by providing a site for cultural content and reproducing Islamic cultural values in digital forms. At the same time, such diasporas are the audiences for digitally produced content from civil society groups in the homeland. New informational linkages between Muslim communities around the developing world have done much to construct a transnational Islamic identity by sharing grievances, language, history, cultural content. Critical Islamists may say there is no such thing as the "Muslim world," but new information technologies have done much to help many Muslims imagine one.

WIRED CITIZENSHIP

There is a vast amount of civic discourse online, and this is where we find politics in the Muslim world today. The internet is valuable during elections, especially rigged ones. Online engagement can mean that community leaders are adopting Western notions of what democracy should looks like, but also that such leaders are building the Islamic variants to civic life online. Today, citizenship means something specific and new—not just informational literacy, but digital literacy.

In part, this is because the system of political communication in many Muslim countries is very different from that of even a few years ago. The meaning and conduct of citizenship is different, especially in countries where the internet provides the only infrastructure for civil discourse. Even in the democracies where the state does provide some of the infrastructure for civic life and acts of citizenship—participation in juries, voting, town hall meetings or their equivalent, and the open fora of newspaper editorials and effective legislatures—the internet greatly supplements the means by which citizens conduct the business of citizenship. In some countries, such as Azerbaijan and Bahrain, open political discourse is barely possible without the digital tools for coordinating meetings, discussing politics in relative ano-nymity, and getting news and information from sources other than the state. In this way, the internet does not simply enable political discourse. In many Muslim countries, the internet embodies political discourse. This has impor-tant implications for the meaning and conduct of citizenship.

Today, several of the most important acts of citizenship are conducted online, and for some Muslim communities, they can only be conducted online. The representation of women in public political spaces, including internet access points, has been shown to be consistently low around the Muslim communities of the developing world. Holding such factors as reli-gion, type of regime, and colonial tradition constant, being in a predomi-nantly Muslim culture is the single most negative predictor of when a woman is elected or appointed to a lower legislative house (Paxton, Hughes, and Green 2006). Particularly in the Gulf region, having an online public sphere has created significant opportunities for women to participate in civic debate with few offline correlates. Civic engagement, in this context, may refer to the ability of women to participate in economic and political exchanges independent of influence from male family members.

The internet is used for much more than business and politics. People socialize online, they flirt and arrange dates, and they shop. Sometimes people debate cultural politics, discussing why gender segregation is necessary, why women should retain the *hajib*, and what love means in communities that sanction or demand arranged marriage. They meet in online clubs to discuss hobbies, play games, or learn the latest strategies in the widespread game of circumventing government censorship. In the Muslim world, internet use is effectively extending citizenship to people who were, before the internet, unable to access news, read about their government, check sources, link with diasporas, talk anonymously. In the most authoritarian of countries, the internet provides the infrastructure for citizenship that is ot provided by an independent civil society, and new information technologies have allowed residents in Muslim countries to develop new citizenship roles.

Many online civil society groups actively work to alter the citizenship roles proscribed for them by ruling elites. They create cultural and political content that can be stored beyond the reach of the state, they engage in online activism, and they form groups independent of the state to solve local collective action problems. Even in countries that have experienced no democratic transition, there exists a small corner of the internet in which civil society is nascent. Ruling elites cannot so easily destroy social movements by excluding them from the system of political communication: movement leaders move overseas, and the movement goes online.

In many Muslim communities, the circle of people who are functioning citizens has been effectively expanded through internet access. In most Western democracies, the population of active citizens is smaller than the number of people. In most Muslim countries, the population of active citizens may be small, but is certainly expanding. It is expanding, and it is the internet that is part of the process of expanding the pool of citizens. When civil society is online, citizens are given more possibilities for memberships in associations that neither the state nor social elites approve of. Moreover, people with some informational sophistication can participate anonymously if they choose, such that their membership is hidden from the state and social elites and beyond restrictions and monitoring.

An important part of this phenomenon is that information technology in many countries outside the West is essentially a collective technology. In the West we all know what a "personal computer" is, and measuring the spread of personal computers has become the fundamental metric for studies of technology diffusion. In Muslim communities around the developing world, such communication technologies may be owned but not exclusively held. That is, the act of ownership is not one of monopolizing the technology from use by others. If anything, the rules of technology ownership are that the owner has the right of first use, but also the right to see that the technology can be used by friends and family in a set of priorities that the owner gets to determine. In Tanzania, for example, the official figures in 2005 suggested that 4 percent of the population owned a mobile phone, while 97 percent of the population said they could access a mobile phone through friends and family. Only 28 percent of the population said they could access a landline (BBC 2005).

The internet is a crucial tool for helping Muslims appreciate the diversity in their own national and spiritual communities. The internet supports learning about the rich cultural heritage in other countries, hearing the variety of musical styles and languages, reading of different political perspectives. As Ghareeb cogently argues for countries in the Middle East, "The new media are encouraging increasing cultural unity among the Arabs by acknowledging their diversity, by helping to reflect and mobilize public opinion on issues of common concern, and by overcoming some narrow regional loyalties (2000, 13)." This applies from North Africa to Indonesia. Moreover, the internet allows young Muslims to learn about life in countries where both faith and freedom coexist.

CONCLUSION

The major difference the internet has made for civil society groups in all Muslim countries has been a vast reduction in the cost of communicating across great distances to domestic constituents and international affiliates. This has resulted in increased dialogue across civil society groups within countries and contacts with international affinity groups and some degree of organizational capacity independent of those international groups. It has improved the capacity of civil leaders to activate and engage citizens interested in specific issues to mobilize large numbers of people in times of systematic crisis, to present public policy alternatives to social elites, and to shape the presentation of news.

The internet has also had a moderating, mediating role in many Muslim communities. In Kuwait, the internet and mobile phones provided the infrastructure through which civic conversations about the role of women in politics evolved into constitutional changes. In international Muslim communities, young people turn to the internet not to learn about organized, institutional Islam, but for spiritual guidance on personal problems. The plethora of electronic fora for debating social norms and behaviors in a civil manner have resulted in demonstrable changes in attitudes toward women and domestic violence (Kort 2005). Fairbanks has argued that pseudo-democratic regimes may be most susceptible to upheaval because they are pretending to be something they are not (Fairbanks 2004). The internet provides dissidents with an additional tool for exposing the corruption and abuses of authoritarian regimes and provides an information infrastructure pretty much independent from the other media, which are closely supervised by the autocratic state. ICTs make it possible for civil society to expose bureaucratic corruption and autocratic practices alike.

It is not just that social movements use new information technologies to learn about successful democratization strategies in other countries, advertising their plight to cultural diasporas and the global community. They also learn how to use new ICTs to improve the organizational capacity and reach of their own movements. A successful online mobilization against an authoritarian regime may only have short-lived outcomes. Or the mobilization may cause enough chaos to allow the regime to entrench itself. But usually, such online mobilizations have an impact on specific aspects of political life: improvements in the justice system of courts; increased political competition within single-party states; more open elections at particular levels of government; more meaningful regime transparency and stakeholder participation during the policy-making process. All of these features of democratic change are very much dependent on the presence and form of information and communication technologies. And, in many of the country cases here, ICTs have been a structural advantage for massive mobilizations against regimes. Foreign support of local democratic movements has taken the form of information infrastructure and the capacity to attract and involve members, raise funds, and express grievances. ICTs have been crucial for the organization of radical youth movements and the use of new protest tactics that undermine authoritarian regimes. Indeed, even campaigns to unite opposition movements, monitor elections, and spread word of fraudulent electoral results have increasingly relied on new information technologies.

Civil society actors participate in politics through activism and protest against the West on the basis of shared grievances. However, many Muslim communities have grievances against each other, and the information technologies have done much to bring coherence to groups and claims of wrongdoing. In important ways, the internet is what has structured the "cognitive liberation" of civil society across the Muslim world: the sense that Muslims have been collectively wronged and that collectively something can be done about it (McAdam 1982). However, this cognitive liberation is much more multifaceted than we usually acknowledge. The process of collective identity formation online has resulted in plenty of discourse within and between Muslim communities, a discourse that is vibrant, mediated by the internet, and on topics that do not always even relate to the West. Most often, civil society actors work to demonstrate the relative deprivation of Muslims within their own communities, targeting their own political and economic elites as much as Western ones.

Certainly, the power gains by non-state actors do not necessarily translate into a loss of power for the state. Yet for a majority of Muslim countries, the closest thing to meaningful civic debate is found online, not in the sited institutions of the territorial state. Bloggers and online multimedia content, produced by diasporas and within authoritarian states, are the opposition in countries like Saudi Arabia, Azerbaijan, and Singapore. In most Muslim countries, neither the state nor political parties monopolize the production of political culture: civic groups and individuals now contribute in significant ways. New ICTs are part of heated debates over the interpretation of Islamic texts. While there is certainly a strong presence of radical Islamic sects and terrorist propaganda online, the number of civic groups and political parties using the internet for democratic discourse and activism is more impressive (and in need of support). There are an important number of cases of protests and activist movements that have led successful democratic insurgencies in the Muslim countries, insurgencies that depended on ICTs for the timing and logistics of protest. It is probably unwise to say that the internet and mobile phones have caused a single democratic revolution. But today, having an active online civil society is a key ingredient of the causal recipe for democratization.

Chapter 6

Censorship and the Politics of Cultural Production

In many Muslim countries, new information communication technologies have significantly improved the capacity of political actors to manage their financial and personnel resources and advance ideological projects at home and abroad. Information technologies such as the internet and mobile phones are also part of the tool kit that political elites use to shape cultural interests and influence public opinion. Yet new ICTs pose a dilemma for government policy makers and mullahs who have developed stringent rules for censoring culture that takes the traditional forms of movies, television and radio programs, magazines, and newspapers. Such rules are crucial to maintaining ideological hegemony, and while the costs of producing these mass media are high, the costs of destroying them are low. For many citizens, the cost of producing digital content with consumer electronics is relatively low. For the state, the cost of destroying such digital artifacts can be high, when it is possible at all. State censors have ways of controlling the production and dissemination of political culture online: sometimes these methods are innovative, sometimes inept. Censors often seem one step behind and reactive, developing restrictions in response to creative maneuvering by citizens armed with mobile-phone cameras, portable flash drives, and basic knowledge of how to use free internet tools.

In this chapter, I will discuss the means of producing and consuming political culture over various media in Muslim communities of the developing world, and review the domains of political culture that ruling elites attempt to manage. I will also survey the techniques for digital surveillance, censorship, and content management. ICTs have two important roles in the distribution of authority in Islamic culture. In some countries, citizens are using ICTs to alter the patterns of cultural production and consumption. In others, these new technologies are giving ruling elites better ways for managing cultural production and the formation of political identity online. In many countries, both roles can be observed simultaneously, but overall, the decentralization of cultural production and consumer electronics is

157

overcoming elite attempts to manage culture through censorship filters on centralized national servers.

FROM EXPRESSION TO REPRESSION

While the internet was certainly an English-language medium in its earliest years of use, the demographic and linguistic diversity of online content has improved in recent years. Today, the internet is a crucial medium of political culture across the Muslim world, despite the limited language options in software, online content, and search engines. In 1996 some 80 percent of the people communicating over the internet were reading, writing, and recording in English; by 2004 this was true for only 35 percent of internet users (UNESCO 2005). Gauging the linguistic diversity of internet content is a complex task, but experts estimate that in 1998, for every eight webpages, six were in English, one was in a Germanic or Romance language, and one was in some other language. By 2003, for every eight webpages, only four were in English, one was in a Germanic or Romance language, and three had content in other languages (UNESCO 2005).[1]

Whereas the American Standard Code for Information Interchange (ASCII) is a set of English alphabet characters, the universal character set makes possible the production of digital text in many different scripts. In a test of how often the universal character set was used in 12 Muslim countries in 2004, only five were found to be using it at all. Almost all the content on Tajikistan's top level domain name servers (*.tj) had text content made up of the universal character set, but at most half the content on servers with top-level domain names in Bangladesh (*.bd), Iran (*.ir), Kuwait (*.kw), and the United Arab Emirates (*.ae) used it. In Brunei (*.bn), Kyrgyzstan (*.kg), Palestine and the West Bank (*.ps), Syria (*.sy), Turkmenistan (*.tm), Uzbekistan (*.uz), and Yemen (*.ye), it was not found at all. Among these Central Asian countries, very little content is accessible in local scripts, meaning that internet users are either communicating in English or Russian, or transferring much of the digital culture they produce onto international *.com, *.org, or *.net servers rather than using servers with their country's top-level domain name. Some internet users who prefer to communicate in languages other than English simply use the Latin character set to construct words in their own language (UNESCO 2005). Use of the universal character set has increased significantly in recent years, though its use is far from universal.

The cultural diversity of digital content increased dramatically with the emergence of a multilingual character code standard for software, and also with global marketing strategies from software companies that increasingly produce versions of their software in other languages. However, the language choices offered by some computer operating systems are not as impressive. For example, observers estimate that Microsoft Windows XP's language options cover just over 80 percent of the global population; the remaining 20 percent would overwhelmingly be speakers of non-European languages and be unable to use this software in their mother tongue. Similarly, with online search engines a crucial tool for using the internet, the search engine coverage is skewed toward the European languages. Not only are instructions for using search engines offered in a limited set of languages and scripts, the content crawled and archived by such search engines is of limited cultural diversity. For example, experts estimate that the language offerings in the 8 billion pages indexed by Google by mid-2005 would cover just over 60 percent of the global population, meaning 40 percent would not be able to find content in their mother tongue (UNESCO 2005).

While the use of Arabic in software, search engines, and content is improving, it is safe to say that the languages of other Muslim populations are significantly underrepresented. Some 43 percent of internet users use a Latin script, 9 percent an Arabic script. While software, search engines, and content are available in major scripts in the Arabic, Hanzi, and Indic language groups, the minor language groups are less likely to be covered. In sum, the minor European languages are likely to be well represented, but the minor non-European languages, mother tongues of large numbers of Muslims, are less likely to be represented (UNESCO 2005).

Yet the evolution in technical standards in software code, search parameters, and the universal character set allow some Muslim communities to produce more culturally relevant content. Improvements in bandwidth and memory mean that this content is not limited to textual production and consumption by the literate. Thus, ICTs have not simply altered the way that major political actors work. They have allowed for a restructuring in the system of cultural production, and many of the people who once could only passively consume political culture by watching TV or listening to the radio are actively producing culture online.

PRODUCING AND CONSUMING POLITICAL CULTURE IN MUSLIM MEDIA SYSTEMS

Political culture includes not just abstract values and ideologies, nor can it simply defined by news content and campaign ads. Political culture is also defined by material aspects of information technologies, which provide very concrete schema that pattern our values and ideologies and, consequently, our voting behavior and public policy opinions. The technical standards described above and the filtering software described below both shape political culture—and are examples of it. At least as important in understanding how media stimuli affect public opinion is understanding where those stimuli come from and how those stimuli may change with new technologies of political communication. Networked information technologies increasingly alter our habits of learning political information and our abilities to express and convey opinions to leaders; our contemporary habits of political learning and means of political expression define this new system of political communication.

Political culture is defined by both social relationships and the material means of transmitting information about those relationships, but we often leave the term undefined and avoid the components of material development—especially communication technologies—that are the most physical manifestations of cultural schema. Everyday cognition relies on cultural schema, knowledge structures that represent objects or events and provide default assumptions about characteristics and relationships when information is incomplete (DiMaggio 1997). Although schema include both representations of knowledge and information-processing mechanisms, in the social sciences we rarely study those mechanisms that are in fact material.[2] Crediting mechanisms with structuration, a hidden and uncontrollable grammar that writes society, is more the task of Harold Innis, Marshall McLuhan, and Jean Baudrillard (McLuhan 1944; Innis and Innis 1972; Baudrillard 1978; Innis 1991). In other words, research into political culture has largely excluded the material dimension of communication technology and treated political culture as ideological repertoires, not technological structures. Telecommunications standards, whether in the form of software search parameters or the filtering settings of a censorship program, are key structural aspects of modern democracy.

Political culture is a set of cognitive and material schema for organizing the movement of socially significant objects through scripted political process in political events and for organizing the way we remember those objects, events, and processes. Political culture consists of cognitive representations, concrete social relations, and the information communication technologies that mediate these representations and relations. These schema, whether ideological or material, constrain some forms of political action and provide capacity for other forms of political action. In sum, political culture usually refers to ideological frames that help filter information. However, I argue that political culture is also defined by material frames—information and communication technologies—that also help filter political content. Political culture is usually treated as a hard deterministic force or as something permitting free will. I argue that political culture provides both capacity and constraint for action. This is certainly true for political life in advanced democracies (Howard 2006). Increasingly, the political culture of Muslim countries is being structured by the material schema of internet architecture.

It is difficult to compare systems of cultural production and consumption in the developing world with those in the developed world. Much more data is available on the developed world, where entertainment firms, industry associations, and governments keep data on the productivity of industries that produce books, movies, and cultural content in digital forms. By 2010 there were, worldwide, approximately 141 million Muslims with some access to the internet, and more with access to mobile phones. The internet was a collection of over 600 million computers, but just over 3 percent of these were registered with the domain name of a Muslim country.[3] However, the pace of change is quick, in terms of both the number of Muslim internet users and the extent of culturally relevant content available. Moreover, the diffusion of digital information technologies has had an impact on cultural production and consumption overall. Over time, how do the new and traditional technologies of cultural consumption and production compare across countries? Recall that Figures 0.1 and 0.2, in the Introduction, give the basic diffusion trends for specific media and technology.

The number of internet hosts has also been on the rise, but, as shown above, in the global context the proportion of internet hosts connected to the internet from Muslim countries is low: 10 percent of the global internet user population is Muslim, while just over 3 percent of the world's internet hosts are registered at the top-level domain name of a Muslim country. These comparative trends reveal that television and radio are the most widely diffused media for consuming culture, and consumption-only cultural media and webpages are the most widely diffusing medium for producing and consuming culture. Books and internet hosts are similar in that they are containers for cultural content. They are also fundamentally different in that readers cannot produce cultural content in book form, whereas internet users can produce cultural content for internet hosts. Is there a better way of comparing these two particular tools for cultural content?

If we assume that a web page or website hosted in a Muslim country has cultural content relevant to that country's population, we can estimate the quick growth in Muslim culture online through counts of top-level domain names. While there is relatively reliable information on the number of hosts connected to the internet, book production is difficult to track over time. Even this patchy data reveals something about the ways in which the internet has become an important means of cultural production in many developing countries and, in particular, developing Muslim countries.

Figure 6.1 presents two important trends: the number of literate adults for every new book title produced, and the number of internet users for every internet host.[4] This figure provides more comparative context for the

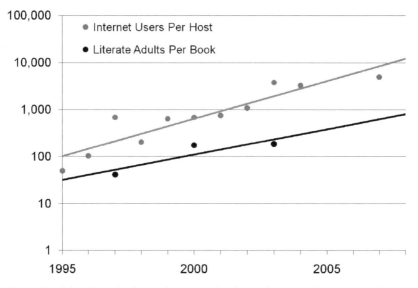

Figure 6.1 Cultural Production and Consumption in Muslim Countries, 1995–2008

Sources and Notes: Based on author's calculations from multiple sources. Data on literate adults from the World Resources Institute, annual book production from UNESCO, internet users from the ITU and Internet World Statistics, and internet hosts from the World Resources Institute and Internet Software Consortium (World Bank 2008; World Resources Institute 2007; ITU 2006; Internet Software Consortium 2007; UNESCO 2007; Internet World Statistics 2007. In 2005, I used Zook's adjustment to the count of internet hosts, which reflects the geographic dispersion of domain names ending in *.com, *.net, and *.org (Zook, 2006). Annual book production provided by UNESCO includes data for the years 1997, 2000, and 2003. Between 1990 and 1995, average is only reported in years for which there is complete data on at least 5 Muslim countries. The WRI provides a literacy rate for the period 2000–2004, which was extended for 2005 and 2006, and the previous years of literacy rates were imputed using the best available data from the World Development Indicators. The WRI provides counts of internet hosts from 1990–2004, 2005 was taken from Zook, and 2006, 2007, and 2008 taken from the Internet World Statistics. Data for internet users was taken from the WDI for 1990–2005, and 2006, 2007, and 2008 taken from the Internet World Statistics.

cultural production trends in Table 6.1—the consumption and production of content online is not just rising, but outpacing that of book production. Books and websites are similar in that there is no minimum or maximum length; they can be hundreds of pages or a few pages. Books, once published, can circulate widely, while consuming cultural content online requires internet skills, infrastructure, and electrical power. Today, there roughly 140 literate Muslim adults for every new book published in countries with large

Muslim communities, and almost 6,000 Muslim internet users for every internet host maintained in the Muslim world. This figure reveals both the high demand and weak domestic infrastructure for cultural content online. The booming numbers of new internet users means that demand for digital cultural content is high, but new users in Muslim countries must be producing and consuming cultural content that resides on hosts in other countries. This high demand also helps explain the booming numbers of new hosts being connected in many Muslim countries—people are eager to have their own cultural content online. This demand is more intense than the demand for cultural content in book form; this helps explain why the rate of hosts being connected to the internet is so much higher than the rate of book production in Muslim countries.

The internet has grown so quickly in Muslim countries that the ratio of internet users for every internet host must be presented on a logarithmic scale. Instead of presenting the number of hosts or internet users per capita, this figure can be said to present the ratio of people who use the internet to the amount of cultural content available for them online. In absolute numbers, there are more books produced each year than internet hosts. On average, 52 million new books have been produced annually in recent years in Muslim countries, while 2 million new servers have annually been connected to the internet.

There are a few people reading lots of books, and lots of internet users visiting relatively few websites. In certain Muslim countries, book production has remained stagnant or even declined over time, but with rising book production in a few key countries such as Egypt, Turkey, and Malaysia, total book production has grown modestly each year. There are two caveats to the generalizations possible from this data. First, it is still based on cultural production and consumption figures for units of nation-states. We must assume that the connectedness rate for cultural subgroups is the same as for whole countries. This is not ideal, given that in some countries Muslim communities are ruling elites, and in others they are impoverished minorities. However, in the absence of more adequate survey data, this assumption needs to be tolerated. Second, we have to assume that the books published in these countries are written in the languages read by much of the population. In some countries, texts may be printed for Arabic readers, even though most of those readers are in other countries.

Together, these figures reveal how important the internet has become as a conduit for cultural content in Muslim communities. In many countries a significant amount of bandwidth carries cultural content in the form of Hollywood and Bollywood movies, networked video games, and pornography. Young people in particular make and exchange music that reflects the latest hip hop sounds but also carries political messages (Drissel 2007).

In what sense does the changing media infrastructure have an impact on political culture? As argued in previous chapters, many of these new webpages also host content that is only implicitly political: blogs for young Muslim men and women, newsfeeds, and Western cultural content. This content may seem innocuous to us, but it is political—indeed politicized—by the social elites who try to manage cultural production through censorship. One way to assess the importance of political culture online is by tracking the kinds of censorship that elites attempt. In surprising ways, censorship is not just the use of firewalls to block overt political content critical of autocratic rule. Several countries, such as China and Cuba, censor only overt political content. But many Muslim countries, even those that are not constitutional monarchies or Islamic republics, use censorship to police the boundaries of cultural norms, terms of cultural interaction. What are the primary domains of political culture and identity formation that ruling elites work most diligently to manage?

MANAGING CULTURAL PRODUCTION AND CONSUMPTION THROUGH CENSORSHIP

The power of political elites in many Muslim countries lies in their ability to manage how their citizens develop political identities. Twenty years ago, ruling elites managed identity formation through tight regulation of television, radio, and film production. Dictators in Central Asia used this media control, for example, to present themselves as benevolent father figures who staved off post-Soviet chaos and preserved national values. In constitutional monarchies and Islamic republics, social elites use the media to preserve the tenets of Islam they value most, and to interpret Islamic edicts in ways that justify the concentration of power. For example, while Sudanese officials may be concerned about the ways that opposition groups use the internet to publish their propaganda and organize their movements, religious leaders worry about the spiritual pollution from Western political culture that might spoil young Sudanese minds. Mohamed Salih Hassan, a Sudanese imam of the powerful Ansar Muslim sect, expressed this viewpoint succinctly, saying that "the Muslim people should respect the faith, and not allow such information to reach their families. If an uncontrollable system like the internet is introduced in society, it will be very difficult for us to preach the Kingdom of Allah." (Global Internet Liberty Campaign Newsletter 1998).

Online censorship has effectively politicized several sets of cultural practices. For example, the Syrian government has attempted to block in-country access to the social networking website Facebook and the blogging application Blogger. Doing so enrages users, generates some international press coverage, and transforms the online social networking software used by high school students and the most innocuous blogs into resistant political culture.

What are the domains of political culture that social elites most aggressively guard? Evidence suggests that censorship tools are used to manage two sensitive aspects of political culture: discussion about the politics of gender; and political identity formation. In these domains of political life, social elites use the state apparatus to help enforce political and social norms. Among the most sensitive topics are the role of women in public and private life, the opportunities given them both in the political and economic realm, and the circumstances in which they can and should encounter men. Ruling elites also use censorship and telecommunications policy to help promulgate an international Muslim identity based on shared grievances and transnational cultural affinities, while at the same time providing interpretations of sacred texts, sympathetic to their needs.

Learning about the Politics of Gender

ICTs mediate gender politics in unexpected ways. In the political economy of media, women are playing more dynamic roles in television and film both in front of and behind the camera. But women have, in the opinion of some observers, aggressively invaded the new public space created by digital media (Mernissi 2004). First and foremost, digital media are allowing citizens to learn about the status of women and gender relations in other countries. Second, they also allow both men and women to debate specific gender issues relevant in their own cultures (Stowasser 2001). Third, the arrival of new ICTs in many Muslim communities and households has become an occasion for renegotiating and restructuring gender relationships. Political elites in some countries restrict internet access to prevent such cultural learning, debate, and renegotiations.

Men and women use the internet, sometimes through anonymizing applications, to discuss gender politics. In Iran, for example, blogs are often used to debate—sometimes hotly—the role of women in society, especially in Islamic republics. Some of the most popular bloggers live not in Iran but in Toronto and Los Angeles, though their readership and impact is certainly in Iran (Slavin 2005; Alexanian 2006).[5] Several studies of the Iranian blogging community suggest that a surprising number of them are women, and within Iran, "coffee-nets" have allowed young men and women to interact in ways not possible in everyday public places where the sexes must remain separated (Rahimi 2003).

Cybercafés have become new social centers where young men and women interact (Wheeler 2001, 2004). Observers have found that some cybercafés are masculine spaces that are inhospitable if not inaccessible to women, including several observed in Lagos, Nigeria (Griswold, McDonnell, and McDonnell 2006). In more traditional Muslim communities, cybercafé interactions are limited and may end at sundown when young women in Dar es Salaam, Baku, and Dushanbe must be at home. Nonetheless, this increased interaction between young men and women in the cybercafés is just as important as the internet itself for increasing the frequency with which men and women converse (al-Saggaf 2004). In Uganda, less than 20 percent of cybercafé users reported doing commercial transactions of some kind. Cybercafés are used as meeting places, as places of shelter and safety, as well as for training women to use ICTs (Etta and Parvyn-Wamahiu 2003).

Within households, women often report being allowed less time online than male family members. For women office workers, reports one Sudanese woman, the workplace becomes part of the ICT solution. "Even if their families refuse it, they can ask for a line and put it in their place of work where they can share the information after working" (IPS/Misa 1998). Research on the impact of ICTs in schools has also found that boys and girls benefit in different ways. A survey of schools in Senegal, Mozambique, and Mauritania found that boys are usually given the most exposure to ICTs in the schoolroom. But when girls and boys have equal exposure, girls actually benefited more than boys in terms of academic outcomes, self-esteem, and communication skills (Gadio 2001). Even considering prohibitive costs and irregular connectivity, benefits accrue differently to boys and girls because they use the internet for different purposes. In a qualitative follow-up study in the same countries, researchers found that when girls can get online, "they tend to look for information on issues that are culturally sensitive, such as reproductive health and sexuality. Girls are interested in information which enables them to control their bodies and to avoid problems such as unwanted pregnancies and sexually transmitted diseases. They are interested in educational activities whereas boys prefer looking at pictures and listening to music" (Gadio 2001, 18).

The arrival of ICTs often becomes an occasion for conversing about and even negotiating gender. Development practitioners find that community conversations about technology access invariably introduces gender as a social construct, not a biological one, giving parents, teachers, and community leaders the opportunity to discuss how traditional beliefs and practices constitute a barrier to girls' education (Gadio 2001). These institutional barriers are not vague cultural precepts that discourage girls from learning to use new information technologies. In the context of ICT diffusion in schools, researchers have found that poverty in Africa means that girls' education cannot be considered important in poor families. Early marriage and predefined work domains (usually not related to ICTs) mean that young women do not encounter ICTs early on. The lack of cultural role models—women who are bright and successful in science and technology-related fields, the absence of female community leaders in policy and planning circles, and the lack of incentives to keep girls in school—all play a part in discouraging girls from enrolling in IT training programs (Sylla 2002). In many Muslim cities, regardless of how safe they feel, most girls must be home by sunset. The cybercafés are taken over by young boys playing video games and watching movies.

The projects that allow young women to encounter the internet are diverse. The Senegalese government has sponsored a multimedia caravan: vans equipped with laptop computers, a digital radio station, power generators, sound systems, chairs, and tents. A small bus runs behind this van for the 30 people who maintain the equipment, set up demonstrations, and teach visitors. The government has a program to give rural women who grow staple crops information about daily market prices over mobile phones. There are community resource centers in poor districts of Dakar managed by young people trained to help even the illiterate to use ICTs (Sylla 2002).

The introduction of new ICTs is not simply providing the opportunity to redress gender disparities in developing communities; it is providing a platform for learning about gender politics. Three factors impede learning about gender politics in Muslim countries. First, new internet users rarely have the ability to conduct sophisticated searches and critically assess the content they find. This comes with practice, along with coaching from friends and family. Second, political elites in some countries actively work to discourage state programs from providing women with ICT training and access, or actively block listservs, blogs, and chat rooms where young Muslims can have some discourse on gender issues. Third, government regulators establish content filters that block websites they judge to be antithetical to the established edicts of gender relations in their country or according to their interpretation of Islam.

Online Information about Islam and Other Muslim Cultures

In the late 1990s several Islamic states embraced the internet, treating it as another way to promote particular approaches to the Islamic faith, Muslim identity and spiritual iconography. Radical Islamic organizations, whether state-entrenched or opposition social movements, competed to display and define spiritual iconography online. For example, the Saui Arabia Ministry of Islamic Affairs, Endowments, Da'wa and Guidance reserved for its own use the domain name islam.org.sa.[6] This URL was used as the exclusive source for streaming prayers from Medina and Mecca online. This Saudi ministry and others have actively used the internet to promote Wahhabist

Islam. Similarly, in Iran's spiritual city of Qom, students at the theological seminary were taught internet skills; then they scanned theological texts for items suitable for distribution online (Peterson 1996; Johari 2002). In countries with large Muslim populations, national libraries were quickly tasked with digitizing treasured documents, organizing photographic collection of spiritual sites, and creating multimedia presentations that link local Islamic narratives to transnational histories. One reason to do this was to create online resources for youth, as a Mauritanian student reports:

> By using the Internet we can communicate in Arabic, French, English and other languages. Now, we even can study the Koran in-depth and learn more about Islam and how it is practiced in various Muslim communities. The Internet has been a powerful communication tool between children of our age living in other places and us. We communicate with them freely about our common teen issues without barriers. We do not know or see each other but the connection makes us very close. I like that!! (Gadio 2001, 24)

Other scholars have hypothesized that satellite news broadcasts have helped to create a transnational Muslim identity through the mass communication of relevant news. However this student suggests that a transnational Muslim identity for contemporary youth may be constructed online, through more personal interactions, unmediated by news organizations. Internet users in advanced democracies are a youthful group, but the average internet user in the Muslim developing world is even younger.

Several scholars have tracked the importance of satellite television broadcasts in creating a transnational Muslim identity. Soap operas, news programs, and religious content have made it possible for disparate Muslim communities, especially those whose mother tongue is not Arabic, to imagine a global spiritual community. Even diaspora communities in cities such as London, New York, and Toronto have used satellite and cable television broadcast systems to create programming for both their diaspora and their homeland, and to consume programming emanating from their homeland. The collective identity of political culture is fashioned by the linkages between diasporic Muslims and the homeland, and linkages between Muslim cultures.

Many countries have allotted significant support for online libraries. Only a few years ago, the majority of public and university libraries had paltry ICT resources. Today, in countries as diverse as Turkey, Egypt, Pakistan, and Malaysia, national libraries have built web-based collections of books, rare manuscripts, theses, journal articles, audio presentations, and 3-D images of Islamic artifacts (Poynder 2004; Hamid Saeed 2000). These online portals to digital artifacts help provide a comprehensive and reliable source of information on the local history of Islam, often in a range of formats and languages. Although these sites claim to exist to help the world better understand Islam, the primary users are scholars, educators, and schoolchildren who explore the content, exchange ideas, and debate Koranic interpretation.

The internet is also used to maintain connections with diaspora communities; family members overseas have become a major news source, forwarding newsletters, clips of stories, links to blogs, funding for civic groups and social movements, and information about the technical opportunities to subvert state censorship. In important ways, the Persian, Jordanian, and Turkish diasporas have been able to participate seriously in domestic politics in ways that make possible democratic entrenchment or transition. At the very least, the new capacity of democratic advocacy groups that are based in the West has allowed them to increase engagement with like-minded groups in-country.

Differences in language, geography, history, and economic wealth contribute to the wide ranging quality of life across Muslim communities. Yet today, what little sense of collective identity that exists is a sense of shared grievances. This collective identity and shared grievances have developed significantly online, and in some cases produce subcultures of terrorists and jihadis, but more often produce subcultures of secular activism. The plight of Palestinians, once an important issue for primarily political leaders in the Arab League, is now followed by Muslims around the world. The security situation in Iraq and Afghanistan, and international relations with Iran, lead the headlines of news content online and offline.

Censoring and Surveilling Political Culture Online

Not all social elites are happy to have citizens developing political identities online, and the primary means of obstructing and managing contemporary identity formation—especially for youth—is through internet censorship. Political elites have several means of cultural management through online censorship: encouraging self-censorship among internet users; regulating and taxing commercial internet service providers; and setting national technical standards. Through intimidation, most authoritarian regimes create a significant amount of self-censorship among their citizens. Some governments advertise the fact that they keep electronic logs of internet use by citizens, claiming to only act on the most excessive cases of pornography or gambling. Knowing that their government may be watching creates an information environment in which Saudis, Iranians, and Uzbeks restrict their online activities or confine their internet activities according to where they suspect the state has less oversight, strategically choosing computers that may provide some anonymity. One strategy is to use shared computers in public settings such as cybercafés or libraries where individual activities are hard to trace electronically, while another is to use personal computers at home where government informants cannot see what is on the screen.

The regulation of ISPs is another organizational form of censorship. ISPs are commonly contracted to help the state preserve moral order, which is often defined by political elites and implicitly means preserving the existing political order. Most governments do not design their own software for regulating the internet. Instead, ISPs are required to use a national proxy server through which commercial filtering software can operate.[7] In some countries, such as Saudi Arabia, users are invited to suggest new sites for blocking and to request that sites be unblocked. Additionally, internet access can be restricted by means of infrastructural and technical standards. Contracted ISPs are often assigned limits on the number of modems and ports they can operate; the filtering software itself can slow down connection speeds. Internet access can be restricted through economic policies: mandated pricing strategies create an information infrastructure that is barely accessible even to the upper middle class. In countries where many people have internet access, the fastest connections, in private homes, belong to social elites.

With patience and perseverance, internet users in Muslim countries can often work around the filtering mechanisms set up by the state. Across these countries, however, there is a pattern to how successful these workarounds are: internet users in democracies have more opportunities to learn about workarounds than their counterparts in constitutional monarchies, who in turn have more opportunity to develop workarounds than users in autocracies. Most of the Islamic democracies have made largely symbolic attempts at censorship. Some will censor violent Islamic opposition groups that threaten a secular government, but rarely will such censorship extend to blocking the anonymizing services and other internet tools that some internet users learn about from friends and family. Most of the constitutional monarchies and Islamic republics have well-funded government agencies to maintain a list of banned websites, and to invent new ways to censor internet use. By comparison, authoritarian regimes are effective censors not because of well-funded government agencies, but because of poorly funded public infrastructure that prevents fast internet connections. In these regimes, streaming news from the BBC, CNN, or Al Jazeera strains the local information infrastructure.

Censorship is not simply a problem of government agencies trying to control online information; it is a complex activity that often involves the direct participation of U.S. based firms, telecommunications policy makers from international agencies, cultural elites, and even foreign governments. Just as the nation-state can manage the physical holdings of its libraries and limit access to books, articles, and other cultural content, the states can manage the multiple choke points and filtering options of the information networks. There are mandatory points of passage in networks; the packets of information transit through the nodes operated by local internet service providers, regional internet exchange points, and the multinational firms who lease services through their undersea trunk cables and satellites. It is at these mandatory points of passage that states block access to information.

Certainly the state can control cultural consumption online through technology and spectrum licensing, ownership of the telecommunications provider and internet exchange points, pricing structures, and the political application of security and decency laws. In many Muslim countries, bloggers, list owners, website managers, and ISPs are themselves responsible for ensuring that their content does not violate such laws. This is an exceptionally difficult task for those who produce cultural content online and those who own the communications infrastructure through which the digital content passes, because censorship efforts in most countries are erratic. Ruling elites developed national security and decency standards to help them regulate cultural content that was more materially sited within a fixed in territory and not easily reproduced and recirculated. Many of the people who produce cultural content online are subject to the same content rules, but these rules are irregularly applied. Today, cultural content is digital, reproducible over a global network, and consumable over mobile phones, computers, radio, and television. Thus, to assist the political elites in cultural management, the state has had to co-opt ISPs and website managers or threaten criminal prosecution to producers and consumers alike.[8]

There is a wide range of censorship strategies among Islamic nations. For example, Iran more aggressively blocks access to Farsi-language content than English content. When 371 major news and information websites were tested for accessibility, 80 percent of the Farsi websites were blocked, but only 45 percent of the English, suggesting that the Iranian regime is less concerned with the impact of internationally produced English-language political content than it is with locally produced Farsi-language political content (Diebert 2008). Ethiopia, Pakistan, Syria, and Uzbekistan have similar strategies for obstructing access to locally produced content while leaving access to international websites fairly unrestricted. In contrast, Oman, Sudan, Yemen, and the United Arab Emirates are more concerned with limiting access to international websites (Faris and Villeneuve 2007). Only recently has the Yemeni government begun making opposition news sites inaccessible to local users, doing so under the guise of preventing terrorism. The cybercafé has become an important social institution in its own right, worthy of targeting by Islamic extremists. In December 2007, police in Tehran warned 170 cybercafés that they ran the risk of being closed down. Subsequently the police closed 24 cafes and arrested 23 people for "immoral behavior." Eleven arrested were women, with two charged for publishing false information, disturbing public opinion, and publicity against the Islamic republic.

It is difficult to know the extent of censorship in Muslim countries: How many megabytes of content are banned? How many URLs and search results are restricted? How many people locate the information they want despite state attempts at censorship? Do the restrictions target Islamic fundamentalists and democrats equally? In 2002, only a few countries were known to have sophisticated internet censorship systems, including Iran and Saudi Arabia, although the most efficient censorship state was probably China. But by 2000, at least 11 Muslim countries had different levels of censorship of content about politics, social issues, and international security, or censorship that prevented the use of internet tools such as search engines and software download sites.[9] By 2008, 20 of the 29 Muslim countries studied had selective, substantial, or pervasive filters for this kind of content (Diebert 2008).

One of the most thorough investigative projects, the OpenNet Initiative (www.opennet.net), found that in these countries, filtering initially dealt with pornographic websites and sexually explicit content, and then was extended to forms of political culture online. This mission creep sometimes occured slowly, as government officials learned to use their censorship systems, but it occurred suddenly during unexpected domestic or international security incidents. For example, Pakistan began by filtering only websites that contained imagery offensive to Islam, but now targets political content, such as websites related to the Balochistan independence movement or Facebook pages connected to "Everybody Draw Mohammad Day". Some countries, such as Singapore, only deny access to pornographic websites, although the government maintains strict controls over traditional media, has heavy penalties for libel, and complex ways of regulating journalists. In contrast, several Gulf States such as Bahrain, Jordan, Syria, Saudi Arabia, and the United Arab Emirates block access to the entire Israeli (*.il) domain. Others, such as Iran, Syria, Pakistan, Tunisia, and Uzbekistan, block entire services, such as YouTube, Skype, and Google Maps. Several types of censorship restrict what we in the West can learn about Muslim politics, and what people in Muslim countries are able to learn about their own political lives. The production and consumption of political culture online can be limited by governments, but the involvement of Western firms and governments also supports these management practices.

The Market for Censorship Services

Many private firms are eager to sell filtering services to governments, and authoritarian governments are not the only ones subscribing to these services. In fact, only a few governments in the Muslim world have the capacity to build and manage their own surveillance and censorship systems. They block access to a set list of URLs, or scan content for a set list of keywords. In either case, a significant number of government officials are needed to maintain up-to-date and accurate lists of banned URLs or targeted keywords.

As Diebert rightly points out, California's Silicon Valley designed not only innovations for information sharing, but also the innovations needed for restricting the flow of information (2008). Kuwait, Oman, Saudi Arabia, Sudan, Tunisia, and the United Arab Emirates use the firm Secure Computing, Yemen uses Websense, and Singapore has SurfControl. In the West, corporate customers use these software applications to prevent employees from gambling or viewing pornography at work. But just as public sector clients can choose to block access to categories of websites that promote vice, they can also choose to block several categories of political content. Websense offers the option to barricade advocacy group websites, which they define as "sites that promote change or reform in public policy, public opinion, social practice, economic activities, and relationships." It is difficult to know how much research either the commercial firms or the public officials put into coding websites according to this definition, or to the category "militancy or extremist groups," formally defined as "sites that offer information about or promote or are sponsored by groups advocating antigovernment beliefs or action" (Websense 2007). The contracting firm does an initial search for websites that fit these definitions, and then government customers can add and delete URLs as needed.

Using commercial filtering software actually affords government censors some flexibility in dealing with public controversy over what gets censored. Some governments are overt about their censorship strategies, while others are more reticent. Internet censors in both Saudi Arabia and the United Arab Emirates publish reports on their activities; when users try to view a blocked URL, they find a page divulging that the content has been blocked. In contrast, Tunisia has been very reluctant to reveal details of its internet censorship programs; blocked websites appear, within Tunisia, as "not found." Uzbekistan uses error pages that claim, falsely, that a blocked website has pornographic content or that redirects users to a "similar" website with false or misleading information.

Censorship by Non-Muslim Governments

Sometimes government policies in Western countries have a direct impact on the kind of information tools available in Muslim countries. There are several good examples of how U.S. government censorship influences what we know about the Islamic cultures, what émigrés can learn about Muslim politics, and what people in other countries can learn about official U.S.

government positions on political and security issues. For example, U.S. trade restrictions on the sale or export of some types of digital content have prevented the use of detailed maps by people in other countries. Aid workers in Sudan cannot use Google maps to study the region, because the company's filtering service identifies the computer's IP address, locates the computer in the Sudan, and denies access to maps of the region (Diebert 2008; Geens 2007).

In December 2003 the *Washington Post* reported that the White House had edited a published press release from earlier in the year. The title "President Bush Announces Combat Operations in Iraq Have Ended" was changed to "Bush Announces *Major* Combat Operations in Iraq Have Ended" (emphasis added) (Milbank 2003; Milbank and Graham 2003). The ability of Western politicians and government leaders to edit their public statements allows them significant power to shape perceptions of what was said, by whom, and when. In October 2003 it was discovered that the White House had added the word "Iraq" to a long list of excluded search terms, effectively preventing search engines such as Google and Yahoo from archiving a significant amount of content about the security situation in Iraq for about six months.[10] During the George W. Bush presidency, the White House regularly used a "robot.txt" file to manage how search engines catalogued content on www.whitehouse.gov. The search engine used by staff within the White House to search the site's contents was not subject to these search restrictions. This meant that outsiders were able to search and view only approved documents (Elmer 2008).

Those are only three examples of how foreign governments can shape what people in other countries can learn about life in the Muslim communities of the developing world using digital media. Editing press releases that have already been "published" and using robot exclusion protocols have a direct effect on the ability to archive online content and create a public record of political life. Indeed, these examples reveal that the censorship of political content about life in Islamic countries is not only something that Islamic governments impose on their citizens. It is also something that non-Islamic countries implement to prevent their citizens from learning about life in the Islamic world. More broadly, these examples reveal how malleable the digital public record really is.

Accidental and Self-Censorship

Software-based censorship is never perfect. Governments who attempt to filter information coming into the country often unwittingly exclude content that has no political implications. Tunisia used commercial filtering software from the United States, "Smartfilter," to block access to streaming pornography, and inadvertently blocked the website DailyMotion and satirical videos about the government's human rights abuses. When this was discovered, the filtering service was able to adjust its settings to correct for this misclassification (Opennet.net 2006).

In many Muslim countries, censorship systems take both a legal and a technical form: codes of social conduct govern what citizens use their computers for; software code governs what websites, tools, and type of content can flow through ISPs and internet exchange points (Gomez 2002). In several countries, the general political climate discourages casual exploration of the internet. In some countries, users at home or in cybercafés feel safe enough to look for content that challenges political or cultural norms, but in more autocratic countries this sense of exploration simply is not pervasive. The general political environment of repression, censorship, and surveillance felt across many domains of social life actually brings about a significant amount of self-censorship, even when there are no specific state-sponsored techniques for monitoring or blocking in place. There is significant statistical evidence that the authoritarian character of a regime suppresses internet use (Milner 2006; Howard and Mazaheri 2009).

CONCLUSION: THE POLITICS OF IDENTITY MANAGEMENT AND COLLECTIVE ACTION

Even though the data presented at the beginning of this chapter is based on estimates of adult technology use in average households, internet users themselves are younger, on average, than internet non-users. This cohort effect is even more evident in Muslim countries. In 2005, 75 percent of internet users in Iran were between 21 and 32 years old; 14 percent of these were online approximately 40 hours a week (Slavin 2005). Hossein Derakhshan reported that a nationwide poll in Iran showed that among various media, people have the most trust in information found online.[11] Given this youthful cohort of internet users, ruling elites consider the management of online cultural production and consumption an urgent priority. Given the proclivity of radical students to use mobile phones and the internet to organize civil disobedience, it is no wonder that some of the toughest dictators have come to fear their young, literate, and tech-savvy citizenry.

New ICTs have significantly increased the capacity of state bureaucracies, political parties, civic groups and journalists to organize and project their ideological perspectives to the domestic and international arenas. Such technologies are also part of the tool kit that political elites have for managing the flow of information and constructing political opinion. Several influential groups of libertarian technologists in the West work actively to monitor and

Table 6.1: Censorship and the Production of Political Culture, 2003–2008

Country	Digital Cultural Production, Relative to Internet User Base	Internet Monitoring and Restrictions	Social Filtering	Political Filtering	Conflict/Security Filtering	Internet Tool Filtering
		Transition				
Albania	•	□				
Algeria	•	■	✕	✕	✕	✕
Bahrain	●	■	○	◉	✕	○
Bosnia	●	□				
Comoros	·					
Djibouti	•					
Egypt	•	◻	✕	✕	✕	✕
Georgia	●	□				
Ghana	·	□				
Indonesia	●	□				
Kenya	·	□				
Kuwait	●		●	○	○	●
Kyrgyzstan	●		✕	✕	✕	✕
Lebanon	●		✕	✕	✕	✕
Liberia	·					
Macedonia	●	□				
Maldives	●					
Mauritania	·					
Montenegro						
Niger	·					
Nigeria	·	□				
Senegal						
Sierra Leone	·					
Suriname	•					
Tanzania	•	□				
Uganda	·	□				
		Entrenchment				
Bangladesh	·	◻				
Benin	•					
Bulgaria	●	□				
Cyprus	●	□				
Guinea-Bissau						
India	●	■	✕	✕	○	○
Israel	●	□	✕	✕	✕	✕
Malawi	·	□				
Malaysia	●	□	✕	✕	✕	✕
Mali	·	□				
Mauritius	●	□				
Mozambique	•	□				
Turkey	●	◻				

Authoritarian

	Cultural production	Internet use	Filtering: tools	Filtering: political	Filtering: social	Filtering: security/conflict
Azerbaijan	•	◘	×	○	×	×
Brunei	●					
Cameroon	•					
CAR	·					
Chad	·	◘				
Eritrea	•					
Ethiopia	·	□	○	◉	○	○
Gambia	·	□				
Guinea	·					
Iran	·		●	●	◉	●
Jordan	·	◘	×	○	×	×
Kazakhstan	●		×	○	×	×
Libya	·		×	◉	×	×
Morocco	●	■	×	×	○	○
Oman	●		●	×	×	◉
Pakistan	●	□	◉	○	●	○
Qatar	·		●	○	○	●
Russia	●	◘				
Saudi Arabia	·		●	◉	○	◉
Singapore	●	■	○	×	×	×
Sudan	·		●	×	×	◉
Syria	·		○	●	○	◉
Tajikistan	•	■	×	○	×	×
Togo	•					
Tunisia	•	■	●	●	○	◉
Turkmenistan	·					
UAE	●	■	●	○	○	◉
Uzbekistan	·	■	○	◉	×	○
Yemen	·		●	○	○	◉

Crisis

	Cultural production	Internet use	Filtering: tools	Filtering: political	Filtering: social	Filtering: security/conflict
Afghanistan	·		×	×	×	×
Burkina Faso	·					
Iraq	·		×	×	×	×
Ivory Coast	•					
Somalia						
West Bank & Gaza			◉	×	×	×
Western Sahara						

Sources: Based on author's calculations from multiple sources: Opennet.net 2008; Internet Software Consortium 2007; World Bank 2008; Privacy International and the GreenNet Educational Trust 2003.

Notes: Digital cultural production relative to internet user population is calculated as the natural log of the ratio of two ratios: the ratio of top level domain named internet hosts in a country to the total number of top level domain names across all 75 countries in 2007; the ratio of internet users in a country to the total number of internet users across all 75 countries in 2007. Cultural production online is indicated as relatively small (·), medium (•), or large (●). Internet use is indicated as being unrestricted (□) monitored (◘), or restricted (■) in 2005. Filtering of internet tools, or of political social, or security/conflict content indicated selective (○), substantial (◉) or pervasive (●) in 2007. If no filtering was found this too is indicated (×).

undermine the censorship activities of the more authoritarian Muslim states. In both the strong and emerging democracies, many political leaders have concluded that the economic value of an information-rich economy and investment in a domestic high-tech sector is worth the risk of an information-rich political life.

Yet it is not clear that elites are able to fully manage cultural production online, and in every authoritarian regime there are examples of how the internet is used by people whose small acts of making home movies, posting pictures to the web, or chatting with friends overseas become politicized by a regime's censorship strategy. In times of crisis, the new media skills that people develop become useful for more explicit political ends such as passing on news and political jokes. For example, when the Azeri national news will not cover student protests, images taken by mobile phone get posted on YouTube and circulated among networks of friends. More recently young Azeris have recorded the video stream of nightly news broadcasts from the official news agency, but posted the broadcasts online with an audio overlay of news that the students consider to be real. In this way, a few creative cyberactivists appropriate the images of prominent Azeri journalists—the official voices of the state—for use in the production of alternative political culture.

Table 6.1 reveals that the regimes most concerned with managing cultural production online are the constitutional monarchies, dictatorships, and Islamic republics. To comparatively measure digital cultural production relative to internet user population, an index is computed using the mathematical expressions described in the introduction. This indicator is the natural log of the ratio of two ratios: the ratio of top level domain named internet hosts in a country to the total number of top level domain names across all 75 countries in 2007; the ratio of internet users in a country to the total number of internet users across all 75 countries in 2007. Using such an index—rather than a simple count of hosts per capita—allows for a weighting of a particular country's number of hosts by the size of its internet user base and relative to other countries with large Muslim communities. Cultural production online is indicated as relatively small, medium, or large, and reveals that comparatively speaking, most of the countries where civil society is producing relatively large volumes of digital content have become more democratic. Monitoring or restricting internet access can clearly constrain civil society online, with clear implications for political parties, journalists, and civil society actors. Moreover, filtering internet tools like search engines or filtering specific kinds of content related to politics, society, or conflict appears to be an activity of those regimes where social elites are working hard to constrain cultural production and consumption online. This table allows for a comparison of content production online across all countries, measured in the number of internet hosts per 10,000 internet users in 2007. This proxy measure should be interpreted carefully. Countries with very few of their own internet hosts may still have a large civil society online, contributing videos to YouTube, writing blog posts, or generating other digital content that actually gets hosted by servers in the West.

Censorship policies play a complex role in political transitions and regime durability. In some authoritarian regimes, ruling elites set censorship policies, and this may help prevent a democratic transition. In other authoritarian regimes, not setting a censorship policy may contribute to a democratic transition. While the censorship policies of all 75 countries are not known, many of the countries that had some form of content filtering experienced little regime change.

New ICTs have presented a dilemma for government policy makers and clerics who have well-developed systems of rules for censoring culture when culture takes the form of movies, TV programs, magazines, and newspapers. Perhaps because mass media cultural content is so closely regulated, people in these countries turn to digital media with enthusiasm. Pirated movies and songs are a growing part of many people's cultural diet. Producing cultural content—videos made by mobile-phone camera, audio mash-ups of copyrighted songs from the West—becomes a deeply political act in regimes that work to suppress independent cultural production. In this way, telecommunications policy in some countries politicizes the activities of people who produce and consume culture with consumer electronics.

These media systems are crucial to maintaining ideological hegemony, and the cost of producing these tangible media are high and the costs of destroying them low. In many Muslim countries, censorship is not simply about protecting political elites, it is about managing cultural production and consumption. The rules and tools of newspaper and television censorship do not easily apply to digital content. That ruling elites and autocratic states work so hard to manage gender politics and identity formation online suggests that digital media are a genuine challenge to the traditional practices of cultural production, consumption, and management.

Conclusion: Information Technology and Democratic Islam

Power has been traditionally linked to the state's tangible ability to control military and media resources. Herein lays the most important transformation in the organization of power through political communication: the last decade has seen the diffusion and distribution of an information infrastructure that is not controlled by individual states, changes in the opportunity structures through which government bureaucracies, journalists, political parties and civic groups serve publics, and alterations in the system by which political culture is produced and consumed. In many countries with large Muslim populations, television and radio long supported the political communications of ruling elites. In contrast, software and hardware applications raise the number of people actively communicating with one another, close cultural distances and diversify the topics of conversation, and facilitate collectivities not centered on national identity and not easily policed by the state. That mobile phones and the internet help political parties compete, journalists investigate, and civic groups organize is a result of technology diffusion. Yet looking across a large number of cases, it appears that state investment in information infrastructure, even to improve its own bureaucratic capacity, may also be one of the key ingredients for contemporary democratization. In spite of the fact that ICTs had an observable role in democratization over the last 15 years in specific cases, we know comparatively little about these roles. Looking across multiple countries, when do ICTs matter in democratization? Understanding the causal conditions for contemporary democratic transition and entrenchment is one of the most important tasks facing scholars of international studies.

Qualitative comparative study reveals that many of the democratic regimes with large Muslim communities became more durable through the diffusion of new information technologies. Other regimes experienced a rapid democratic transition, with significant improvements in democratic practices in short periods of time. A few regimes became interesting hybrid states, when authoritarian governments became less so through ICTs that brought accountability to lower levels of government or when emerging democracies used ICTs as part of new censorship strategies. Yet how can the full set of causal explanations for these outcomes be summarized in meaningful ways? Which countries really became more democratically durable than others? Which regimes experienced a democratic transition, and what kinds of hybrids regimes did they become?

Each chapter in this book has analyzed components of an overall argument about the ways in which ICTs can support both democratic institutions that are already in place and the construction of new practices in political communication. Each chapter began with the best instances of how wired governments, political parties online, journalists equipped with new media technologies, and tech-savvy civic groups have had an impact on political transitions within particular countries. Then each chapter considered countries in a comparative perspective. An important part of that process involved understanding examples in which democratic transitions occurred in countries where ICTs did not have much of a role, and examples in which the absence of ICTs may have had a role in the rise of authoritarianism. Rather than treating nations as stable cases, free of historical context, and modeling relationships between independent variables, this argument used a significant amount of qualitative and comparative evidence and a method for simplifying complex trends to reveal the development of contemporary Muslim media systems.

Some states have actively developed e-government programs that increase the range of services offered to citizens, and invested in information infrastructure so that branches of government work more effectively and efficiently. Outcomes of wiring up the nation-state have included greater flows of international remittances, the development of domestic ICT industries, and improved capacity of state agencies to serve the public. Some of this improved capacity has very direct implications for democracy: state officials become better at collecting and counting votes during elections; legislators become better at writing effective laws and justice officials become better at enforcing them; and government censors become better equipped to prevent citizens from consuming unfavorable political or cultural content. Some of this improved capacity has more indirect implications for democracy: revenue authorities become better at collecting taxes, managing state budgets and personnel resources, and uncovering corruption. Many other kinds of government agencies develop online portals that help the public understand how their government works, and archives that help entrepreneurs, students, and journalists find the information they need. Perhaps most important, states that invested in public telecommunications infrastructure also created the fundamental informational architecture for political parties, journalists, and civil society groups.

Many political parties have developed online portals for their members, not simply for propaganda purposes, but also for enabling party organizations to become more competitive. Party competition is one of the key democratic practices, and increasingly, the internet and mobile phones are part of the communications network that parties use to marshal supporters to vote, volunteer, and contribute funds. Recent experience with elections in Turkey, Pakistan, Bangladesh, Malaysia, and Indonesia demonstrates how important digital technologies are in opening up political contests. Mainstream parties are better able to read and respond to public opinion, and the digital political communication strategies of mainstream parties activate large networks of voters Activating these networks has allowed mainstream parties to trounce extremist Islamist parties on election day. In countries where political parties are illegal, the internet is actually *more* important, because it provides the only infrastructure for political communication. The most wired political parties develop complex multimedia content that is not just designed to appeal to domestic voters, but is meant to be accessible to international observers, whether foreign journalists and diplomats or diaspora communities. Political parties that do not take advantage of internet infrastructure do not just appear less "modern" in the domestic political discourse, but they miss out on strategic opportunities that other political parties exploit.

Both the work of journalism and the organization of journalists significantly changed over the last decade. In dictatorships, Islamic republics, and constitutional monarchies, independent journalism is a serious challenge to state-dominated news media. Journalists use the internet to file stories for foreign news agencies, to fact-check stories before reporting them domestically, and to appeal for international help when persecuted by government agents. News consumers rely on the internet to corroborate what they hear from official government news agencies; in many emerging democracies and less authoritarian regimes, the international news websites are an important source of content. Digital information infrastructure permits greater circulation of stories, and creates alternative sources of news and perspective during times of political and military crisis. Citizen-journalists who do not feel their story is being suitably told are now doing their own digital storytelling. These patterns of political expression and learning are fundamental to developing democratic discourses.

ICTs have also had a role in supporting the flourishing population of civil society groups. Some civil society groups within established democracies have become very active organizations for mobilizes public engagement and others remained small nonpartisan political actors working on public policy recommendations. NGOs sometimes even offer ISP services to citizens, and telecommunications policy has become a domain in which civil society groups are active. There is a growing variety of faith-based charities, unions, and public interest groups operating in many Muslim countries. Some are linked to groups in the West, using the internet to build bridges with affinity groups in neighboring countries, sharing strategies for improving service delivery and engaging with government officials, and reaching out to the news media. Many of these civil society groups are not avowedly political, but they are important for democracy because they are a form of social organization that is outside the direct management of the state. ICTs have enabled this independence.

When civil society groups act, they do not just conceive of what democratic discourse should be, they define and follow—as much as possible—plans of action. Increasingly, the strategic action plans of civil society groups are predicated on the use of new media. Information technologies are not only important because some civil society actors wish it would be so, but because their media outreach strategies, membership drives, fund-raising, and service delivery are ever more contingent on effective use of such technologies. Moreover, social movement leaders have rapidly adapted their tactics based on new information supplies and online strategizing in moments of crisis.

Many countries that were already well along the path to democratization have experienced democratic entrenchment, in which ICTs helped deepen democratic practices and solidify democratic institutions. In a few countries, ICTs have allowed for more effective dictatorships, while in still others the absence of such technologies has allowed for greater repression. Given all of the intriguing stories, particular country experiences, and democratic outcomes analyzed in previous chapters, what is the best way of adding it all up, assessing the trends, and drawing conclusions that advance our understanding of the contemporary recipe for democratization?

The goal of this concluding chapter is to identify the recipes for democratization, with particular attention to how information technologies serve as ingredients—or in combinations and permutations of ingredients. This will allow for conclusions about the ways in which ICTs have been sufficient or necessary causes of democratic transitions in 75 countries with significant Muslim populations, between 1994 and 2010.

A TECHNOLOGICAL THEORY OF DEMOCRACY

The qualitative, empirical evidence reviewed lends itself to a set-theoretic argument, because the evidence revealed that many of the countries experiencing high levels of ICT diffusion have almost all experienced significant changes in their systems of political communication. The claim is based on the parsimoniously summarized relations between properties and cases, rather than modest correlations between technology diffusion and democratization. Examining cases with the same causal conditions to see if they also share the democratization outcome is appropriate for identifying

sufficient conditions, and sufficient conditions often appear as combinations of conditions. Identifying the causal conditions shared by cases that
have democratized is appropriate for identifying the necessary conditions
of democratization. It other words, if information technologies are a sufficient cause of democratization, then the presence of information technologies implies the presence of democratization (though democratization
does not imply the presence of information technologies). If information
technologies are a necessary cause of democratization, then the presence of
democratization implies the presence of information technologies (though
information technologies do not imply that democratization will occur).

It is likely that there are several recipes for contemporary democratization,
and many possible ingredients and combinations of ingredients. One way to
assemble the accumulated country experience is by comparing the recent histories of countries that share the common outcome of a significant period of
democratic transition or entrenchment. Analyzing the relationships in this
set-theoretic manner exposes the key ingredients for democratization.
Moreover, treating the institutional outcomes as fuzzy sets avoids selecting
cases on the outcome because countries will actually vary in their degree of
membership in the set displaying democratic transition or entrenchment.

A set-theoretic argument assembles the empirical evidence to show the
ways that democratic transitions or entrenchment has been the outcome of
technology diffusion. Fuzzy set theory allows for gradations of membership
in the set of countries that had a democratic transition, or the set of countries in which information technologies have diffused. This set-theoretic
approach generates valid general knowledge based on our direct observation
of many country cases, explicates the different conditions that enable or
constrain political outcomes, and identifies the common ingredients of the
various contemporary recipes for democratization.[1] The chapters on states,
parties, journalists, civic groups, and cultural elites demonstrated the explicit
connections between information technologies and democracy building in
countries with large Muslim communities. Set theory allows us to examine
cases with the same causal conditions to see if they also share the same outcome. More important, if we assume that there is not just one recipe for
contemporary democratization, but several, we can use fuzzy set analysis to
identify combinations of causal conditions that share the same outcome.

Infrastructural and Contextual Conditions

Several contextual factors might exacerbate or mitigate the causal role of
particular aspects of technology diffusion, and reducing the set of causal
attributes to a few important ones must also respect the significant diversity
among these countries. The cases that appear as examples in previous chapters

differ in important ways, yet there may still be causal patterns and shared attributes that explain membership in the set of countries that have democratized. Along with the impact of technology diffusion on the system of political communication involving states, journalists, political parties, civil society groups, and cultural elites, additionalcontextual conditions should also be evaluated on a case by case basis:

- average incomes within the country (measured as GDP per capita, adjusted for purchasing power parity);
- how equitably economic wealth is distributed across the population (measured as gini coefficients for income distribution);
- average levels of education (measured as the gross percentage of the population enrolled in secondary school);
- how important fuel exports are to the national economy (measured as the percentage of merchandise exports consisting of fuel);
- the size of the Muslim community in each country (measured as the percentage of the total population practicing Islam);
- the size of each country's population.

In each case, data is used for 2010 or the best available year. If the data taken from large datasets were incomplete, supplementary data from secondary sources were sought. Patching by hand significantly reduced the number of missing cases.

Education and economic wealth—especially inequities in the distribution of wealth—can play significant causal roles in social unrest. Wealth disparities can be exploited by political leaders during elections. In regimes where political parties cannot work to improve the quality of life for their membership, such disparities can be the motivation for social rebellion. Poverty is most likely to motivate people to rebel when there is also a perception of relative deprivation, with an enormous gulf between rich and poor that seems insurmountable to the poor. Concomitantly, countries in which most of the population is well off may be less likely to experience radical, violent democratization movements. In countries where the population is literate and well educated, citizens are likely to have a better understanding of the causes and consequences of their poverty, and some awareness of political alternatives that might be available. Authoritarian regimes can collapse when social elites defect from supporting the autocrat, so the population's ability to evaluate the risks and benefits of supporting a dictator a pursuing such alternatives is key. While many of the oil-rich states in the Gulf region have significant economic wealth, about two out of five people in the region live on $2 or less a day. Among the ten wealthiest heads of state around the world, seven are the heads of state of poor Arab countries (Talbi and Spencer 2000).

Another sizeable group of Muslim countries are unique in that they are economically dependent on oil and natural gas exports. This attribute has several implications for a path to democracy (Weiffen 2008). Many of the oil-rich Muslim countries are constitutional monarchies and somewhat authoritarian regimes where the ruling elites are also extended family members. Fuel-dependent economies that may appear to be wealthy in terms of GDP per capita may have a skewed distribution of such wealth, since the benefits of oil revenues often accrue to ruling families. Moreover, oil wealth can bring independence from the multilateral lending institutions. Accepting loans from the international community often means that the beneficiary statemust agree to international demands for political accountability. Consequently, ruling elites may have fewer funds to use in co-opting client groups and maintaining patronage networks. So agreeing to loan conditions risks domestic destabilization, and having oil revenues can mean financial independence from the multilateral lending community.

Some of these 75 countries are culturally homogenous, others have significant diversity. For many countries in North Africa and the Gulf, Muslims make up the bulk of the population, and diversity lies in the aspects of Islamic faith practiced. Outside of this region, Muslim communities are often large but one of several minorities within a nation-state. For countries where a large majority of the population is Muslim—especially those where the majority of Muslims are of the same sect—political discourse is very different from that in countries where Muslims are in the minority. Political conversations in countries such as Kuwait and Iran are organized around madrassa schools and *diwaniyya* clubs, and can involve much of the (usually male) population in traditional discursive contexts. In countries such as Nigeria and Malaysia, Muslim community leaders must negotiate pacts with the leaders of other ethnic and religious groups to compose a domestic political agenda of shared goals. In countries such as Georgia and Uganda, where Muslim communities are relatively small, the leaders of these communities have a difficult time shaping the national political agenda. Sometimes aggrieved populations are attracted to violence as a means of achieving political aims. But it can also mean that minority groups benefit through democratic practices that accommodate political representation and give them access to state resources. Theologists and Islamists might argue that some interpretations of Islam might be more amenable to participation in democratic discourse than others, but this possibility is not tested here.

Population size varies greatly across the Muslim world, making for very different domestic political environments. Countries such as India and Indonesia are among the most populous in the world, and countries such as Djibouti and Qatar have barely a million inhabitants. In large countries, governments have many more client groups, larger populations of urban intellectual elites, and larger populations of poor in urban slums. The physical distances separating citizens and resources across the subcontinent of India and the islands of Indonesia are a significant logistical challenge for state administration. Running an election in these countries is an organizational triumph. Complex humanitarian disasters in Bangladesh and Ethiopia have an impact on tens of millions of people, and the sheer numbers of poor, dispossessed people can be a source of political instability. In small states the political dynamics are different: elite circles are dense and in close physical proximity, ruling families have social networks that can include most of the political interests and client groups in a national community. The resources of the state may be more modest but easier to distribute in patronage networks and co-option strategies.

Several additional factors are worth considering, but were rarely found in the causal recipe for democratization for more then a few cases. For example, membership in the core community of nations and integration with the global economy may have an impact on the pace of democratization. Globalization has the effect of drawing some authoritarian regimes into a community of democratic regimes, and research has suggested that such contact often results in institutional isomorphism among state agencies as government officials share norms and learn public policy solutions from each other (Henisz, Zelner, and Guillen 2005; Haas 1990). However, in working toward solution sets for explaining transition or entrenchment, the amount of foreign direct investment and the percent of national income deriving from trade were rarely relevant. This should not be interpreted as evidence that integration with the global economy does not result in democratic transitions, only that there is not strong set-theoretic evidence either way. Large countries often also have a "youth bulge," with significant numbers of people under the age of 15 who must be accommodated in schools and the labor force. If they are not accommodated, cohorts of disaffected youth can cause trouble for a regime. This variable was tested, however, and consistently dropped out of the reduced causal sets as a factor that neither contributed to nor detracted from membership in the set of countries that democratized.

In addition, membership in the set of post-Soviet and Warsaw Pact countries was tested as a possible causal connection to democratization. All of the countries studied here share some Islamic cultural history and have important Muslim communities today. Thirteen of these countries also share a recent history of association with Russia, either through the Warsaw Pact or through membership in the Soviet Union. This shared history is an important aspect of the democratization path in several respects. In these countries, religion was formally illegal, and in several of them Islam practices were violently repressed by the state. With the collapse of the Soviet Union, these states were left with

strong dictators and a state apparatus ill-equipped to accommodate the interests of Muslim communities. Today, the strongest, most authoritarian dictators
run countries that are in the set of post-Soviet regimes. Many of these countries are also among the most culturally isolated from the West. Not only do
they have large Muslim populations slowly adapting to new domestic political
conditions, they have the weakest information infrastructure. For these reasons,
being fully in the set of post-Soviet countries is not a very plausible explanation
for democratic entrenchment. By contrast, full non-membership in this set
might contribute democratic entrenchment. However, this attribute rarely
appeared in any of the solution sets, and when it did appear, its causal effect
was unidirectional: being a member of this category negatively contributed to
membership in the set of transition or entrenchment countries; not being a
member was neither a negative nor positive contributor. In the final analysis,
membership in this set did not need to be tested.

Political Outcomes

The previous chapters advanced the argument that in many countries,
e-government, wired political parties, digital journalism, and online
civic groups have brought about democratic transitions or entrenchment. Many of the states that invested in information technologies have
become better equipped to serve citizens. Such information technologies are now the fundamental infrastructure for party competition and
contemporary journalism. The important impact of new media journalism has been to allow for cultural connections between cultural diasporas and homelands, spiritual connections between religious leaders
and the faithful, and political connections between communities with
similar grievances. In particular, pan-Arab news media has helped create a wide news audience, mediated by satellite broadcasts that particular
states are often unable to effectively regulate. Mobile phones and the
internet have quickly become the fundamental infrastructure for civil
society, giving nonprofit groups and clubs of all kinds a system of communication independent of the state. This very information infrastructure, however, has been effectively used by some states to manage the
production and consumption of political culture, making ruling elites
better censors. So in evaluating the causal conditions of regime change,
this study of countries with large Muslim communities has revealed four
plausible conditions that have had positive causal roles in democratic
transition and entrenchment, and one plausible condition that has had
negative consequences for democratic institutions and practices.

The recipe for contemporary democratization increasingly probably involves some combination of ingredients regarding the information infrastructure

used by states, political parties, journalists and civil society. Additionally, important contextual factors need to be evaluated in assessing the most prominent and parsimonious recipes for contemporary democracy.

Each case of democratization has unique features that are not shared by any other case. Since the goal of this book is to understand the role of ICT diffusion in democratization, any general conclusions must apply to as many cases of democratization as possible, and should be contextualized with other plausible, relevant causes of democratization that might be shared across the set of cases. For example, Bosnia's path to democracy has involved significant investment from the international community, both in the form of direct financial aid and armed security personnel to help maintain peace. A few other Muslim countries have had similar levels of support, but not many. Iraq and Afghanistan are receiving international support for democratic governance, but not at the same levels of investment. Montenegro has also benefited from the largesse of regional governments, but only became an independent democracy after a successful referendum and withdrawing from Serbia. While all the details of particular paths to democracy are important parts of each case history, it is likely that the contextual factors identified above are the most important in most cases.

Institutional Consequences

Democratic outcomes can take several forms. If a country is somewhat authoritarian, it can experience a democratic transition where there are marked improvements in regime transparency over a relatively short period of time. If a country is already somewhat democratic, it can experience the entrenchment of those political practices as each election produces legitimate leaders. Membership in both outcome categories can be defined by countries that have experienced a major political transformation toward open political institutions, fair elections, and the protection of civil liberties. Recall from the introduction that the basis for deciding what counts as a major democratic transition is a three-point, positive change on the Polity IV scale of democratic institutions. With some adjustments to this scoring system for particular countries, and the addition of observations since the dataset was completed, it is possible to describe different levels of membership in the overall set of countries that have experienced a democratic transition since 1994. For full membership in the set of countries experiencing democratic entrenchment, countries must have become stronger, more practiced democracies in recent years. Countries such as Turkey, Bulgaria, and India are examples of such countries and are full members of the set. At the threshold of full membership in this theoretical set is a group of countries that are fully transitioned though young democracies, and countries that are entrenched authoritarian regimes are out of this set. Emerging democracies have experienced a very significant leap out of authoritarianism only in recent years. Then there is a group of countries that are mostly in the set of countries that have experienced a democratic transition—countries such as Georgia, Bangladesh, and Malaysia are increasingly durable democracies that are still developing their open and transparent political practices and have low but positive scores on the Polity IV index. Just barely in this set are countries such as Algeria and Singapore, which have a few democratic institutions, but because of a political transition in recent years have at least moved out of the authoritarian side of most indices.

There are other countries that, to different degrees, do not belong in the set of countries that have experienced a major democratic transition. Egypt and Uganda, for example, have experienced a major three-point transition toward democracy, but for the most part these countries just became less authoritarian. Thus, they are more out of the set than in it. Countries such as Morocco and Yemen are mostly out of the set, because while they may have become less authoritarian, they did so only through modest political transitions, perhaps moving up only one or two points toward the democratic end of the scale. At the threshold for full non-membership in the set of countries that have democratized are cases with only a few hopeful signs of political transition. For the most part these countries have been consistently authoritarian and have shown no movement toward systematic democratic practices. Many Gulf and North African countries are at the threshold of full exclusion from the set, countries such as Kuwait and Tunisia. Fully excluded countries include many states in crisis, such as Iraq and Afghanistan, countries that have become more authoritarian over time, such as Azerbaijan, and countries that are well entrenched authoritarian regimes, such as Saudi Arabia.

Figure 7.1 presents the relationships between important infrastructural and causal conditions, the primary political outcomes, and observed institutional consequences. Policy reforms in the telecommunications sector, including explicit digital development policies, privacy policies, and public spectrum allocation policies set the conditions. For many states, the political outcomes include cash flow from remittances, economic growth in the domestic ICT industries, and improving administrative capacity for government agencies. Digital technologies allow political party leaders to reach out to voters, diaspora communities, and citizens in countries where voting is not allowed. Outcomes can include improved fund-raising, rising administrative capacity for the party bureaucracy, the ability to efficiently target campaign messages or activate party members, and less vulnerability to state interference with the political communication. For journalists, ICTs provide additional outlets for individual writers, additional sourcing, and the opportunity to develop professionally. The observed outcomes of ICT use by journalists include greater

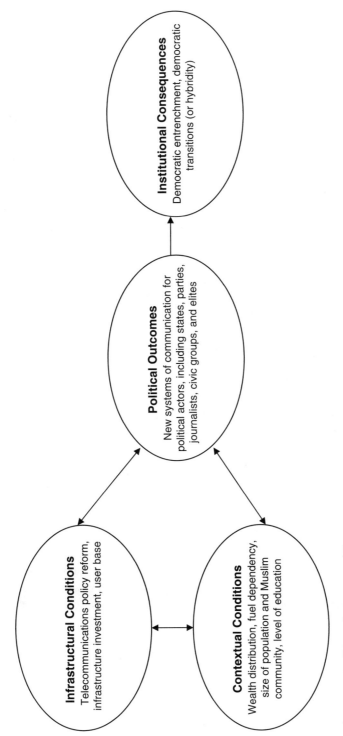

Figure 7.1 Conditions, Outcomes, and Consequences

publication reach and better research tools. As with political parties and journalists, civil society groups that build or take advantage of infrastructural conditions often see valuable outcomes: the ability to organize independently of
the state, make international linkages with affinity groups, bridge and bond
with other groups, raise funds to support the services they provide, and activate members in times of crisis. For ruling elites, the condition of information
infrastructure can provide them with the technical capacity to monitor and
restrict political culture online and administrative control over informational
choke points in digital networks. But such infrastructure also supports new
systems of producing and consuming political culture. So while one outcome
can include more effective censorship, it often includes debate over the interpretation of Islamic texts, the formation of new and individuated political
identity online (especially among youth), and the active deliberation of gender
roles and pan-Islamic identity (Anderson 2003).

Recipes for Contemporary Democratization

Table 7.1 identifies the simplified solution sets for the conditions that have
proven to be sufficient causes of either a democratic transition or entrenchment among countries with large Muslim populations since 1994. Certainly,
there are more complex formulations of conditions that would also explain
democratization, and each case could be described with a unique combination
of causal factors. The combinations reported here are not the only plausible
ones, but they do cover the widest spectrum of Muslim experience around
the developing world, and the cases are largely consistent with causal conditions for democratic outcomes. Coverage refers to the percentage of cases
explained by that recipe. Consistency refers to the degree to which cases
adhere to a particular causal recipe. Appendix A offers a detailed technical
discussion of the fuzzy set analysis, along with more complete details about
all parsimonious solution sets and notes on the more complex solution sets.

The combinations of sufficient causes are chosen for having the best and
second-best coverage of all the parsimonious solutions. Having determined
which causes are sufficient, the causes were tested both on their own and in
combination to measure the degree to which they also serve as necessary
conditions for transition or entrenchment. Table 7.1 presents two of the best
necessary causes or combinations of causes: one is chosen for having the
highest degree of coverage, and one is chosen for having the highest degree
of consistency. As might be expected, a solitary necessary cause covers lots of
cases but with low consistency, while combinations of necessary causes
describe fewer cases with greater consistency.

Across both kinds of democratic outcomes, information technologies are
an important ingredient. For states to have become more democratic they

Table 7.1: The Prominent, Parsimonious Causes of Democratic Transitions and Entrenchment

Causal Conditions	Percentage of Cases Covered by Solution	Percentage of Solution Consistent across Covered Cases	Causal Outcomes
Sufficient Causes			
Having a comparatively active online civil society in countries with a relatively small population	65	82	
Having a comparatively active online civil society in countries with a relatively well educated population	63	74	Democratic Transitions
Necessary Causes			
Having a comparatively small population	76	85	
Having a comparatively active online civil society in countries with a relatively small and well educated population	68	91	
Sufficient Causes			
Having a state with a comparatively well developed information infrastructure, and an economy not dominated by fuel exports	56	87	
Having a comparatively well educated population, and an economy not dominated by fuel exports	51	87	Democratic Entrenchment
Necessary Causes			
Having an economy not dominated by fuel exports	77	73	
Having a state with a comparatively well developed information infrastructure, an economy not dominated by fuel exports and a relatively well educated population	54	96	

Notes: Coverage refers to the percentage of cases explained by that recipe. Consistency refers to the degree to which cases adhere to a particular causal solution. See Appendix A for additional notes and the full list of cases explained by causal solutions.

often have to experience technology diffusion that affects political actors, particularly civil society groups and state bureaucracies. Technology use by journalists, civil society groups, and state censors is relevant for other solution sets, but these seem less prominent across all the cases. Indeed, the contextual factors also have prominence in some of the minor solution sets and a few combinations of necessary and sufficient conditions have nothing to do with technology diffusion. But most of the solutions with good coverage and consistency demonstrate that an active online civil society and good state information infrastructure in small countries with well educated populations has resulted in democratic transitions. These causal recipes chosen for their high levels of case coverage and consistency.

The two most prominent and parsimonious sufficient causes of democratic transition share one ingredient—having a comparatively active online civil society. Having such an active online civil society, along with having a comparatively small population or a comparatively well-educated population, proves to represent almost two-thirds of the cases studied. Testing all three sufficient causes for their possible role as a necessary cause reveals that having a comparatively small population is the solitary cause with the greatest case coverage, while all three causes in combination explain 68 percent of the cases with 91 percent consistency. On its own, having a large civil society may not be the active ingredient, because education dropped out of many causal recipes. It is the relatively large internet and mobile phone user base—a wired civil society—that consistently serves as a causal condition across multiple democratization recipes.

Having a state with a well-developed information infrastructure and an economy not dominated by fuel exports is a sufficient cause of democratic entrenchment. The second best set of sufficient causes is having a comparatively well-educated population and an economy not dominated by fuel exports. Thus, the two most prominent and parsimonious sufficient causes of democratic entrenchment include one solution set that involves state information infrastructure, and one that involves no technology diffusion factors. Both solution sets have a common ingredient—having an economy that is comparatively not dominated by fuel exports. Testing all three sufficient causes for their possible role as a necessary cause reveals that having an economy not dominated by fuel exports is the solitary condition with the greatest case coverage, while all three causes in combination explain 54 percent of the cases with 96 percent consistency.

Set relations in social research have three analytical advantages over correlational treatments: set relations involve explicitly causal connections between social phenomena, they are fundamentally asymmetric, and they can have significant explanatory power despite weak correlations (Ragin 2009). Among the countries with large Muslim communities, those with a rapidly expanding information infrastructure experienced either democratic transitions or entrenchment. This conclusion makes an explicit link through which technology diffusion can contribute to democratization.

Transitions to Democracy—or Regime Hybridity

Democratic transitions are not always successful, and a set-theoretic perspective allows us to learn from the partial successes. A growing number of Muslims living around the developing world inhabit a new kind of media environment, and are subjects of a new system of political communication. Many have been relieved from a situation in which they mostly consumed news and political culture over information and communication technologies owned by the state, and are now in a situation where they have significantly more choices to make as consumers and can even become producers of political culture. Information infrastructure *is* politics, and culture is the battleground for the future of democratic Islam. Moreover, this research suggests that the way to support democratic Islam is through open information infrastructure. Many of the regimes that were already somewhat democratic became more so through the diffusion of information technologies. Other regimes transitioned to democracy rapidly, in part because information technologies supported the work of investigative journalists, political parties, and civic groups.

Some regimes, however, did experience democratic improvements in specific political practices and institutions, but all in all just became less authoritarian. For example, technology diffusion has had identifiable consequences for systems of political communication in Bahrain and Egypt, but these countries are not fully in the set of countries that transitioned to democracy. Obvious members of this group include Georgia, Indonesia, and Tanzania. But rather than concluding that Bahrain and Egypt just became less authoritarian through technology diffusion, it might be more nuanced to conclude that information technologies have increased the hybrid nature of those regimes. So while Egypt remains under a fairly strong dictator at the executive level and political parties do not openly compete for elected office, the vibrant blogging community there has greatly improved the level of conversation in the country and helped social movement leaders score some notable political victories. These online citizens will make future elections highly contested. In Bahrain, the concessions to political transparency have been very modest. Yet a vibrant public sphere for that country has formed online, and while virtual, its existence has had real-world consequences for the system of political communication in that country.

There is easy evidence that the internet has been a tool for recruiting young disaffected Muslims for extremist causes, and this book has sought to organize the compelling evidence that the internet is more broadly and effectively the tool for civic Islam. Indeed, some conservative analysts are beginning to identify the negative consequences of overreacting to the few cases of online radicalization, and to argue for public policy initiatives to strengthen the information infrastructure and online presence of mainstream and open Muslim communities (Stevens and Neumann 2009).

Consequences for Foreign Policy

The conclusions reached here lend themselves to some practical foreign policy objectives. First, countries that want to encourage democratization elsewhere must more actively discourage the export of censorship software. The experience of countries with ruling Islamic elites has been that the state begins censoring pornographic websites with the pretense of protecting cultural values, and expands to political content whenever it faces a political or security-related crisis. As the cost of commercial censorship drops and services expand, it is safe to predict that more states ruled by cultural elites will be among the best customers of censorship software.

Second, the international lending community must be more willing to finance the construction of public information infrastructure in developing nations. Such infrastructure not only supports the work of the state, but has observed implications for political parties, journalists, and civic groups. Allowing, and indeed encouraging, the development of applications and content for democratic discourse will not only counteract the reach and appeal of Islamic fundamentalists online, but it will create the opportunity for citizens to imagine democratic variations that are best suited to their needs—and less authoritarian overall. Debates over telecommunications reform over the last two decades have been dominated by efforts to privatize existing information infrastructure and develop new infrastructure within the marketplace. Many Muslim countries have retained close state control of this infrastructure primarily out of the fear of surrendering a tool for propaganda and moral control. Censorship aside, looking across the 75 countries, there are some important lessons for why public investment in information infrastructure has positive outcomes. Telecommunications policies that are well articulated, while at the same time receptive to innovation from the commercial services sector, have the effect of creating an environment of stability and certainty for the private sector. Countries where the national infrastructure saw significant public investment and where commercial ISPs were founded and managed by local entrepreneurs seem to have the healthiest internet access markets (Wilson 2004; Howard and Mazaheri 2009).

Third, as Muslim media systems are dynamically evolving, this may be the moment to encourage internet use among civic actors (including journalists and political parties). Supporting an information infrastructure for civil Islam is likely to undermine the appeal of fundamentalist discourse. Countries such as Turkey and Indonesia are good examples of the way democratic governance and accessible information infrastructure may help combat Islamic fundamentalism it ways that secular authoritarianism does not. In both countries, radical Islamists compete for electoral office alongside more secular candidates, but rarely have fundamentalists received more than a fifth of the popular vote in recent years, even in the regions in which they are most concentrated. And almost all of the cases in this study have peripheral regions in which violent, fundamentalist political movements fester. Elections—even rigged ones—will have significant implications on the future of Chechnya, Dagestan, Ingushetia, Darfur, and Mindinao. Information and communication technologies have had a demonstrable role in changing the opportunity structures for political communication in large nations; they may also contribute to localized institution-building as well. The formal democratic institution of voting does not replace informal political relations, it builds upon them. So even in countries where elections are rigged, strengthening the communication networks among non-state actors builds upon the political capacity of those actors. Satellite television still delivers much of the political content consumed by voters, but increasingly the competition for popular opinion occurs over mobile phone networks and the internet.

THE CONTEMPORARY RECIPES FOR DEMOCRATIZATION

Comparative analysis demonstrates that having an active online civil society is both a necessary and sufficient cause of transitions out of authoritarianism. Moreover, having a state with a well-developed information infrastructure proves to be both a necessary and sufficient cause of institutional entrenchment in countries that were already somewhat democratic. The causal role of technology diffusion operates in conjunction with two additional contextual factors. Democratic transitions of countries with large Muslim communities have often, over the last 15 years, also been an artifact of how large and well-educated the population is. Institutional entrenchment in countries that already have some democratic processes is an artifact of how well-educated the population is and how dependent the economy is on fuel exports.

In recent years, wired states, parties, journalists, and civic groups have contributed to the spread of democracy in countries that were not very democratic, and improved the durability of regimes that were emerging democracies. Based on the evidence offered in the previous chapters, it is safe to assert that there is a close causal connection between information infrastructure and contemporary democratization, and that the set of countries with lots of ICTs constitutes a subset of the set of democracies. There are countries with few ICTs that also display democratic features, so there are certainly other paths to democracy. Yet this does not undermine the claim that technology diffusion has political outcomes, including wired political parties, a wired state, journalists with internet access, and a large online civil society. Nor does it undermine the claim that changing systems of political communication have consequences for the institutions of democratic or authoritarian power.

Some of these wired Muslim polities are also among the set of countries that experienced a democratic transition in recent years. In some cases, the transition was "completed" in a way that satisfies political pundits: a full and fair set of national elections with a nonviolent change in executive authority. In other cases, the transition was toward some hybrid status: modest steps toward democratization symbolized by the legalization of political parties, or the involvement of more client groups in political decision making, or the relaxation of authoritarian controls. In other cases, the transition has been slight, and better described as "liberalization" than democratization. A few countries became more authoritarian, and a few had multiple, complex transitions, becoming less authoritarian through a transition to a hybrid regime in which a few political actors are able to operate much as their peers in other more fully democratic countries operate.

A crucial failing of much work on technology diffusion and democratization has been in the way that the potential for democratic uses of information technologies are described as if such uses are real and consistent across the contemporary operation of actors in systems of political communication. In contrast, the arguments made here emphasize the observed outcomes for political actors and both democratic and authoritarian uses of information technologies.

Information technologies matter inasmuch as they reinforce—and redirect—local variations in political practices. What does the evidence presented in previous chapters teach us about political change in Muslim countries since the arrival of information and communication technologies? First, there is significant evidence of "modularity" in political action: successful internet or mobile phone activation strategies in one country are tested— when the opportunity arises—in other countries. In this study, significant demonstration effects of the use of ICTs in democratization are evident, and steps toward or away from democratic practices have been incremental. Rather than trying to explain the role of ICTs in significant democratic revolution and upheaval, it would be more useful to offer a causal explanation of the role of information technologies in incremental change in multiple facets of political life. Information and communication technologies are the infrastructure for transposing democratic ideals from community to community. They support the process of learning new approaches to political representation, of trying out new organizational strategies, and of cognitively extending the possibilities and prospects for political transformation from one context to another.

ICTs reduce uncertainty, whether among elites deciding to back authoritarian dictators or democratic activists, or parties forming coalitions, or journalists corroborating stories. ICTs introduce new information to the calculus that citizens aspiring for democracy use in deciding whether to contest a shady election or join a political group not sanctioned by the state. More than that, ICTs structure the demand and supply of information. ICTs provide new channels for mediating political discourse, drawing in community members from elite groups, distant diaspora communities, and impoverished locals. By introducing new information and channels for mediation, states, parties, civic groups, journalists, and citizens in Islamic countries are able to learn about past patterns of behavior of the other actors.

ICTs allow states to collectively manage resources, people, and conflict. One of the great paradoxes of international relations is that organizations for the collective management of conflict only fail when members behave in such a fashion as to impede the realization of rules of conduct enshrined in their charters (Haas 1987). In important ways, the same can be said for the behavior of actors within a system of political communication. When actors misbehave, they are by definition not following the norms, rules, and patterns of behavior expected of them by other political actors. In this way, ICTs have already had an important, demonstrable impact on the capacity of the state to manage its affairs and conduct its business in an open or exposed manner. Similarly, ICTs have already had an important, demonstrable impact on the ability of civil society groups to monitor what their state is doing, to compete with radical groups for members, and to offer social services independent of the state. Overall, ICTs improve the administrative capacity of the state, and improve the capacity of civil society groups to be independent of the state.

Regular communication ties between family and friends, and between home and diaspora, means that the community is resilient in times of political and military crisis. New media technologies like the internet and mobile phones affect how individuals decide to participate or not participate in democratic actions. For individuals with internet access and regular connection to family and friends over mobile phones, the social risks of nonparticipation approaches that of participation. News groups, text messages from friends in plight, digital videos with cultural content unavailable on broadcast media—all keep a supply of information open and direct. In the past, collective action was hampered by the fact that Muslim communities did not always have good information about what was happening across their neighborhoods and regions. Now the infrastructure for relaying that information is solid, decentralized, and in important ways, out of state control.

The new information and communication technologies have allowed for different capacities and constraints in social movement organizing. The organizers of collective action in developing countries often faced a simple and central communication challenge: radio and television stations were easy for the state to seize and blow up; newspapers and magazines could be starved of paper and ink in times of crisis. Certainly the power can be cut and mobile phone towers turned off, but with so much of the cyber infrastructure residing outside of many Muslim countries, it is impossible for a state to take action against the online democratic activists in a diaspora. Democratic activists in a diaspora used to only be able to raise funds and send resources home to family and opposition leaders; today the diaspora is capable of running its own very effective propaganda campaigns, producing cultural content for people in the home country, and strengthening private connections between family and friends.

ICTs enable states to participate better in international relations, and enable communities to participate in intercultural learning. Secular Islam is alive and well, and online. In the context of the Islamic world, many ideologues and entrepreneurs have taken to the internet. With media systems so tightly controlled, either by authoritarian governments or powerful firms, people hungry for more flexible and interactive communications tool have turned to new ICTs. Movies, television, and news had an important role in shaping democratic values in the West. In many Muslim countries, it is ICTs such as satellite television, video games, the internet, and mobile phones that have this role, particularly for youth. Such technologies are not simply media for propaganda, but the infrastructure for political culture itself. Already these new informational linkages between Muslim countries have done much to mediate a transnational Islam based on shared grievances.

The subtitle of this book is a reference to Barrington Moore's *The Social Origins of Dictatorship and Democracy*. In it, Moore argued that the strongest democratic institutions of the twentieth century resulted from the most violent civil wars of the previous centuries. His is a story involving centuries of time, a comparative method, and does not suppose a singular path to democracy. The analysis here is also comparative, and though it has a shorter time frame, it demonstrates the digital origins of contemporary dictatorships and democracies. In many of the countries studied here, systems of political communication have evolved to the point where civic discourse no longer has to be copresent with the organizations of the state, or even sited in political territories.

Countries where civil society and journalists made active use of the new information technologies subsequently experienced a radical democratic transition or significant solidification in their democratic institutions. While there certainly are examples of how ICTs are used to facilitate graft, there are far more examples of how ICTs are used to catch graft. While there certainly are examples of how states use ICTs to control information and manipulate the public, there are far more examples of how ICTs are used by the public to get around the informational controls set up by states. Citizens of the countries studied here are no longer just consumers of political content, they manage the means of cultural production through consumer electronics. There are several recipes for democratic transition and entrenchment, and it is best to think of such political change in terms of evolution rather than revolution. It is clear that, increasingly, the route to democratization is a digital one.

Appendix A: Countries in This Study

The full dataset of all variables in the causal recipes described in the Conclusion is available at www.pitpi.org, as are the technical scripts for secondary solution sets not described here, the calibration points for specific membership sets. The fuzzy sets analyzed here were composed from the data presented in the chapters in the book, and replication data is available on the website. For more on fuzzy set calibrations see the codebook for the fs/QCA 2.0 software and Ragin (2009).

Preparing data for treatment as fuzzy set required several steps. First, I computed indices for causal attributes analyzed in each chapter, and then I computed the indices for additional context variables often recommended by the literature on democratization in the developing world. Then I calibrated the indices, a process that evens out the distribution of cases between the thresholds for full inclusion in each set, full exclusion from the set, and the crossover point at which cases go from being partially in the set to being partially out of the set.

FUZZY CALIBRATIONS

Calibrating the fuzzy set membership of a group of countries requires judgments for the threshold of full membership in the set, full exclusion from the set, and the transition midpoint at which a country is neither in nor out of the set. For example, among the 75 countries there are a few very populated countries and many countries with a small population. Figure A.1 reveals a skewed curve that comes from organizing countries by population. India is at the top of this set, and obviously helps define the category of "populated country." In fact, India has such a large population that if the set were left uncalibrated, Indonesia and Pakistan would be barely in the set, and most of the countries would be fully out of the set. Yet the important attribute is that some countries are comparatively more populated than others, so calibration makes the differences between the populous countries more comparable to those between smaller countries. The very populated countries still define the set by being almost full members, while the rest of the cases get indexed by their degrees of membership in the set. In this case, the threshold value for full membership in the set of populated countries is established just below the actual population of India. At the lowest points in the curve are countries such as the Maldives, Brunei, Western Sahara, and Suriname, and these are definitely not very populated countries. So the threshold for full exclusion is set at 470,000 people because these countries have even smaller populations than that. The crossover threshold has been set at 7 million people, which roughly splits countries into two groups. Since Tajikistan and Bulgaria have slightly larger populations, these two countries are just barely in the category of "populated country." The recalibration around these thresholds allows for fuzzy set values that more meaningfully reveal the degree to which each country can be included in the theoretical set of populated countries.

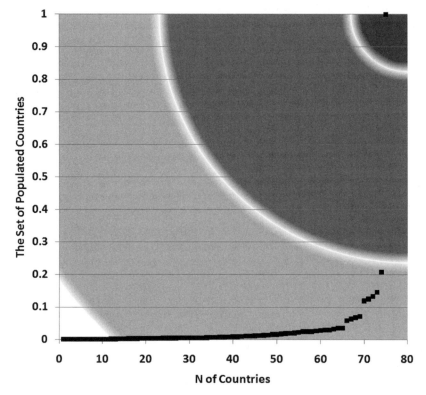

Figure A.1 Membership in the Set of Populated Countries: Uncalibrated
Source: World Bank, 2010.

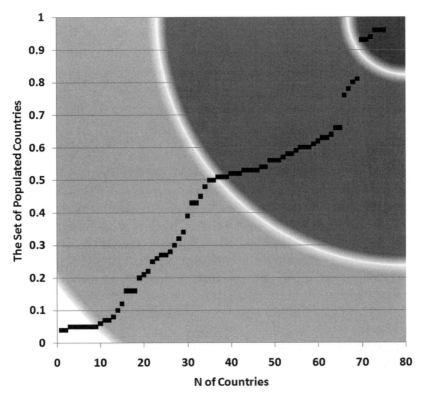

Figure A.2 Membership in the Set of Populated Countries: Calibrated
Source: See Figure A.1.

Calibrating the Infrastructural Conditions

For membership in the category of countries with well-developed state information infrastructure, the threshold for full membership is defined as improvement in government communications infrastructure, with points allotted for the number of telecommunications sector reforms, whether or not the state had a privacy policy, whether or not the state had a public spectrum allocation policy, the number of executive agencies with internet portals, and the e-government score determined by West (2008). Tanzania and Jordan are full members of this category. The threshold for full non-membership excludes the West Bank and Western Sahara from the category. The transition point barely excludes Montenegro and barely admits Oman to the category.

For membership in the category of countries that experienced significant improvements in the information infrastructure of political parties, with points allotted for having a high ratio of political parties with internet portals, whether those political parties maintained their information infrastructure in-country, and the gigabytes of content found at party websites. Turkey and Bulgaria are full members of this set, while the threshold for full non-membership effectively excludes a number of countries where political parties are effectively banned. The transition is defined at a point that barely excludes Togo, and barely admits Bosnia to the category.

For membership in the category of countries that experienced significant improvements in the information infrastructure of news media, the threshold for full membership is set to include Pakistan, Russia, and India, based on the number of online news websites serving people in each country. The threshold for full non-membership excludes Guinea-Bissau and the Ivory Coast. The transition is defined by Tanzania, which is barely out of the set, and Libya, which is barely in the set of countries that experienced significant improvements in digital news media.

For membership in the category of countries that experienced significant improvements in the information infrastructure of civil society, the full membership is defined by Singapore and Israel, based on a technology distribution index described in the Introduction and Chapter 5. Non-membership is defined by Iraq and Liberia, while Togo is barely out of the set and Pakistan barely in the set.

For membership in the set of countries using ICTs to censor political content and manage cultural identity, a variety of sources on censorship were consulted. The well-respected sources on censorship, even when assembled together, provided comparative information on only two-thirds of the cases. So to help determine membership in the set of countries that censor their population's internet use, some general information about press censorship was taken from a Reporters Without Borders index. Still, the membership values for the majority of cases are heavily weighted by data specifically about internet freedoms. Iran and Turkmenistan define full membership, while Israel, Cyprus, Ghana, and Mali define non-membership. Sierra Leone is barely excluded from the category, while Afghanistan is barely in the category of countries that use ICTs for censorship.

Calibrating Contextual Conditions

For membership in the category of wealthy countries, the threshold for full membership is set to include the UAE and Qatar, where the average annual income was US$50,000 in 2008. Liberia, Guinea-Bissau, and Somalia define full non-membership in the category of wealthy countries, because in these countries the average annual income is below US$500. The transition is defined by Cameroon and Yemen, where average annual income is just over US$2,000 a year, and these countries are barely admitted to the category of wealthy countries.

For membership in the category of countries with income inequalities, the threshold for full membership is set to include Bosnia, the Central African Republic, and Sierra Leone, where the gini coefficient is above 0.56. Albania, Cyprus, Montenegro, and Ethiopia define full non-membership in the category of countries with income inequalities, because in these countries the gini coefficient is below 0.30. The transition is defined by Mauritania and Malawi, where the gini coefficient is just over 0.39, and these countries are barely admitted to the category of countries with income inequalities.

For membership in the category of countries with an educated population, the threshold for full membership is set to include Bahrain, Uzbekistan, Qatar, and Bulgaria, where close to 100 percent of the population has completed secondary education. Niger, Guinea-Bissau, Somalia, Liberia, and Western Sahara define full non-membership in the category of countries with an educated population because less than 11 percent of the population has completed secondary education. The transition is at the 50 percent mark, with Ghana just outside the category and Tanzania barely in the category.

For membership in the category of countries where fuel exports are an important part of the economy, Algeria and Nigeria define the set because fuel exports are almost 100 percent of the merchandise exports for these countries. Full non-membership is defined by Ethiopia and Malawi, and the transition to partial membership is marked by Gambia and Somalia. The former is barely excluded from the set, while the later is barely included.

For membership in the category of Muslim countries, the threshold for full membership is set to include the 11 countries where more than 98 percent of the population self-identifies as being practicing Muslims. Full non-membership is defined by countries such as Georgia and Kenya, where Muslims make up less than 20 percent of the population. The transition is defined by Albania and the Sudan, countries that are barely in the set because just over 70 percent of the population are practicing Muslims.

As described in the example above, the threshold for full membership in the set of populated countries is defined by India, easily the largest country in the set. Full non-membership is defined by countries such as the Maldives and Brunei, where there are fewer than 500,000 people. The transition is defined by Tajikistan and Bulgaria, countries that are barely in the set with a population of just over 7 million.

Calibrating Institutional Outcomes

The Polity IV index provides a good starting point for comparing democratization trends. The original dataset extends to 2007, and the author has made some adjustments to the original dataset and has extended coverage to 2008. The size of the Muslim community is based on the proportion of the population practicing Islam, according to the World Bank World Development Indicators. The size of the Muslim community in each country is judged as a small minority if it is between 10 and 49 percent (•), majority if it is between 50 and 89 percent (●) and a totality if it is more than 90 percent (•) of the total. Information and communication technology distribution is based on an index of the distribution of information technology resources, weighted by economy size, as described in the introduction. Index values were computed using data from the World Bank World Development Indicators for mobile phones, internet users, internet hosts, personal computers, internet bandwidth, and internet subscribers, and then averaged. Technology diffusion is judged as slow (·) if the country is in the bottom third of the index, medium (□) if the country is in the middle third of the index, or rapid (○) if it is in the top third of the index.

Multiple sources were used to inform the decisions on if and when a Muslim country experienced a political transition, whether the transition was for better or worse, and how the degree of shift might compare to other countries. The primary source was the Polity IV dataset, which tracks regime change up to 2007 and includes most of the states with large Muslim communities. The dataset ranks countries on a 21-point index from -10 (completely authoritarian) to +10 (completely democratic), with a 0 score representing neither an authoritarian nor democratic regime, but a chaotic state of transition usually involving war, anarchy, or state collapse. The index itself has several components, including assessments of the competitiveness of political participation, the openness and competitiveness of executive recruitment, and the constraints on the chief executive, whether president, prime minister, or monarch (Marshall and Jaggers 2008). Working from this index, countries that experienced a democratic transition are those for which experts find a 3-point transition toward the positive democratic end of the scale. Countries that experienced one or two points of improvement, if they already ranked as strong democracies, are categorized as experiencing entrenchment. The remaining countries are ones that continued to be ruled by authoritarian regimes, or experienced only temporary regime transitions. Crisis states include those embroiled in the chaos of war, invasion, or state failure. While interesting examples from these states are presented in chapters on specific types of political actors, these states are ultimately dropped from fuzzy set analysis. Additional sources, regional experts, and fieldwork allow for rankings to be updated to 2008 and for some adjustments to the Polity IV rankings. These adjustments are described in the tables below.

Thirteen countries experienced democratic entrenchment, and steadily received a democracy score of 6 or higher over the period of study. A country is consistently somewhat democratic if it received a score of between 1 and 5 over the period of study. A country is consistently authoritarian if it was steadily scored between -6 and -10. A country is consistently somewhat authoritarian if it received a score of between -1 and -5. A country is a crisis state if it suffered from an extended period of lawlessness, civil war, foreign invasion, or other form of state collapse. Territories with unresolved status, Western Sahara, the West Bank, and Gaza strip, are included as crisis states.

Table A.1: Proportion of Population Practicing Islam, Rate of ICT Diffusion, and Countries Experiencing a Democratic Transition

Country	Muslim Population	Rate of Technology Diffusion	Transition Years, Magnitude and Notes on Author Adjustments to Polity IV Ranking
Albania	•	+	2001–2005; 4 points.
Algeria	●	+	1994–2004; 9 points.
Bahrain	●	+	1992–2002; 3 points.
Bosnia	·	✚	2006–2008; 6 points. Bosnia has become more democratic, with recent elections, significant reduction in EU troop presence, and the changing mission of these troops from peacekeeping to civil policing.
Comoros	●	+	2003–2006; 5 points.
Djibouti	●	+	1998–1999; 8 points.
Egypt	●	+	2004–2005; 3 points. Transitioned from being authoritarian to being only somewhat authoritarian, but in author's judgment still a democratic transition.
Georgia	·	✚	1994–2004; 3 points.
Ghana	·	+	2000–2004; 6 points.
Indonesia	•	+	1998–1999; 11 points.
Kenya	·	+	2001–2002; 10 points.
Kuwait	•	+	2006–2008; 4 points.
Kyrgyzstan	•	✚	2004–2006; 7 points.
Lebanon	•	✚	2004–2008; 7 points. Lebanon has been plagued by violence, war, and foreign interference. Between 2005–2006 there were signs of democratic stability, then in 2007 more political violence, and in 2008 a successful round of elections.
Liberia	·	+	2002–2006; 6 points.
Macedonia	·	+	2001–2002; 3 points.

(*continued*)

Table A.1: Continued

Country	Muslim Population	Rate of Technology Diffusion	Transition Years, Magnitude and Notes on Author Adjustments to Polity IV Ranking
Maldives	●	+	2005–2008; 5 points. Transitioned from being authoritarian to being only somewhat authoritarian, but in author's judgment still a democratic transition. Maldives has long been a dictatorship, but has recently transitioned to being less authoritarian with the legalizing of political parties and the drafting of a constitutional document.
Mauritania	●	+	2004–2006; 3 points. Transitioned from being authoritarian to being only somewhat authoritarian, but in author's judgment still a democratic transition.
Montenegro	·	+	2006–2008; 4 points. Montenegro, in recent years, has appealed for independence from Serbia, held a referendum and chose independence, and successfully elected a head of state.
Niger	●	+	1998–1999; 11 points.
Nigeria	·	+	1997–1999; 10 points.
Senegal	●	✚	1999–2000; 9 points.
Sierra Leone	·	+	2000–2002; 5 points.
Suriname	·	+	2005–2008; 3 points. Suriname has been governed by a coalition of political parties since 1991, and the coalition expanded in 2005.
Tanzania	·	✚	1999–2005; 3 points. Tanzania has become more democratic, with the two-term president not challenging the constitutional ban on a third term, and 2005 elections being judged by international observers as having some cases of intimidation and logical irregularities, but on the whole free and fair.
Uganda	·	+	2004–2005; 3 points. Transitioned from being authoritarian to being only somewhat authoritarian, but in author's judgment still a democratic transition.

Table A.2: Proportion of Population Practicing Islam, Degree of ICT Diffusion, and Countries Experiencing Democratic Entrenchment

Country	Muslim Population	Technology Diffusion	Democracy Status
Bangladesh	•	+	Consistently democratic.
Benin	·	+	Consistently democratic.
Bulgaria	·	✚	Consistently democratic.
Cyprus	·	✚	Consistently democratic.
Guinea-Bissau	·	✚	Had a non-linear transition: Guinea-Bissau was slightly democratic until 2002 when it became slightly authoritarianism for two years (-6), then returned to be a stronger democracy (+7).
India	·	✚	Consistently democratic.
Israel	·	✚	Consistently democratic.
Malawi	·	+	Had a non-linear transition: Malawi has been democratic, but briefly became somewhat democratic between 2001-4 (-2), after which it returned to being more democratic (+2).
Malaysia	•	✚	Consistently somewhat democratic. Even though Malaysia does not rank as a strong democracy up to 2007, successful elections in 2008 are evidence of democratic entrenchment (+2).
Mali	●	+	Consistently democratic.
Mauritius	·	✚	Consistently democratic.
Mozambique	·	✚	Consistently democratic.
Turkey	●	✚	Consistently democratic.

Table A.3: Proportion of Population Practicing Islam, Degree of ICT Diffusion, and Countries That Remained Authoritarian

Country	Muslim Population	Technology Diffusion	Authoritarian Status
Azerbaijan	●	+	Became more authoritarian.
Brunei	·	✚	Consistently authoritarian. Brunei is consistently authoritarian, run as a constitutional monarchy with some recent improvements, but not enough to call a transition.
Cameroon	·	+	Consistently somewhat authoritarian.
CAR	·	+	Became more authoritarian.
Chad	·	+	Consistently somewhat authoritarian.
Eritrea	·	✚	Consistently authoritarian.
Ethiopia	·	+	Remained authoritarian. Consistently scored +1 in Polity IV over the period of study, but in author's judgment this country is not in the set of transition or entrenchment countries.
Gambia	●	+	Consistently authoritarian.
Guinea	·	+	Consistently somewhat authoritarian.
Iran	●	+	Had a non-linear transition: Iran became slightly less authoritarian in 1996–1997 (+3) but returned to authoritarianism in 2004 (-3).
Jordan	●	✚	Consistently somewhat authoritarian.
Kazakhstan	·	+	Became more authoritarian.
Libya	●	+	Consistently authoritarian.
Morocco	●	✚	Consistently authoritarian.
Oman	●	+	Consistently authoritarian.
Pakistan	●	+	Became more authoritarian.
Qatar	·	+	Consistently authoritarian.
Russia	·	✚	Experienced a +3 point transition towards democracy according to Polity IV, but in author's judgment this country is not in the set of transition or entrenchment countries. Russia has had difficulty with executive turnover and has developed a strong presidentialist regime.
Saudi Arabia	●	+	Consistently authoritarian.
Singapore	·	✚	Consistently somewhat authoritarian.

Sudan	•	+	Experienced a +3 point transition towards democracy according to Polity IV, but in author's judgment this country is not in the set of transition or entrenchment countries.
Syria	●	+	Consistently authoritarian.
Tajikistan	●	+	Consistently somewhat authoritarian.
Togo	·	✚	Consistently somewhat authoritarian.
Tunisia	●	+	Consistently somewhat authoritarian.
Turkmenistan	•	+	Consistently authoritarian.
UAE	•	+	Consistently authoritarian.
Uzbekistan	•	✚	Consistently authoritarian.
Yemen	●	+	Consistently somewhat authoritarian.

Table A.4: Proportion of Population Practicing Islam, Degree of ICT Diffusion, and Countries Experiencing an Extended Period of Interruption from Foreign Powers, Interregnum, or Anarchy

Country	Muslim Population	Technology Diffusion	Crisis Status
Afghanistan	●	+	
Burkina Faso	•	+	Had a non-linear transition: Burkina Faso became slightly democratic 1999–2001 but returned to chaos in 2002.
Iraq	●	+	
Ivory Coast	·	+	Had a non-linear transition: Ivory Coast became a slight democracy between 1998–2001 (+10), but has been in anarchy since 2002.
Somalia	●	✚	
West Bank	•	+	
Western Sahara	●	+	

For membership in the category of countries that had experienced entrenchment, the threshold for full membership is defined as an 11-point improvement in democratic institutions during the period of transition, which uses Indonesia and Niger to define full membership in the category. The threshold for full non-membership is defined by Pakistan and the Central African Republic, which experienced a -13 and -6 drop in their democracy score over the study period. Many other countries had a consistent regime with no transition in either direction. The transition point between categories was set at a 1-point improvement, which barely excludes Guinea-Bissau and barely admits Oman into the category.

For membership in the category of countries that had experienced democratic entrenchment, the threshold for full membership is defined as at least 36 years of durability as a democratic regime, which sets Malaysia, Mauritius, India and Israel as full members of the category. The threshold for full non-membership is defined as at least 50 years of durability as an authoritarian regime, which includes Oman, Libya, and Saudi Arabia. The transition point between categories was set at one year as a democratic regime, which barely excludes Pakistan and barely admits the Comoros into the category.

Several other kinds of calibrations and manipulations help get the data into shape for fuzzy set analysis. For example, the fuzzy category of countries experiencing a democratic transition includes 34 countries that, relying on Polity IV data alone, are neither in nor out of the set. Both Yemen and Turkey are neither in nor out of this category, but for different reasons, so it makes sense to adjust the membership values of each so that they "lean" in a sensible direction. Thus Turkey was recoded to be barely in the set of countries experiencing a democratic transition, and Yemen recoded to be barely out of the set.

Western Sahara and the Palestinian Territories of the West Bank and Gaza are treated as countries in some datasets but not others. Given their prominent role in international Islamic politics, they are treated as units of analysis here. Since data on these two units of analysis are patchy, the fuzzy set variables were patched with additional sources, or by hand with information about neighboring countries. Depending on the variable, Mauritania was often a reference point for the Western Sahara, while Egypt or Lebanon served as reference points for the West Bank and Gaza. For example, the fuzzy set of countries with large online civil societies had missing data in these instances, so given the author's knowledge of these cases, Western Sahara was coded as having a slightly smaller online civil society than Mauritania, and the West Bank and Gaza was graded with a slightly larger online civil society than Egypt. Since the crisis states are unlikely to teach us much about the recipe for democratization, they have been removed from the analysis.

SELECTING CAUSAL SETS

As in all social science, the researcher must make difficult decisions about what to include in a causal explanation that covers most of the cases and for which most of the cases are consistent. The fs/QCA program renders complex, parsimonious, and intermediate solutions. In the concluding chapter, the parsimonious solutions were presented because they reveal which conditions are essential to distinguishing between the positive and negative cases of democratic transition. Parsimonious solutions tend to sacrifice some set-theoretic consistency and include cases with missing data, but yield better case coverage overall. However, only the West Bank and Western Sahara were missing data, and these cases were dropped in the final analysis. Moreover, the consistency cutoff was set to be relatively high. The complex solutions provide a more complete account of the causal mechanisms behind democratization, but supplement without contradicting the key findings. For these reasons, the parsimonious explanations are offered in the conclusion.

Removing the crisis states left 68 countries in the comparison set. With 12 causal variables, there are 4,096 possible combinations of ingredients for the democratization recipe. However, only a much smaller number of these combinations actually describe real cases; a few combinations explain many cases, some combinations only explain one unique case, most combinations have no real examples. So fs/QCA identifies a series of minimal solutions. If two solutions differ in only one causal condition but have the same outcome, then the causal condition that distinguishes the two solutions can be removed to create a simple, combined expression. The concluding chapter discusses the most prominent causal recipes for democratic transition as determined by the number of cases covered and the degree to which cases are consistent with the solutions.

For the sufficient causes of institutional change, cases are noted if they have greater than 0.5 membership in the outcome for that specific causal configuration. This may mean that some of the noted cases are not fully consistent with other causal conditions. Some cases can be explained by several recipes, so the countries that best fit with membership in the outcome are listed in descending order of fit. Since these set relations are fuzzy, there are additional cases that would be explained, though perhaps with less consistency. The noted cases have the same causal conditions and also share, to varying degrees, membership in the outcome. The necessary conditions are shared by the cases that have democratized.

The Solution Sets for Sufficient Causes

The solution set for sufficient causes of democratic transition had a consistency cutoff of 90 percent, meaning that cases with full membership in the outcome had to be at least 90 percent consistent. There were 41 causal combinations containing real cases of democratic transition. Table 7.1 presents the two parsimonious solutions with the highest case coverage, though there were 38 parsimonious solutions all in all that covered 96 percent of the cases with 69 percent consistency.

The solution set for sufficient causes of democratic entrenchment had a consistency cutoff of 95 percent. There were 41 parsimonious causal combinations containing real cases of democratic entrenchment. Table 7.1 presents the two parsimonious solutions with the highest case coverage, though there were 28 solutions all in all that covered 82 percent of the cases with 77 percent consistency.

Membership in the outcome of democratic transition caused by having a comparatively active online civil society with a comparatively small population includes the following countries, in order of consistency (with consistency and coverage for each case in brackets): Brunei (0.95, 0.75), Cyprus (0.95, 0.5), Mozambique (0.93, 0.75), Bahrain (0.89, 0.69), Kuwait (0.89, 0.75), Mauritania (0.88, 0.5), Pakistan (0.87, 0.39), Lebanon (0.83, 0.85), Maldives (0.81, 0.69), Niger (0.8, 0.54), Turkey (0.79, 0.39), Bosnia (0.78, 0.85), Sierra Leone (0.78, 0.5), Georgia (0.77, 0.69), Sudan (0.69, 0.69), Kyrgyzstan (0.67, 0.89), Jordan (0.65, 0.5), Israel (0.62, 0.54), Albania (0.62, 0.75), and Djibouti (0.52, 0.91). Membership in the outcome of democratic transition caused by having a comparatively active online civil society with a comparatively well-educated population includes: Sierra Leone (0.94, 0.5), Brunei (0.94, 0.75), Bulgaria (0.94, 0.5), Cyprus (0.93, 0.5), Turkey (0.92, 0.39), Israel (0.92, 0.54), Kuwait (0.9, 0.75), Bahrain (0.89, 0.69), Mozambique (0.88, 0.75), Mauritania (0.88, 0.5), Pakistan (0.87, 0.39), Qatar (0.87, 0.62), Lebanon (0.85, 0.85), Tunisia (0.84, 0.5), Bosnia (0.83, 0.85), Georgia (0.81, 0.69), Maldives (0.81, 0.69), Russia (0.81, 0.39), Niger (0.8, 0.54), and Kazakhstan (0.76, 0.16).

Membership in the outcome of democratic entrenchment caused by having a state with comparatively well-developed information infrastructure and an economy not dominated by imports includes: Jordan (0.93, 0.25), Mauritania (0.93, 0.9), Tajikistan (0.93, 0.66), Malawi (0.9, 0.67), Bangladesh (0.83, 0.7), Liberia (0.68, 0.51), and Ethiopia (0.53, 0.66).

Membership in the outcome of democratic entrenchment caused by having a state with a comparatively well-educated population and an economy not dominated by fuel exports includes: Israel (0.92, 0.96), Jordan (0.9, 0.25), Mauritania (0.9, 0.9), and Lebanon (0.85, 0.53).

The Solution Sets of Necessary Causes

The two solution sets for the sufficient causes of democratic transition each suggest three variables that should be tested for their possible role as necessary causes. Indeed, each of the causes appear in many of the other solution sets not presented here, so these are certainly among the most important ingredients for democratization. For each institutional outcome—transition or entrenchment—the candidates were tested on their own, in pairs, and all together. The necessary causes with the greatest case coverage were ones that had little to do with information technology diffusion, though the factors that did concern technology diffusion had only slightly lower levels of case coverage. Putting all three causes together yielded a necessary combination of causes with excellent consistency and some sacrifice in coverage.

Whereas the best two sufficient causes were selected on the basis of case coverage, the necessary conditions were chosen in a different way. It is important to distinguish between trivial and non-trivial necessary causes, because a solitary condition may appear in almost all causal recipes, whether or not these cases display democratic outcomes. Indeed, every one of the causal conditions could be tested for necessity, but the most theoretically useful ones have high case coverage, may also double as sufficient conditions, and in combination with other conditions have good consistency. For example, a well-educated population may be a necessary condition for democratization, but if well-educated populations are always present then the absence of an educated population will never be found to constrain democratic outcomes. Alone it is a somewhat trivial finding. But in combination with other necessary causes, the cases that exhibit democratic outcomes have much greater consistency. It turns out that having an active online civil society and a small, well-educated population is a non-trivial causal condition for democratic transitions. Moreover, having a well-developed state information infrastructure, an economy not dominated by fuel exports, and a relatively well-educated population is a non-trivial necessary cause of democratic entrenchment. Rather than list all seven causes and causal combinations, the conclusion highlights the necessary causes with the greatest coverage and greatest consistency.

Appendix B: Annotated References

This appendix offers reference annotations, organized by country as well as the four major profiles of political actors used in the book: states, political parties, journalists, and civic groups. I have added a "general" category to catch other kinds of political and internet themes. The "general" category includes items on censorship, the digital divide, diasporic activities online, and the political implications of other ICTS such as video games, digital art, and online humor. The items below represent the material covered in research for the comparisons made in this book. The list therefore would not be useful for other aspects of Muslim media systems, such as television, radio, and newspapers, that are not covered here.

This collection of references covers research published up to 2009 in major peer review journals and books (both authored and edited). There are a growing number of graduate dissertations on single countries, a plethora of long form journalism in newspapers and magazines, and much published on telecommunications by such industries in each country. Many of these kinds of reports are "grey literature" items and are archived at www.wiareport.org.

Table B.1: Study Population: Countries Experiencing a Democratic Transition

Country	States	Political Parties	Journalism and News Media	Citizens and Civil Society	General
Albania				Saunders 2005	
Algeria		Mellahi and Frynas 2003	Quandt 2002	Mellahi and Frynas 2003	
Bahrain					Palmer 2000
Bosnia			Bieber 2000		
Comoros	Farrell, Isaacs, and Trucano 2007				
Djibouti	Farrell, Isaacs, and Trucano 2007				
Egypt	Farrell, Isaacs, and Trucano 2007		Dimitrova and Connolly-Ahern 2007; Hamdy 2009; Armbrust 2003	Warschauer, Said, and Zohry 2002; Shapiro 2009; Khalifa 1995; Ayyad 2009	Abdulla 2007, 2005
Georgia					Fairbanks 2004; Beissinger 2007
Ghana			Kafewo 2006		
Indonesia	Luwarso 2004	Hill, 2003; Hameed 2007; Hefner 2003; Hill 2008	Fox 2006; Laksmi and Haryanto 2007; Lim 2005	Bräuchler 2003; Hill 2002; Hill and Sen 2002; Lim 2002, 2003; Nilan 2003; Sen and Hill 2003; Barendregt 2008	Idris 2000; Kloet 2002; van Dijk and Szirmai 2006; Hill and Sen 2005

Country				
Kenya	Etta and Elder 2005; Waema 2009; Farrell, Isaacs, and Trucano 2007	Nyabuga and Mudhai 2009		Goldstein and Rotich 2008; Khasiani 2000; Ogola, Schumann, and Olatunji 2009
Kuwait			Al-Roomi 2007	Wheeler 2001, 2004, 2006
Kyrgyzstan				
Lebanon			Gonzalez-Quijano 2003	Nasser and Abouchedid 2001
Liberia	Farrell, Isaacs, and Trucano 2007			
Macedonia				
Maldives				
Mauritania	Farrell, Isaacs, and Trucano 2007			
Montenegro	Schuler 2008			
Niger	Farrell, Isaacs, and Trucano 2007			
Nigeria	Mabawonku 2001; Farrell, Isaacs, and Trucano 2007; Mudhai 2009; Gaither 2007		Okwori and Adeyanju 2006	Jagboro 2003; Ogola, Schumann, and Olatunji 2009

(continued)

Table B.1: Continued

Country	States	Political Parties	Journalism and News Media	Citizens and Civil Society	General
Senegal	Farrell, Isaacs, and Trucano 2007		Seck 2006	Gueye 2003	Wilson 2004; Thioune and Camara 2004; Etta and Parvyn-Wamahiu 2003
Sierra Leone	Farrell, Isaacs, and Trucano 2007		Tam-Bryoh 2006		Kargbo 1997
Suriname					
Tanzania	Sawe 2005; Farrell, Isaacs, and Trucano 2007		Jones and Mhando 2006		
Uganda	Farrell, Isaacs, and Trucano 2007; Obot; Kintu, and Elder 2005		Khamalwa 2006	Amuriat and Okello 2005; Dralega 2009	Katahoire, Baguma, and Etta 2004; Etta and Parvyn-Wamahiu 2003; Gitta and Ikoja-Odongo 2003

Table B.2: Study Population: Countries Experiencing Democratic Entrenchment

Country	States	Political Parties	Journalism and News Media	Citizens and Civil Society	General
Bangladesh	Hasan 2003; Press 1999; Rahman 2005; Taifur 2004; Akther, Onishi, and Kidokoro 2007		Rahman 2007; Sarkar 2003	Chowdhury 1999; Huq 2003	
Benin					
Bulgaria					
Cyprus					
Guinea-Bissau	Farrell, Isaacs, and Trucano 2007				
India	Agarwala and Tiwari 2007; Bhatnagar and Schware 2000	Tekwani and Shetty 2007	Sen 2007; Rao 2003		Bhatnagar and Schware ; Franda 2002
Israel	Wolcott 1999			Jamal 2009	Franda 2001
Malawi	Farrell, Isaacs, and Trucano 2007				
Malaysia	Mendoza 2005; Bunnell 2004; Siong 2004; Karim and Khalid 2003; Bahfen 2009	Gong 2009; Chin and Huat 2009	Gan 2002; George 2006; Seneviratne 2007; Chin 2003	Boellstorff 2003; Gan 2001; Lasimbang and Goh 2006	Evers 2005; Abbott 2001
Mali	Farrell, Isaacs, and Trucano 2007				
Mauritius	Farrell, Isaacs, and Trucano 2007				Etta and Parvyn-Wamahiu 2003

(continued)

Table B.2: Continued

Country	States	Political Parties	Journalism and News Media	Citizens and Civil Society	General
Mozambique	Farrell, Isaacs, and Trucano 2007; Macueve 2008		Andre 2006		Ephraim Sluma 2004; Etta and Parvyn-Wamahiu 2003
Turkey	Wolcott and Cagiltay 2001; Yesil 2003			Ogan and Cagiltay 2006; Torenli 2005; Altintas, Aydin, and Akman 2002; Yavuz 2003	Wolcott and Goodman 2000; Sevdik and Akman 2002

Table B.3: Study Population: Countries Experiencing Authoritarianism

Country	States	Political Parties	Journalism and News Media	Citizens and Civil Society	General
Azerbaijan					Rogers 2000
Brunei			Tizireen 2003		
Cameroon	Farrell, Isaacs, and Trucano 2007		Alobwede 2006		Zeitlyn and Barone 2004
CAR	Farrell, Isaacs, and Trucano 2007				
Chad	Farrell, Isaacs, and Trucano 2007				
Eritrea	Farrell, Isaacs, and Trucano 2007				
Ethiopia	Farrell, Isaacs, and Trucano 2007		Gebretsadik 2006		
Gambia	Farrell, Isaacs, and Trucano 2007				
Guinea	Farrell, Isaacs, and Trucano 2007				
Iran			Rahimi 2003; Kelly and Etling 2008	Alavi 2005; Heuvel, May 30, 2005; Alexanian 2006; Doostdar 2004; Rahimi 2003; Etling and Kelly 2008; Khiabany and Sreberny 2009	Johari 2002

(continued)

225

Table B.3: Continued

Country	States	Political Parties	Journalism and News Media	Citizens and Civil Society	General
Jordan	Ein-Dor, Goodman, and Wolcott 1999; Blakemore and Dutton 2003			Wheeler 2006	
Kazakhstan					
Libya					
Morocco	Farrell, Isaacs, and Trucano 2007; Ibahrine 2004			Kriem 2009; Davis 2005	
Oman					
Pakistan	Khan 2004; Wolcott 1999		Khan and Joseph 2008	Saeed et al. 2000	Wolcott 1999
Qatar					
Russia					
Saudi Arabia	Wolcott 1999; Alwabel			Teitelbaum 2002; al-Saggaf 2004; Fandy 1999; Kraidy 2006	Echchaibi 2009

Country				
Singapore	Mendoza 2005; Hogan 1999; Government of Singapore 2006; Lee 2004; Shariff 2004	Kluver 2008	George 2006; Keong 2003	Ho, Lee, and Shahiraa Sahul Hameed 2008; Ibrahim 2006	Yang 2005; Guillén and Suarez 2001; Lee 2005; Evers 2004; Gomez 2002
Sudan	Farrell, Isaacs, and Trucano 2007				Geens 2007
Syria					
Tajikistan					
Togo	Farrell, Isaacs, and Trucano 2007				
Tunisia			Ayish 2003		Opennet.net 2006
Turkmenistan					
UAE					
Uzbekistan					
Yemen					

Table B.4: Study Population: Crisis States and Other

Country	States	Political Parties	Journalism and News Media	Citizens and Civil Society	General
Afghanistan					Ghashghai and Rosalind 2002
Burkina Faso					
Iraq					
Ivory Coast	Farrell, Isaacs, and Trucano 2007			Ogola, Schumann, and Olatunji 2009	
Somalia	Farrell, Isaacs, and Trucano 2007		Ismail 2006		
West Bank and Gaza				Souri 2007; Aouragh 2008; Khoury-Machool 2007	Ein-Dor, Goodman, and Wolcott 2000
Western Sahara					

Table B.5: Study Population: Comparative Case Studies

Comparative Unit	States	Political Parties	Journalism and News Media	Citizens and Civil Society	General
Arab World	Ghareeb 2000; Wheeler 2008; Nour 2002; Murphy 2006	Lynch 2003	Rugh 2004; Al-Shehri and Gunter 2002; Hanley 1999; Dimitrova and Connolly-Ahern 2007; Dimitrova et al. 2005	Michaeal 2000; Mamoun 2000; Lynch 2007; Hofheinz 2006, 2007; Fandy 2000	Machin and Suleiman 2006; Ghareeb 2000; Franda 2001; Eid 2004
Middle East Central Asia		McLaughlin 2003		Gher and Amin 2000	Franda 2001, 2002 Mcglinchey and Johnson 2007
North Africa	Danowitz, Nassef, and Goodman 1995			Newsom and Lengel 2003	
Muslim World			Nisbet 2004	Nisbet 2004; Cooke and Lawrence 2005	Eickelman and Anderson 2003
Islam and Islamic Sects				Bunt 2002, 2003	Barzilai-Nahon and Barzilai 2005
Southeast Asia					
Transnational Islam				Kanat 2005	Thompson 2002
Muslims in the West				Torenli 2006	

Notes

INTRODUCTION

1. The number of Muslim households is estimated using the percentage of the population that is Muslim in each of the countries in this study and the number of households in each country. The indicators for radio and television sets are the percentages of households equipped with at least one of these. The indicators for personal computers, home satellites, mobile phones, and internet users are given as a rate of penetration per 100 households. The number of countries with complete data varies from indicator to indicator; averages are always computed from the countries with available data; since 2000 the majority of countries analyzed in this study report this data. Because of the nature of the data, these three ways of presenting the trends are necessary, as they are slightly different. For example, the graph allows the reader to say that by 2000, fully 69 percent of Islamic households in the developing world had a television. In 2000, the ratio of internet users to households was 9 to 100, but that does not strictly mean that 9 percent of Islamic households in the developing world had an internet user in the household. However, informational resources such as mobile phones, the internet, and computers are collective resources, so such an can person his sonemeaning. Thus, it is conceptually reasonable to estimate that 9 percent of Islamic households in the developing world had an internet user in the household.

2. See Karatzogianni (2006), 98–108, for the "panic school" on cyber-terrorism.

CHAPTER 1

1. Author's calculations using data on 73 Muslim countries and 124 non-Muslim developing countries in 2000 and 2010, from the World Development Indicators (2010) and Internet World Statistics (2010).

2. For example, Kenya's internet user base increased from under 100,000 people in 2000 to 3.4 million by 2010. This could be expressed as a growth of 3,360 percent, a compound annual growth rate of 42 percent, or a doubling time of 26 months. The latter two figures are more intuitively useful, especially in a comparative context.

3. Author's calculations, based on data from Internet World Statistics (2010) and the United Nations Population Revision (2005). There are several reasons why this is a rough estimate only. First, the country-specific estimates of internet use come from national ISPs who sometimes report their known subscriber base, sometimes report

an estimate of the number of people in households that subscribe to services, and sometimes report an estimate of the number of users in cybercafés and other public internet access points. Second, it is unlikely that the distribution of internet users among the national population is the same as the distribution of internet users among Muslim subgroups. There are several countries in which Muslims are a small wealthy elite, many of whom would have regular internet access; there are several countries in which Muslims are a poor subpopulation, for whom internet access is not available, or even a priority.

4. One estimate is that as much as 80 percent of internet access in Arab countries takes place in such internet access points (Wheeler 2008).

5. Etta and Parvyn-Wamahiu point out that these "places" have a wide range of names: telecenter, telecottage, telekiosk, teleboutique, phone shop, infocenter, telehaus, telestugen, digital clubhouse, cabinas publicas, multipurpose access center, community technology center, multipurpose community telecenter, community access center, multipurpose community center, community media center, community learning center, community multimedia center, electronic village hall, tele-village or cybercafé.

6. Polity IV data has been critiqued for having a minimalist definition of democracy that undervalues participation, being a composite index of several redundant indicators, and a questionable aggregation procedure (see Munck and Verkuilen 2002). It remains, however, a well-considered and respected index in comparison to some of the alternatives, and it has been kept up to date. Thus, this dataset is only the basis for comparative set descriptions, and where needed the author made corrections and additions, describing these decisions in the chapters ahead.

CHAPTER 2

1. Indeed, making it difficult to discover what a government's reforms have been and what kinds of internet privacy policies or restrictions are in place is also evidence of a government's lack of interest in disseminating such information.

2. Traceroute was used to identify the path of packets from a Seattle-based internet query to a host server with content. Traceroute results require some interpretation. First, the path of packets will be different with every query, though on average the number of hops is fairly consistent. In cases where the final destination host computer was the United States, we assume that if the website is that of a wealthy OECD country, that the country is paying for additional mirror services to help handle the internet queries. In cases where the final destination host computer for a poor country website was in the United States, we assume that the poor country has no domestic infrastructure and has paid for commercial services within the United States.

3. Emerging democracies with large Muslim communities include: Bosnia and Herzegovina, Cameroon, Central African Republic, Chad, Ethiopia, Gambia, Guinea, Kyrgyzstan, Liberia, Macedonia, Malaysia, Maldives, Montenegro, Niger, Nigeria, Pakistan, Sierra Leone, Singapore, Suriname, Tajikistan, Tanzania, Togo, Tunisia, Uganda, and Yemen.

4. Dictatorships with large Muslim communities include: Azerbaijan, Egypt, Eritrea, Kazakhstan, Libya, Mauritania, Morocco, Sudan, Turkmenistan, and Uzbekistan.

5. Crisis states with large Muslim communities include: Afghanistan, Burkina Faso, Ivory Coast, Guinea-Bissau, Iraq, Malawi, Somalia, the West Bank and Gaza, and Western Sahara.

6. The developed world includes: Australia, Austria, Belgium, Canada, Denmark, Finland, France, Germany, Greece, Iceland, Ireland, Italy, Japan, South Korea, Luxembourg, Netherlands, New Zealand, Norway, Portugal, Spain, Sweden, Switzerland, United Kingdom, and United States.

CHAPTER 3

1. This conservative estimate is taken by subtracting the number of Islamic fundamentalist parties and parties of unknown ideology from the total number of parties in 2008.

CHAPTER 4

1. Wheeler (2009) offers good examples of what the Egyptian blogosphere provides by way of critique. Egyptian blogger Abdul-Moneim Mahmud reports "arbitrary arrests and acts of torture by the [Egyptian state] security services" as a way to criticize the excesses of state coercion (http://www.ana-ikhwan.blogspot.com). Similarly, Egyptian Abdel Kareem Nabil Suleiman has used his blog to "condemn the government's authoritarian excesses" (http://www.karam903.blogspot.com). Both have been arrested for their critical posts. Another Egyptian blogger explains the importance of blogs: "It's really different to read a piece of news, opinion, or thought on a weblog than on a 'traditional' news site. The difference I guess is that they mostly reflect personal opinions, provide lots of freedom for everyone to voice their opinion, and to hear opinions and news those are not channeled through mainstream media. They also allow for contribution where everyone is actually contributing to the news delivery" (From Cairo With Love, "The Blogging Effect," February 11, 2005 (http://fromcairo.blogspot.com/2005/02/blogging-effect.html), accessed April 22, 2007. As cited in Wheeler in Howard and Chadwick.

2. To identify online news sites for these countries, a base list was compiled from onlinenewspapers.com, national online newspaper listings at Wikipedia, and an internet search. Links were checked to verify that the site was still valid. Thus "online newspapers" are updated with content every few days, as opposed to "online magazines" that see longer articles, but less regular posting.

3. The Pew Global Values study consistently report high levels of trust in online news sources. However, there is certainly variation among countries. In the Central Asian countries of Kazakhstan, Kyrgyzstan, Tajikistan, and Uzbekistan, surveys by the Central Asia and ICT Project find that Russian language media, national televised media, and print media trump internet sources for trustworthiness (CAICT Project 2006).

CHAPTER 5

1. Small-sized online civil societies are countries where between 0 and 0.18 percent of the population are online in 2007, medium-sized online civil societies are those where between 0.19 and 8 percent of the population are online, and large-sized

civil societies are those where between 9 and 60 percent of the population are online.

2. In Figure 5.1, the relative growth rate of civil society online is determined by tertiles. Between 2000 and 2007, slow-growth online civil societies are countries with annual growth rates between 8 and 27 percent each year, medium-growth online civil societies are countries with annual growth rates between 28 and 42 percent each year, and rapid-growth online civil societies are countries with annual growth rates between 43 and 125 percent each year.

3. Based on author's calculations from data available in World Bank 2001. Countries in this estimate include Algeria, Djibouti, Egypt, Arab Republic of Iran, Islamic Republic of Iraq, Jordan, Lebanon, Morocco, Syrian Arab Republic, Tunisia, Republic of Yemen, and the West Bank and Gaza.

4. See Cavelty 2007, footnote 2 for examples of such media coverage in the United States.

5. While Islamic scholars debate online, there is some evidence that scholarly publishing in other research domains has been slow to take to the internet (Nasser and Abouchedid 2001). Arab and Lebanese journal editors have been accused of assessing articles for publication based on patron relations, and the financial constraints of many universities prevent much institutional support for journal publishing. Arabic journals have limited international circulation, so many Arab scholars seek publication in Western journals, and in some countries secret police oversight effectively discourages and certainly self-censors publishing in the social sciences. These should be reasons that academic discourse would take to the internet in a big way, but there is little evidence that this has happened, and many Arab researchers have held negative attitudes toward digital scholarship (Nasser and Abouchedid 2001).

6. In August 2000, Saudi Arabia disappeared from the internet for 17 hours because of a coordinated DOS attack; in February 2001, connectivity over two days was severely hampered by further attacks.

7. Many governments are still threatened by hactivists, preferring to call their work cyber dissidence. See Karatzogianni (2006), 145–149, on the ways governments in the Muslim world crack down on cyber dissidence.

8. Even one of Al-Qaeda's Arabic Web sites, alneda.com, has been found hosted on servers in Malaysia, Texas, and Michigan (Kelley 2002).

9. Iran is an interesting case because it is one of the most wired of Muslim countries, has a well-organized and articulate democratic movement, yet no democratic revolution appears in sight. If new information technologies have a role in democratization elsewhere, why not Iran? Indeed, much of the research on ICTs and politics in Iran fail to demonstrate much in the way of democratic outcomes, preferring to say instead that the internet is important for providing rhetorical space for dissent. In many authoritarian states political parties are simply outlawed, while in others they are tolerated but must take the label of an "organization" or "social movement." One of the opposition organizations in Iran, the Mojahedin-e Khalq Organization, is a socialist group considered by some to support terrorist activities, but which has effectively used ICTs within Iran in its campaign against the country's Islamic regime. The organization has long maintained a web presence, and in the late 1990s was successfully beaming critical satellite programming into Iran using an Israeli satellite system (Goodman et al. 1998).

10. See http://www.opennetinitiative.net/special/kg/.

11. Examples include Buzzell 2005; Pax 2006; Riverbend 2006, 2005; Alavi 2005.

12. Terrorist groups often use the internet to claim responsibility for an attack, communicate to members, or otherwise publicize their activities to journalists. It is rare for reporters in the West to be handed recordings of beheadings, hostage footage, or training camp activity: usually these are found online by experts who surveille terrorist websites. Many of the groups conducting terrorist campaigns are very media conscious, and they respond quickly online when they want to dispute a claim made in or by the Western media. For example, on June 7 2006 the U.S. military claimed that it had killed the leader of Al-Qaeda in Iraq, Abu Musab al-Zarqawi, and terrorist websites confirmed this quickly by posting eulogies praising his achievements. Indeed, the fact that some terrorists groups do use the internet to communicate makes it easier to track their activities. Several for-profit and nonprofit organizations watch terrorist chat rooms, website, and listserv traffic 24 hours a day. Examples include the Terrorism Research Center (www.terrorism.com), the Search for International Terrorist Entities (SITE) Institute (www.siteinstitute.org), the Project for the Research of Islamist Movements (www.e-prism.org), and Global Terror Alert (www.globalterroralert.com). Conducting so much business online makes it possible to do some fairly comprehensive counter-terrorist measures. Several firms translate Arabic and Muslim media by collecting information online and distributing translations the same way. Analysts will gain access to terrorist websites by posing as sympathetic activists, and then sharing jihadist declarations and chat that is intended for a closed social circle over listservs of counterterrorism security analysts. Civil society and counterterrorism strategists to deliberate and work out their interpretations through blogs. Examples include Juan Cole's Informed Comment, Marc Lynch's Abu Aardvark, Martin Kramer's On the Middle East, Tony Badran's The Syria Monitor, and Jashua M.Landis' Syria Comment. Many of these specialized bloggers are not widely read in the West, but are an important resource for both journalists and security analysts. As with any blogging community, these experts often disagree with each other's commentary, but the internet makes it possible to share insight and, on occasion, reach points of useful consensus.

CHAPTER 6

1. For more information on linguistic diversity online, see the FUNREDES project, http://funredes.org/lc.

2. A notable exception is emerging in the field of the social studies of science and technology, which takes as its foci the co-constitution of cultural forms, material objects, and political culture. See also Zarubavel's study (1992) of how information about the New World was diffused by early mapmakers.

3. In 2007, 2.47 percent of the world's internet hosts were located in Muslim countries. Adjusting for geographic dispersion of top-level domain names that are not country-specific—websites ending in *.com, *.net, or *.org that might actually be registered in a Muslim country—puts the proportion of the world's hosts within Muslim countries at 2.39 percent in 2005.

4. The data points are the averages among the pool of countries that had data available that year. If a country was missing data in a particular year, and a

reasonable imputation from the previous or subsequent year could not be made, the country was dropped from the average. Data is patchy in earlier years, especially for trends such as book production and literacy. So the average levels of cultural production and consumption in the early years involves six countries with significant Muslim populations. In the case of book production, this is a problem of missing data and not much can be done. In the case of internet host production, many Muslim countries did not even have domain names until the mid-1990s, so cases are not really missing and the average rate of internet users per host is based on those countries with hosts. Beginning in 1998, this graphic represents the average levels of literature users per book produced across at least 22 Muslim countries and the average levels of internet hosts online across at least 50 Muslim countries.

5. One of the most well-respected Farsi bloggers, Hoder.com, is maintained by Hussein Derakhshan, who writes from Toronto and asserts that there were 100,000 Persian bloggers in 2005 (Slavin 2005).

6. One expert observed that "Saudi Arabia invests in the propaganda of the Saudi Arabian-style Islam, the Wahhabi-style Islam, much more than the whole Soviet Union for the whole Soviet history spent on the propaganda of the Communist ideology" (Schwirtz 2007).

7. In 1998 for Saudi Arabia this was proxy.isu.net.sa.

8. Many authoritarian states simply do not have a legal regime capable of criminalizing the act of cyber-dissidence: trouble-making bloggers are simply jailed. The Arab states, however, do have these mechanisms, allowing for just enough transparency to observe the state in action. In Bahrain, Galal Olwi was arrested in March of 1997 and detained for 18 months, charged with supplying information via the internet to "The Bahrain Liberal Movement." In Algeria, journalist Ahmed Fattani was arrested in October 2003 for "posting articles online" after the newspaper he edited, *Expression,* had been suspended. In Syria, Abdel Rahman Shagouri was arrested in February 2003 for emailing a newsletter Lavant News from the banned website www.thisissyria.net. He is still being held on charges that he "endangered Syria's reputation and security." In Tunisia, journalist Zohair al-Yahyaoui was arrested in June 2004 and sentenced to 28 months in prison for "disseminating false news" on the internet through his website TUNISIANE (Wheeler 2008).

9. In 2000, these were Azerbaijan, Ethiopia, Iran, Oman, Pakistan, Saudi Arabia, the Sudan, Syria, Tunisia, the UAE, Uzbekistan, and Yemen.

10. The original discovery is noted at http://home.bway.net/keith/whrobots/. Excluding directories from search engine crawlers is a useful way of avoiding the duplication or retrieval of multiple copies of the same content. Up to April 2003, 10 instances of "Iraq" were excluded from search engines, and by October 2003, 754 instances. The current list of White House directories excluded from external search engines is accessible at http://www.whitehouse.gov/robots.txt.

11. Derakhshan reported that 46 percent trust information from the internet, 44 percent trust information from television and radio, 25 percent trust information from satellite channels, 23 percent trust newspapers, and 20 percent trust foreign-based radio.

CONCLUSION

1. As mentioned in the introduction, there is a significant debate in the social sciences over the value of qualitative, comparative, and quantitative research. The arguments made here seek to contribute to the debate by offering an example of how set theory can be practically applied, but the nuances of the debate are not reproduced here. For the argument that qualitative and comparative methods work best when they adopt the correlational assumptions of quantitative research, see King et al. (King, Keohane, and Verba 1994). For full discussion of the value of set theory, see Ragin (2009).

References

Abbott, Jason. "Democracy@Internet.Asia? The Challenges to the Emancipatory Potential of the Net: Lessons from China and Malaysia." *Third World Quarterly* 22, no. 1 (2001): 99–114.

Abdul-Mageed, Muhammad M. "Online News Sites and Journalism 2.0: Reader Comments on Al Jazeera Arabic" tripleC 6 no. 2 (2008): 59–76.

Abdulla, Rasha A. *The Internet in the Arab World: Egypt and Beyond.* New York: Peter Lang, 2007.

Abdulla, Rasha A. "Taking the E-Train: The Development of the Internet in Egypt." *Global Media and Communication* 1, no. 2 (2005): 149–165.

Abou El Fadl, Khaled, Joshua Cohen, and Deborah Chasman. *Islam and the Challenge of Democracy.* Princeton, NJ: Princeton University Press, 2004.

African Media Development Initiative. "Research Summary Report." In *African Media Development Initiative,* edited by Gerry Power. London: BBC World Service Trust, 2006.

Agarwala, Kamalesh N., and Murli D. Tiwari. *IT and E-Governance in India.* Delhi: Macmillian, 2007.

Akther, Mohammad Shakil, Takashi Onishi, and Tetsuo Kidokoro. "E-Government in a Developing Country: Citizen-Centric Approach for Success." *International Journal of Electronic Governance* 1, no. 1 (2007): 38–51.

Al Jazeera. "War on Gaza—Experimental Beta." http://labs.aljazeera.net/warongaza/, 2009.

Al-Obaidi, Jabbar. "Communication and the Culture of Democracy: Global Media and Promotion of Democracy in the Middle East." *International Journal of Instructional Media* 30, no. 1 (2003).

Al-Roomi, Samar. "Women, Blogs, and Political Power in Kuwait." In *New Media and the New Middle East,* edited by Philip M. Seib, 139–155. New York: Palgrave Macmillan, 2007.

Al-Saggaf, Yeslam. "The Effect of Online Community on Offline Community in Saudi Arabia." *Electronic Journal of Information Systems in Developing Countries* 16, no. 2 (2004).

Al-Shehri, Fayez, and Barrie Gunter. "The Market for Electronic Newspapers in the Arab World." *Aslib Proceedings* 54, no. 1 (2002): 56–70.

Alavi, Nasrin. *We Are Iran: The Persian Blogs.* Vancouver: Soft Skull Press, 2005.

Alexanian, Janet A. "Publicly Intimate Online: Iranian Web Logs in Southern California." *Comparative Studies of South Asia, Africa and the Middle East* 26, no. 1 (2006): 134–145.

Allawi, Ali A. *The Crisis of Islamic Civilization*. New Haven, CT: Yale University Press, 2009.

Alobwede, Charles Esambe. "Cameroon: Reseach Findings and Conclusions." In *African Media Development Initiative*, edited by Gerry Power. London: BBC World Service Trust, 2006.

Altintas, Kemal, Tolga Aydin, and Varol Akman. "Censoring the Internet: The Situation in Turkey." *First Monday* 7, no. 6 (2002).

Alwabel, S. A. and Zairi Mohamed. *The Web and Its Impact on the Provision of Financial Services : A Benchmarking Perspective of Saudi Banks*. Bradford: University of Bradford, 2005.

Amin, H. "Freedom as a Value in Arab Media: Perceptions and Attitudes among Journalists." *Political Communication* 19, no. 2 (2002): 125-136.

Amuriat, Goretti Z., and Dorothy Okello. "Women on ICT Policy Making in Uganda." In *At the Crossroads: ICT Policy Making in East Africa*, edited by Florence Eba Etta and Laurent Elder. Ottawa: International Development Research Center, 2005.

Anderson, Jon W., and Dale Eickelman. "Media Convergence and Its Consequences." *Middle East Insight* 14, no. 2 (1999): 59-61.

Anderson, Jon W. "The Internet and Islam's New Interpreters." In *New Media in the Muslim World: The Emerging Public Sphere*, edited by Dale Eickelman and Jon Anderson. Bloomington, IN: Indiana University Press, 2003.

Andre, Fernando. "Mozambique: Reseach Findings and Conclusions." In *African Media Development Initiative*, edited by Gerry Power. London: BBC World Service Trust, 2006.

Aouragh, Miriyam. "Everyday Resistance on the Intenet: The Palestinian Context." *Journal of Arab and Muslim Media Research* 1, no. 2 (2008): 109-130.

Armbrust, Walter. "Bourgeois Leisure and Egyptian Media Fantasies." In *New Media in the Muslim World*, edited by Dale F. Eickelman and Jon W. Anderson, 102-128. Bloomington: Indiana University Press, 2003.

Arunachalam, S. "Information Technology: What Does It Mean for Scientists and Scholars in the Developing World? How Technology Enhances Existing Inequalities." *Bulletin of the American Society for Information Science* 25, no. 6 (1999): 21-24.

Ayish, Muhammad. I. "Political Communication on Arab World Television: Evolving Patterns." *Political Communication* 19, no. 2 (2002): 137-154.

Ayish, Muhammad I. "Media Convergence in the United Arab Emirates: A Survey of Evolving Patterns." *Convergence: The Journal of Research Into New Media Technologies* 9, no. 3 (2003): 77-89.

Ayyad, Khayrat. "The Use of the Internet by NGOs to Promote Government Accountability: The Case of Egypt." In *African Media and the Digital Public Sphere*, edited by Okoth Fred Mudhai, Wisdom J, Tettey, and Fackson Banda, 89-104. New York: Palgrave MacMillan, 2009.

Bahfen, Nasya. "Modems, Malaysia, and Modernity: Characteristics and Policy Challenges in Internet-Led Development." In *Internationalizing Internet Studies: Beyond Anglophone Paradigms*, edited by Gerard Goggin and Mark Mclelland, 163-177. New York: Routledge, 2009.

Banisar, D. "National Freedom of Information Laws." Privacy International, http://www.privacyinternational.org/issues/foia/foia-laws.jpg.

Barendregt, Bart. "Sex, Cannibals, and the Language of Cool: Indonesian Tales of the Phone and Modernity." *The Information Society* 24, no. 3 (2008): 160–170.

Barkho, L. "The Arabic Al Jazeera vs Britain's BBC and America's CNN: Who Does Journalism Right?" *American Communication Journal* 8, no. 1 (2006): 1–15.

Barzilai-Nahon, Karine, and Gad Barzilai. "Cultured Technology: The Internet and Religious Fundamentalism." *Information Society* 21, no. 1 (2005): 25–40.

BBC. "Mobile Growth 'Fastest in Africa.'" *BBC News* (2005), http://news.bbc.co.uk/2/hi/business/4331863.stm.

Beissinger, Mark R. "Structure and Example in Modular Political Phenomena: The Diffusion of Bulldozer/Rose/Orange/Tulip Revolutions." *Perspectives on Politics* 5, no. 2 (2007): 259–276.

Bennett, W. Lance, and Philip N. Howard. "Evolving Public-Private Partnerships: A New Model for E-Government and E-Citizens." *Partnerships for Technology Access.* Redmond, WA: Microsoft Corporation, 2007.

Bhatnagar, Subhash, and Robert Schware, eds. *Information and Communication Technology in Development: Cases from India.* New Delhi: Sage, 2000.

Bieber, Florian. "Globally Wired: Politics in Cyberspace (Third in a Series)—Cyberwar or Sideshow? The Internet and the Balkan Wars." *Current History* 99, no. 635 (2000): 124–128.

Blakemore, Michael, and Roderic Dutton. "E-Government, E-Society and Jordan: Strategy, Theory, Practice, and Assessment." *First Monday* 2009, Special Issue no. 8: A Web Site with a View—The Third World on First Monday (2003).

Boczkowski, Pablo J. "Rethinking Hard and Soft News Production: From Common Ground to Divergent Paths." *Journal of Communication* 59, no. 1 (2009): 98–116.

Boellstorff, Tom. "I Knew It Was Me : Mass Media." In *Mobile Cultures: New Media in Queer Asia*, edited by Christopher Allen Berry, Fran Martin, and Audrey Yue, 21–51. Durham, NC: Duke University Press, 2003.

Bonde, Bent Norby."How 12 Cartoons of the Prophet Mohammed were Brought to Trigger an International Conflict." *Nordicom Review* 28, no. 1 (2007): 33–48.

Bräuchler, Birgit. "Cyberidentities at War : Religion, Identity, and the Internet in the Moluccan Conflict." *Indonesia* no. 75 (2003): 123–151.

Brunet, Patrick J, Oumarou Tiemtoré, and Marie-Claude Vettraino-Soulard. *Ethics and the Internet in West Africa.* Ottawa: International Development Research Centre, 2004.

Baudrillard, Jean. *Critique of the Political Economy of the Sign.* St. Louis: Telos, 1978.

Bunnell, Tim. "Cyberjaya and Putrajaya: Malaysia's "Intelligent" Cities." In *The Cybercities Reader*, edited by Stephen Graham, 348–353. New York: Routledge, 2004.

Bunt, Gary R. *Imuslims: Rewiring the House of Islam*, Islamic Civilization and Muslim Networks. Chapel Hill: University of North Carolina Press, 2009.

Bunt, Gary R. *Islam in the Digital Age: E-Jihad, Online Fatwas and Cyber Islamic Environments*, Critical Studies on Islam. London: Pluto Press, 2003.

Bunt, Gary R. *Virtually Islamic: Computer-Mediated Communication and Cyber Islamic Environments.* Cardiff: University of Wales Press, 2002.

Burkhart, Grey E., and Susan Older. *The Information Revolution in the Middle East and North Africa.* Washington, DC: Rand, 2003.

Butler, D. "Internet May Help Bridge the Gap." *Nature* 397 no 6, 714 (7 January 1999): 10–11.

Buzzell, Colby. *My War: Killing Time in Iraq.* New York: G. P. Putnam's Sons, 2005.

CAICT Project. "2006 Caict Survey: Topline Results." CAICT Project, 2006.

Canclini, N. G. "Unequal Partners: Threat of New Communications Media to Non-Western Culture." *UNESCO Courier* (1996): 29–31.

Cavelty, Myriam Dunn. "Cyber-Terror—Looming Threat or Phantom Menace? The Framing of the U.S. Cyber-Threat Debate." *Journal of Information Technology and Politics* 4, no. 1 (2007): 19–36.

Chadwick, Andrew, and Philip N. Howard, eds. *Handbook of Internet Politics.* London: Routledge, 2009.

Chen, Hsinchun, Wingyan Chung, Jailun Qin, Edna Reid, Marc Sageman, and Gabriel Weimann. "Uncovering the Dark Web: A Case Study of Jihad on the Web." *Journal of the American Society for Information Science and Technology* 59, no. 8 (2008): 1347–1359.

Chin, James. "Malaysiakini.Com and Its Impact on Journalism and Politics in Malaysia." In *Asia.Com: Asia Encounters the Internet*, edited by Kong-Chong Ho, Randy Kluver and Kenneth Yang, 129–142. London: RoutledgeCurzon, 2003.

Chin, James, and Wong Chin Huat. "Malaysia's Electoral Upheaval." *Journal of Democracy* 20, no. 3 (2009): 71–85.

Chowdhury, Nuimuddin. "Putting Bangladesh's Poor Women on the World Wide Web: Towards a Global Economic Village." Ottawa: International Development Research Center, 1999.

CIA. "World Factbook." Central Intelligence Agency, 2007–2010.

Cleaver, H. "The Zapatista Effect: The Internet and the Rise of an Alternative Political Fabric." *Journal of International Affairs* 51, no. 2 (1998): 621–640.

Cooke, Miriam, and Bruce B. Lawrence. *Muslim Networks from Hajj to Hip Hop*, Islamic Civilization and Muslim Networks. Chapel Hill: University of North Carolina Press, 2005.

Cragin, Kim, Peter Chalk, Sara A. Daly, and Brian A. Jackson. *Sharing the Dragon's Teeth: Terrorist Groups and the Exchange of New Technologies.* Sanda Monica, CA: Rand Corporation, 2007.

Danowitz, A. K., Y. Nassef, and S. E. Goodman. "Cyberspace across the Sahara: Computing in North Africa." *Communications of the ACM* 38, no. 12 (1995): 23–29.

Dartnell, Michael Y. *Insurgency Online: Web Activism and Global Conflict*, Digital Features. Toronto: University of Toronto Press, 2006.

Davis, Susan Schaefer. "Women Weavers Online: Rural Moroccan Women on the Internet." In *Gender and the Digital Economy: Perspectives from the Developing World*, edited by Cecilia Ng and Swasti Mitter, 159–185. New Delhi: Sage, 2005.

Diamond, Lawrence. "Rethinking Civil Society: I. Toward Democratic Consolidation." *Journal of Democracy* 5, no. 3 (1994): 4–17.

Diebert, Ronald. "The Geopolitics of Internet Control." In *Routledge Handbook of Internet Politics*, edited by Andrew Chadwick and Philip N. Howard. London: Routledge, 2008.

Dimitrova, Daniella and Colleen Connolly-Ahern. "A Tale of Two Wars: Framing Analysis of Online News Sites in Coalition Countries and the Arab World." *Howard Journal of Communications* 18, no. 2 (2007): 153–168.

Dimitrova, Daniela V., Lynda Lee Kaid, Andrew Paul Williams, and Kaye D. Trammell. "War on the Web: The Immediate News Framing of Gulf War II." *Harvard International Journal of Press/Politics* 10, no. 1 (2005): 22–44.

Djankov, Simeon, Caralee McLiesh, Tatiana Nenova, and Andrei Shleifer. "Who Owns the Media?" *Journal of Law and Economics* 46, no. 2 (2003): 341–382.

Doostdar, Alireza. "The Vulgar Spirit of Blogging: On Language, Culture, and Power in Persian Weblogestan." *American Anthropologist* 106, no. 4 (2004): 651–662.

D'Orazio, Vittorio. *Market Trends: Banking, Middle East, 2007.* Vol. G00150114. Stamford, CT: Gartner Dataquest, 2007.

Dralega, Carol Azungi. "ICTs, Youths, and the Politics of Participation in Rural Uganda." In *African Media and the Digital Public Sphere*, edited by Okoth Fred Mudhai, Wisdom J Tettey, and Fackson Banda, 125–142. New York: Palgrave MacMillan, 2009.

Drissel, David. "Online Jihadism for the Hip-Hop Generation: Mobilizing Diasporic Muslim Youth in Cyberspace," *The International Journal of Interdisciplinary Social Sciences* 2, no. 4 (2007): 7–20.

Dunleavy, Patrick. *Digital Era Governance: IT Corporations, the State, and E-Government.* Oxford: Oxford University Press, 2006.

Echchaibi, Nabil. "Hyper-Islamism? Mediating Islam from the Halal Website to the Islamic Talk Show." *Journal of Arab and Muslim Media Research* 1, no. 3 (2009): 199–214.

Economist. "A World Wide Web of Terror." *The Economist* 384, no. 8, 537 (2007): 28–30.

Edejer, T. T. "Disseminating Health Information in Developing Countries: The Role of the Internet." *British Medical Journal* 321, no. 7, 264 (2000): 797–800.

Eickelman, Dale F., and Jon W. Anderson. *New Media in the Muslim World: The Emerging Public Sphere.* 2nd ed., Indiana Series in Middle East Studies. Bloomington: Indiana University Press, 2003.

Ein-Dor, Philip, Seymour Goodman, and Peter Wolcott. "The Diffusion of the Internet in the Hashemite Kingdom of Jordon." In *The Global Diffusion of the Internet Project.* Omaha: University of Nebraska, 1999.

Ein-Dor, Phillip, Seymour Goodman, and Peter Wolcott. "From Via Maris to Electronic Highway: The Internet in Canaan." *Communications of the ACM* 43, no. 7 (2000): 19–23.

El-Kashef, Injy. *Islam Dot Com.* New York: Palgrave Macmillan, 2009.

Eld, Gamal. "The Internet in the Arab World a New Space of Repression?" The Arabic Network for Human Rights Information, http://anhri.net/en/reports/net2004/.

Elmer, Greg. "Exclusionary Rules? The Politics of Protocols." In *The Handbook of Internet Politics*, edited by Andrew Chadwick and Philip N. Howard. London: Routledge, 2008.

Ephraim Sluma, Daniel Brode, Nicky Roberts. "Internet Para as Escolas in Mozambique." In *Information and Communication Technologies for Development in Africa*, edited by Tina James. Ottawa: International Development Research Center, 2004.

Esselaar, Steve, Cristoph Stork, Ali Ndiwalana, and Mariama Deen-Swarray. "ICT Usage and Its Impact on Profitability of SMEs in 13 African Countries." *Journal of Information Technology and International Development* 4, no. 1 (2007): 87–100.

Etling, John, and Bruce Kelly. "Mapping Iran's Online Public: Politics and Culture in the Persian Blogosphere." In *Internet and Democracy Case Study Series.* Cambridge, MA: Berkman Center for Internet and Society, 2008.

Etta, Florence Eba, and Laurent Elder. "The Policy Making Landscape in Kenya." In *At the Crossroads: ICT Policy Making in East Africa*, edited by Florence Eba Etta and Laurent Elder. Ottawa: International Development Research Center, 2005.

Etta, Florence Eba, and Sheila Parvyn-Wamahiu. "Information and Communication Technologies for Development in Africa: Volume 2, The Experience with Community Telecentres." Ottawa: International Development Research Centre, 2003.

Etta, Florence Ebam, and Sheila Parvyn-Wamahiu. "Telecenters in Mozambique." In *Information and Communication Technologies for Development in Africa*, edited by Florence Ebam Etta and Sheila Parvyn-Wamahiu, 60-69. Ottawa: International Development Research Center, 2003.

Etta, Florence Ebam, and Sheila Parvyn-Wamahiu. "Telecenters in Uganda." In *Information and Communication Technologies for Development in Africa*, edited by Florence Ebam Etta and Sheila Parvyn-Wamahiu, 72-113. Ottawa: International Development Research Center, 2003.

Etta, Florence Ebam, and Sheila Parvyn-Wamahiu. "Timbuktu Telecentre, Mali." In *Information and Communication Technologies for Development in Africa*, edited by Florence Ebam Etta and Sheila Parvyn-Wamahiu, 37-60. Ottawa: International Development Research Center, 2003.

Evers, Hans-Dieter. "Transition Towards a Knowledge Society: Malaysia and Indonesia in Global Perspective." In *Governing and Managing Knowledge in Asia*, edited by Thomas Menkhoff, Hans-Dieter Evers, and Yue Wah Chay, 91-110. Singapore: World Scientific Pub., 2005.

Fahmy, Shahira. "Emerging Alternatives or Traditional News Gates: Which News Sources Were Used to Picture the 9/11 Attack and the Afghan War?" *Gazette* 67, no. 5 (2005): 381-398.

Fairbanks, Charles H. "Georgia's Rose Revolution." *Journal of Democracy* 15, no. 2 (2004): 110-124.

Fandy, M. "Cyberresistance: Saudi Opposition between Globalization and Localization" *Comparative Studies in Society and History* 41, no. 1 (1999): 24-47.

Fandy, Mamoun. "Information Technology, Trust, and Social Change in the Arab World." *Middle East Journal* 54, no. 3 (2000): 378-394.

Faris, Robert, and Nart Villeneuve. "Access Denied." In *Access Denied: The Practice and Policy of Global Internet Filtering*, edited by Ronald J. Deibert, John G. Palfrey, Rafal Rohozinski and Jonathan Zittrain. Boston: MIT Press, 2007.

Farrell, Glen, Shafika Isaacs, and Michael Trucano, eds. *Survey of ICT and Education in Africa: Country Case Studies*. Washington, DC: *info*Dev, World Bank, 2007.

Fattah, Alaa Abd El. "In Egypt, YouTube Trumps Facebook." In *PostGlobal: Need to Know*. Washington, DC: The Washington Post/Newsweek, 2008.

Fink, Carsten., and Charles Kenny. "W(H)Ither the Digital Divide?" *Info* 5, no. 6 (2006): 15-24.

Fischer, Claude S. *America Calling: A Social History of the Telephone to 1940*. Berkeley: University of California Press, 1992.

Fleishman, Jeffrey. "Facebook Reflects Struggle over Islam's Role." Los Angeles Times, http://www.latimes.com/news/nationworld/world/la-fg-facebook19-2008sep19, 0,1968535.story.

Foot, Kirsten A., and Steven M. Schneider. *Web Campaigning* Cambridge, MA: MIT Press, 2006.

Fountain, Jane E. *Building the Virtual State: Information Technology and Institutional Change*. Washington, DC: Brookings Institution Press, 2001.

Fox, Richard. "Strong and Weak Media? On the Representation of 'Terorisme' in Contemporary Indonesia." *Modern Asian Studies* 40, no. 4 (2006): 993–1052.

Franda, Marcus F. *China and India Online: Information Technology Politics and Diplomacy in the World's Two Largest Nations*. Lanham, MD: Rowman & Littlefield, 2002.

Franda, Marcus F. *Governing the Internet: The Emergence of an International Regime*, Ipolitics. Boulder, CO: L. Rienner Publishers, 2001.

Franda, Marcus F. *Launching into Cyberspace: Internet Development and Politics in Five World Regions*, Ipolitics. Boulder, CO: Lynne Rienner Publishers, 2002.

Gadio, Coumba Mar. "Exploring the Gender Impacts of World Links in Some Selected Participating African Countries: A Qualitative Approach." 36. Washington, DC: World Links, 2001.

Gaither, Thomas Kenneth. *Building a Nation's Image on the World Wide Web : A Study of the Head of State Web Sites of Developing Countries*. Youngstown, NY: Cambria Press, 2007.

Gan, Siowck Lee. *IT and Education in Malaysia: Problems, Issues and Challenges*. Petaling Jaya: Pearson Education Malaysia, 2001.

Gan, Steven. "Virtual Democracy in Malaysia: The Internet Has Helped Put Press Freedom on the Front Burner." *Nieman Reports* 56, no. 2 (2002): 65–67.

Gebretsadik, Gebremedhin Simon. "Ethiopia: Reseach Findings and Conclusions." In *African Media Development Initiative*, edited by Gerry Power. London, UK: BBC World Service Trust, 2006.

Geens, Stefan. "Google Earth Ban in Sudan Is Due to U.S. Export Restrictions." *Sudan Tribune*, 22 April 2007.

George, Cherian. *Contentious Journalism and the Internet: Towards Democratic Discourse in Malaysia and Singapore*. Singapore: Singapore University Press in association with University of Washington Press, 2006.

Ghareeb, Edmund. "New Media and the Information Revolution in the Arab World: An Assessment." *Middle East Journal* 54, no. 3 (2000): 395–418.

Ghashghai, Elham, and Lewis Rosalind. *Issues Affecting Internet Use in Afghanistan and Developing Countries in the Middle East*. Edited by Rand Corporation. Santa Monica, CA: Ft. Belvoir Defense Technical Information Center, 2002.

Gher, Leo A., and Hussein Y. Amin. *Civic Discourse and Digital Age Communications in the Middle East*, Civic Discourse for the Third Millennium. Stamford, CT: Ablex, 2000.

Gitta, Samuel, and J. R. Ikoja-Odongo. "The Impact of Cybercafes on Information Services in Uganda." *First Monday* 8, no. 4 (2003).

Giustozzi, Antonio. *Koran, Kalishnikov, and Laptop: The Neo-Taliban Insurgency in Afghanistan*. New York, NY: Columbia University Press, 2001.

Goldstein, Joshua, and Juliana Rotich. "Digitally Networked Technology in Kenya's 2007–2008 Post-Election Crisis." Berkman Center for Internet & Society at Harvard University, http://cyber.law.harvard.edu/sites/cyber.law.harvard.edu/files/Goldstein&Rotich_Digitally_Networked_Technology_Kenyas_Crisis.pdf.pdf.

Global Internet Liberty Campaign Newsletter, Volume 2, Issue 4. March 24, 1998. http://gilc.org/alert/alert24.html

Gomez, James. *Internet Politics: Surveillance and Intimidation in Singapore.* Bangkok: Think Centre, 2002.

Gong, Rachel. "Internet Politics and State Media Control: Candidate Blogging in Malaysia." www.cprsouth.org. Singapore: Communication Policy Research South, 2009.

Gonzalez-Quijano, Yves. "The Birth of a Media Ecosystem: Lebanon in the Internet Age." In *New Media in the Muslim World*, edited by Dale F. Eickelman and Jon W. Anderson, 61–79. Bloomington: Indiana University Press, 2003.

Goodman, Seymour E., Grey E. Burkhart, William A. Foster, Laurence I. Press, Zixiang (Alex) Tan, and Jonathan Woodard. "The Global Diffusion of the Internet Project: An Initial Inductive Study." http://mosaic.unomaha.edu/GDI1998/GDI98.html: The Mosaic Group; SAIC, 1998.

Gore, Al. *Remarks Prepared for Delivery by Vice President Al Gore*, International Telecommunications Union, March 21, 1994.

Government of Singapore. "Singapore E-Government 2006." 2006.

Grant, Emanuel S. "Towards an Internet-Based Education Model for Caribbean Countries." *Journal of Educational Media* 25, no. 1 (2000): 21–30.

Griswold, Wendy, Erin Metz McDonnell, and Terence Emmett McDonnell. "Glamour and Honor: Going Online and Reading in West African Culture." *Information Technology and International Development* 3, no. 4 (2006): 37–52.

Gueye, Cheikh. "New Information and Communication Technology Use by Muslim Mourides in Senegal." *Review of African Political Economy* 30, no. 98 (2003): 609–625.Guillén, Mauro, and Sandra Suarez. "Developing the Internet: Entrepreneurship and Public Policy in Ireland, Singapore, Argentina, and Spain." *Telecommunications Policy* 25, (2001): 349–371.

Guillén, Mauro, and Sandra Suarez. "Explaining the Global Digital Divide: Economic, Political and Sociological Drivers of Cross-National Internet Use." *Social Forces* 84, no. 2 (2005): 681–708.

Gurr, Ted R. Peoples versus States: Minorities at Risk in the New Century, Washington D.C: Unites States Institute for Peace Press, 2000.

Haas, Ernst. "The Collective Management of International Conflict, 1945-1984." In *The United Nations and the Maintenance of International Peace and Security*, edited by United Nations Institute for Training and Research and Columbia University, School of International and Public Affairs. Boston, MA: Kluwer Academic Publishers, 1987.

Haas, Peter M. *Saving the Mediterranean: The Politics of International Environmental Cooperation*, New York: Columbia University Press, 1990.

Hafez, Kai. "Journalism Ethics Revisited: A Comparison of Ethics Codes in Europe, North Africa, the Middle East, and Muslim Asia." *Political Communication* 19, no. 2 (2002): 225–250.

Hafkin, Nancy, and Nancy Taggart. "Gender, Information Technology, and Developing Countries: An Analytic Study." edited by Academy for Educational Development. Washington, DC: Office of Women in Development, U.S. Agency for International Development, 2001.

Hamdy, Naila. "Building Capabilities of Egyptian Journalists in Preparation for a Media in Transition." *Journal of Arab and Muslim Media Research* 1, no. 3 (2009): 215–243.

Hameed, Shahiraa Sahul. "Internet Deployment in the 2004 Indonesian Presidential Elections." In *The Internet and National Elections: A Comparative Study of Web Campaigning*, edited by Nicholas Jankowski Randolph Kluver, Kirsten Foot, and Steven Schneider, 194–209. New York: Routledge, 2007.

Hamid Saeed, Muhammad Asghar, Muhammad Anwar, Muhammad Ramzan. "Internet Use in University Libraries of Pakistan." *Online Information Review* 24, no. 2 (2000): 154.

Hanley, Delinda C. "The New Arab Media, Satellite TV, and the Internet." *The Washington Report on Middle East Affairs* XVIII, no. 4 (1999).

Hasan, Sadik. "Introducing E-Government in Bangladesh: Problems and Prospects." *International Social Science Review* 79, no. 3–4 (2003): 111.

Herbst, Susan. *Reading Public Opinion : How Political Actors View the Democratic Process*. Chicago, University of Chicago Press, 1998.

Hefner, Robert W. "Civic Pluralism Denied? The New Media and Jihadi Violence in Indonesia." In *New Media in the Muslim World*, edited by Dale F. Eickelman and Jon W. Anderson, 158–179. Bloomington: Indiana University Press, 2003.

Henisz, Witold, Bennet Zelner, and Maurio Guillen. "The Worldwide Diffusion of Market-Oriented Infrastructure Reform, 1977–1999." *American Sociological Review* 70, no. 6 (2005): 871–897.

Hill, David T. "Communication for a New Democracy: Indonesia's First Online Elections." *The Pacific Review* 16, no. 4 (2003): 525–548.

Hill, David T. "East Timor and the Internet: Global Political Leverage in/on Indonesia." *Indonesia: Modern Indonesia Project* no. 73 (2002): 25–51.

Hill, David T. "Indonesia: Electoral Politics and the Internet." In *Making a Difference: A Comparative View of the Role of the Internet in Election Politics*, edited by Stephen Ward, Richard Davis, and Diana Owen. New York: Rowman & Littlefield, 2008.

Hill, David T. *The Internet in Indonesia's New Democracy*. London: Routledge.

Hill, David T., and Krishna Sen. *The Internet in Indonesia's New Democracy*, Asia's Transformations. London: Routledge, 2005.

Hill, David T., and Krishna Sen. "Netizens in Combat: Conflict on the Internet in Indonesia." *Asian Studies Review* 26, no. 2 (2002): 165–187.

Ho, Shirley S., Waipeng Lee, and Shahiraa Sahul Hameed. "Muslim Surfers on the Internet: Using the Theory of Planned Behaviour to Examine the Factors Influencing Engagement in Online Religious Activities." *New Media Society* 10, no. 1 (2008): 93–113.

Hoffman, D., and T. Novak. "Bridging the Racial Divide on the Internet." *Science* 280, no. 5362 (1998): 390–391.

Hofheinz, Albrecht. "Arab Internet Use: Popular Trends and Public Impact." In *Arab Media and Political Renewal: Community, Legitimacy, and Public Life*, edited by Naomi Sakr, 56–79. London: I. B. Tauris, 2007.

Hofheinz, Albrecht. "The Internet in the Arab World: Playground for Political Liberalization." *Zeitschrift: Internationale Politik und Gesellschaft* 3, no. 3 (2006): 78–95.

Hogan, Sarah. "To Net or Not to Net: Singapore's Regulation of the Internet." *Federal Communications Law Journal* 51, no. 2 (1999): 429–446.

Horwitz, Robert Britt. *Communication and Democratic Reform in South Africa*, Communication, Society, and Politics. Cambridge and New York: Cambridge University Press, 2001.

Howard, Philip N. *New Media Campaigns and the Managed Citizen*. New York: Cambridge University Press, 2006.

Howard, Philip N. "Testing the Leap-Frog Hypothesis: Assessing the Impact of Extant Infrastructure and Telecommunication Policy on the Global Digital Divide." *Information, Communication & Society* 10, no. 2 (2007): 133-157.

Howard, Philip N., and Adrienne Massanari. "Learning to Search and Searching to Learn: Income, Education and Experience Online." *Journal of Computer Mediated Communication* 12, no. 3 (2007).

Howard, Philip, Laura Busch, Dawn Nafus, and Ken Anderson. "Sizing up Information Societies—Towards a Better Metric for the Cultures of ICT Adoption." *The Information Society* 25, no. 3 (2009): 208-219.

Howard, Philip N., Lee Harrison Rainie, and Steve Jones. "Days and Nights on the Internet: The Impact of a Diffusing Technology." *American Behavioral Scientist* 45, no. 3 (2001): 383-404.

Howard, Philip N., and Nimah Mazaheri. "Telecommunications Reform, Internet Use and Mobile Phone Adoption in the Developing World." *World Development* 37, no. 7 (2009): 1159-1169.

Howard, Philip N. and WIA Project. "Ownership Diversity in Muslim Media Systems." www.wiaproject.org Seattle: University of Washington, 2008.

Howard, Philip N., and WIA Project. "World Information Access Report 2008—Politics Online in the Muslim World." www.wiaproject.org. Seattle: University of Washington, 2008.

Howard, Philip N., and WIA. "World Information Access Report 2007—Wired States." www.wiaproject.org. Seattle: University of Washington, 2007.

Hughes, Thomas Parke. *Networks of Power: Electrification in Western Society, 1880-1930*. Baltimore: Johns Hopkins University Press, 1983.

Huq, Maimuna. "From Peity to Romance: Islam-Oriented Texts in Bangladesh." In *New Media in the Muslim World*, edited by Dale F. Eickelman and Jon W. Anderson, 129-187. Bloomington: Indiana University Press, 2003.

Ibahrine, Mohammed. "Towards a National Telecommunications Strategy in Morocco." *First Monday* 9, no. 1 (2004).

Ibrahim, Yasmin. "Capital Punishment and Virtual Protest: A Case Study of Singapore." *First Monday* 10, no. 2 (2006).

Idris, Naswil. "Telecommunications, Broadcasting, and Computer Industries in Indonesia." In *Electronic Communication Convergence: Policy Challenges in Asia*, edited by Mark Hukill, Ryota On, and Chandrasekhar Vallath, 197-215. New Delhi: Sage, 2000.

Innis, Harold. The Bias of Communication. Toronto: University of Toronto Press, 1991.

Innis, Harold. Empire and Communications. Toronto: University of Toronto Press, 2007.

International Fund for Agricultural Development. "Sending Money Home: Worldwide Remittance Flows to Developing and Transition Countries." Rome, Italy, 2007.

Internet Software Consortium. "Domain Name Survey." Internet Software Consortium, 2010.

Internet World Statistics. "Usage and Population Statistics." Internet World Statistics, 2010. Retrieved on February 18, 2010 from: http://www.internetworldstats.com/stats.htm

InterPress Service / Media Institute of Southern Africa "'Uncontrollable' Internet Immoral in Sudan." March 17, 1998.

Ismail, Jamal Abdi. "Somalia: Reseach Findings and Conclusions." In *African Media Development Initiative*, edited by Gerry Power. London: BBC World Service Trust, 2006.

ITU. "International Telecommunications Union Database." Geneva: International Telecommunications Union, 2006–2010.

Jagboro, Kofoworola. "A Study of Internet Usage in Nigerian Universities: A Case Study of Obafemi Awolowo University, Ile-Ife, Nigeria." *First Monday* 8, no. 2 (2003).

Jamal, Amal. "Media Culture as Counter-Hegemonic Strategy: The Communicative Action of the Arab Minority in Israel." *Media, Culture, and Society* 31, no. 4 (2009): 559–577.

James, J. "Bridging the Digital Divide with Low-Cost Information Technologies." *Journal of Information Science* 27, no. 4 (2001): 211–217.

Jimba, S. W. "The Influence of Information Technology Access on Agricultural Research in Nigeria." *Internet Research* 10, no. 1 (2000): 63.

Johari, Abbas. "Internet Use in Iran: Access, Social, and Educational Issues." *Educational Technology Research and Development* 50, no. 1 (2002): 81–83.

Jones, John Muthee, and Nandera Mhando. "Tanzania: Reseach Findings and Conclusions." In *African Media Development Initiative*, edited by Gerry Power. London: BBC World Service Trust, 2006.

Kafewo, Samuel. "Ghana: Reseach Findings and Conclusions." In *African Media Development Initiative*, edited by Gerry Power. London: BBC World Service Trust, 2006.

Kalathil, Shanthi, and Taylor C. Boas. *Open Networks, Closed Regimes: The Impact of the Internet on Authoritarian Rule*. Washington, DC: Carnegie Endowment for International Peace, 2003.

Kanat, Kilic. "Ethnic Media and Politics: The Case of the Use of the Internet by Uyghur Diaspora." *First Monday* 10, no. 7 (2005).

Karatzogianni, Athina. *The Politics of Cyberconflict*, Routledge Research in Information Technology and Society. London: Routledge, 2006.

Kargbo, John Abdul. "The Internet in Sierra Leone: The Way Forward?" *First Monday* 2, no. 2 (1997).

Karim, Muhammad Rais bin Abdul, and Nazariah Mohd Khalid. *E-Government in Malaysia : Improving Responsiveness and Capacity to Serve*. Sebang Jaya, Malaysia: Malaysia Pelanduk Publications, 2003.

Karouny, M. "Hizbollah Computer Game Recalls Israeli Battles, Reuters, 18 March, Quoted from www.Specialforce.Net." *Reuters*, March 18, 2003.

Katahoire, Anne Ruhweza, Grace Baguma, and Florence Etta. "Schoolnet Uganda: Curriculumnet." In *Information and Communication Technologies for Development in Africa*, edited by Tina James, 215–247. Ottawa: International Development Research Center, 2004.

Kaufmann, Daniel, Aart Kraay, and Massimo Mastruzzi. "Governance Matters VII: Aggregate and Individual Governance Indicators, 1996–2007." In *World Bank Policy Research Working Paper No. 4654*. Washington, DC: World Bank, 2008.

Kelley, Jack. "Militants Wire Web with Links to Jihad." *USA Today*, July 10, 2002.

Kelly, John, and Bruce Etling. "Mapping Iran's Online Public: Politics and Culture in the Persian Blogosphere." http://cyber.law.harvard.edu/sites/cyber.law.harvard.edu/files/Kelly&Etling_Mapping_Irans_Online_Public_2008.pdf.

Keong, Lee Chu. "Singapore." In *News Media and New Media*, edited by Madanmohan Rao, 301–311. Singapore: Eastern Universities Press, 2003.

Khalifa, Aymen M. "Reviving Civil Society in Egypt." *Journal of Democracy* 6, no. 3 (1995): 155–163.

Khamalwa, John Wotsuna. "Uganda: Reseach Findings and Conclusions." In *African Media Development Initiative*, edited by Gerry Power. London: BBC World Service Trust, 2006.

Khan, Zafarullah. "Cyber Jihad: Fighting the Infidels from Pakistan." In *Asian Cyberactivism: Freedom of Expression and Media Censorship*, edited by Steven Gan, James Gomez, and Uwe Johannen, 442–473. Bangkok: Friedrich Naumann Foundation, 2004.

Khan, Zafarullah, and Brian Joseph. "The Media Take Center Stage." *Journal of Democracy* 19, no. 4 (2008): 32–37.

Khasiani, Shanyisa Anota. "Enhancing Women's Participation in Governance: The Case of Kakamega and Makueni Districts, Kenya." In *Gender and the Informaiton Revolution in Africa*, edited by Eva M. Rathgeber and Edith Ofwona Adera, 215–238. Ottawa: International Development Research Centre, 2000.

Khiabany, Gholam, and Annabelle Sreberny. "The Internet in Iran: The Battle over an Emerging Virtual Public Sphere." In *Internationalizing Internet Studies: Beyond Anglophone Paradigms*, edited by Gerard Goggin and Mark Mclelland, 196–216. New York: Routledge, 2009.

Khoury-Machool, Makram. "Palestinian Youth and Political Activism: The Emerging Internet Culture and New Modes of Resistance." *Policy Futures in Education* 5, no. 1 (2007): 17–36.

Kiernan, Peter. "Middle East Opinion: Iran Fears Aren't Hitting the Arab Street." *World Politics Review* 594 (2007). Retrieved from http://www.worldpoliticsreview.com/article.aspx?id=594.

Kimmage, Daniel. "The Al-Qaeda Media Nexus: The Virtual Network Behind the Global Message." Radio Free Europe / Radio Liberty, http://docs.rferl.org/en-US/AQ_Media_Nexus.pdf.

King, Gary, Robert O. Keohane, and Sidney Verba. *Designing Social Inquiry: Scientific Inference in Qualitative Research*. Princeton, NJ: Princeton University Press, 1994.

Kloet, Jeroen. "Digitisation and Its Asian Discontents: The Internet, Politics and Hacking in China and Indonesia." *First Monday* 7, no. 9 (2002).

Kluver, Randolph. "Singapore: Elections and the Internet-Online Activism and Offline Quiescence." In *Making a Difference: A Comparative View of the Role of the Internet in Election Politics*, edited by Stephen Ward, Richard Davis and Diana Owen. New York: Rowman & Littlefield, 2008.

Kohn, Melvin. "Cross-National Research as an Analytic Strategy." *American Sociological Review* 52, no. 6 (1987): 713–731.

Kort, Alexis. "Dar Al-Cyber Islam: Women, Domestic Violence, and the Islamic Reformation on the World Wide Web." *Journal of Muslim Minority Affairs* 25 (2005): 363–383.

Kraidy, Marwan M. "Hypermedia and Governance in Saudi Arabia." *First Monday* 9, no. 7 (2006).

Kranzberg, Melvin. "The Information Age: Evolution or Revolution?" In *Information Technologies and Social Transformation*, edited by Bruce R. Guile, 35-55. Washington, DC: National Academy Press, 1985.

Kriem, Maya S. "Mobile Telephony in Morocco: A Changing Sociality." *Media, Culture, and Society* 31, no. 4 (2009): 617-632.

Kulikova, S. V. & Perlmutter, D. D. (2007). "Blogging Down the Dictator? The Kyrgyz Revolution and Samizdat Websites." *Gazette*, 69(1), 29-50.

Laksmi, Shita, and Ignatius Haryanto. "Indonesia: Alternative Media Enjoying a Fresh Breeze." In *Media Pluralism in Asia: The Role and Impact of Alternative Media*, edited by Kalinga Seneviratne, 53-85. Singapore: Nanyang Technological University, 2007.

Lasimbang, Jenifer, and Debbie Goh. "Indigenous People's Experiments with ICT as a Tool for Political Participation and Other Socio-Cultural Struggles in Sabah, Malaysia." In *Internet, Governance, and Democracy: Democratic Transitions from Asian and European Perspectives*, edited by Jens Hoff. Copenhagen: Nordic Institute of Asian Studies, 2006.

Lee, Terence. "Emulating Singapore: Towards a Model for Internet Regulation in Asia." In *Asian Cyberactivism: Freedom of Expression and Media Censorship*, edited by Steven Gan, James Gomez and Uwe Johannen, 162-199. Bangkok: Friedrich Naumann Foundation, 2004.

Lim, Merlyna. "From Real to Virtual (and Back Again): Civil Society, Public Sphere, and the Internet in Indonesia." In *Asia.Com: Asia Encounters the Internet*, edited by K. C. Ho, Randolph Kluver and Kenneth C. C. Yang, 128-133. London: Routledge, 2003.

Lim, Merlyna. "From Walking City to Telematic Metropolis : Changing Urban Form in Bandung, Indonesia." In *Critical Reflections on Cities in Southeast Asia*, edited by Tim Bunnell and Lisa B. W. Drummond, 75-100. Singapore: Times Academic Press, 2002.

Lim, Merlyna. *Islamic Radicalism and Anti-Americanism in Indonesia: The Role of the Internet*, Policy Studies. Washington, DC: East-West Center, 2005.

Luwarso, Lukas. "Manufacturing Control: New Legislations Threaten Democratic Gains in Indonesia." In *Asian Cyberactivism*, edited by Steven Gan, James Gomez and Uwe Johannen. Bangkok: Friedrich Naumann Foundation, 2004.

Lynch, Marc. "Beyond the Arab Street: Iraq and the Arab Public Sphere." *Politics & Society* 31, no. 1 (2003): 55-92.

Lynch, Marc. "Blogging the New Arab Public." *Arab Media & Society* 1, no. 1 (2007).

Mabawonku, Iyabo. *Potentials of Internet Use in Information Provision to Policy Makers in Nigeria*, Working Paper / Development Policy Centre. Ibadan: Nigeria Development Policy Centre, 2001.

Machin, David, and Usama Suleiman. "Arab and American Computer War Games: The Influence of a Global Technology on Discourse." *Critical Discourse Studies* 3, no. 1 (2006): 1-22.

Macueve, Gertrudes. "Assessment of the Outcomes of E-Government for Good Governance: A Case of the Land Management Information System in Mozambique." *International Journal of Electronic Governance* 1, no. 4 (2008): 363-384.

Mamoun, Fandy. "Information Technology, Trust, and Social Change in the Arab World." *The Middle East Journal* 54, no. 3 (2000): 379-394.

Mann, C. L., and D. Rosen. *The New Economy and A.P.E.C.* Washington, DC: Peterson Institute for International Economics, 2002.

Margolis, Jane, and Allan Fisher. *Unlocking the Clubhouse: Women in Computing.* Cambridge, MA: MIT Press, 2002.

Marshall, Monty G., and Keith Jaggers. "Polity IV Project: Political Regime Characteristics and Transitions, 1800-2007." In *Polity IV Project.* Arlington, VA: George Mason University, 2008.

McAdam, Doug. *Political Process and the Development of Black Insurgency, 1930-1970.* Chicago: University of Chicago Press, 1982.

Mcglinchey, Eric, and Erica Johnson. "Aiding the Internet in Central Asia." *Democratization* 14, no. 2 (2007): 273-288.

McGrath, Cam. "Egypt: Cyber Insurgency Rattles Regime." InterPress Service, http://ipsnews.net/news.asp?idnews=47064.

McLuhan, Marshall. Understanding Media: The Extensions of Man. Cambridge: MIT University Press, 1994.

McLaughlin, W. S. "The Use of the Internet for Political Action by Non-State Dissident Actors in the Middle East." *First Monday* no. 11 (2003).

McMahan, David T., and James W. Chesebro. "Media and Political Transformations: Revolutionary Changes of the World's Cultures." *Communication Quarterley* 51, no. 2 (2003): 126-153.

Mellahi, Kamel, and Jedrzej George Frynas. "An Exploratory Study into the Applicability of Western HRM Practices in Developing Countries: An Algerian Case Study." *International Journal of Commerce and Management* 13, no. 1 (2003): 61-80.

Mendoza, Lunita. "Malaysia: Emerging Regional Test-Hub for Advanced Wireless Services." In *Asia Unplugged: The Wireless and Mobile Media Book in the Asia-Pacific,* edited by Madanmohan Rao and Lunita Mendoza, 389-401. New Delhi: Response Books, 2005.

Mendoza, Lunita. "Singapore: Powered by Infocomm." In *Asia Unplugged: The Wireless and Mobile Media Book in the Asia-Pacific,* edited by Madanmohan Rao and Lunita Mendoza, 337-345. New Delhi, India: Response Books, 2005.

Mernissi, Fatema. "The Satellite, the Prince, and Scheherazade: The Rise of Women and Communicators in Digital Islam." *Transnational Broadcasting Studies* 12 (2004). Retrieved from: http://www.tbsjournal.com/Archives/Spring04/mernissi.htm.

Michaeal, Dunn. "New Media, New Politics? From Satellite Television to the Internet in the Arab World / New Media in the Muslim World: The Emerging Public Sphere / Arabizing the Internet." *The Middle East Journal* 54, no. 3 (2000): 465.

Milbank, Dana. "White House Web Scrubbing: Offending Comments on Iraq Disappear from Site." *Washington Post,* December 18 2003, Dec 17, A05.

Milbank, Dana, and Bradley Graham. "Bush Revises Views on 'Combat' in Iraq 'Major Operations' Over, President Says." *Washington Post,* Tuesday, August 19, 2003.

Miller, Flagg. *The Moral Resonance of Arab Media: Audiocassette Poetry and Culture in Yemen.* 1st ed., Harvard Middle Eastern Monographs. Cambridge, MA: Center for Middle Eastern Studies of Harvard University, 2007.

Milner, Helen. "The Digital Divide: The Role of Political Institutions in Technology Diffusion." *Comparative Political Studies* 39, no. 2 (2006): 176–199.

Mudhai, Okoth Fred. "Implications for Africa of E-Gov Challenges for Giants South Africa and Nigeria." In *African Media and the Digital Public Sphere*, edited by Okoth Fred Mudhai, Wisdom J. Tettey, and Fackson Banda, 21–40. New York: Palgrave MacMillan, 2009.

Murphy, Emma. "Agency and Space: The Political Impact of Information Technologies in the Gulf Arab States." *Third World Quarterly* 27, no. 6 (2006): 1,059–1,083.

Naficy, Hamid. The Making of Exile Cultures: Iranian Television in Los Angeles. Minneapolis: University of Minnesota Press, 1995.

Nasr, Seyyed Vali Reza. "The Rise of "Muslim Democracy" *Journal of Democracy* 16, no. 2 (2005): 13–27.

Nasser, Ramzi, and Kamal Abouchedid. "Problems and the Epistemology of Electronic Publishing in the Arab World: The Case of Lebanon" *First Monday* 6, no. 9 (2001).

Newsom, Victoria Ann, and Laura Lengel. "The Power of the Weblogged Word: Contained Empowerment in the Middle East North Africa Region." *Feminist Media Studies* 3, no. 3 (2003): 360–363.

Nilan, Pam. "The Social Meanings of Media for Indonesian Youth." In *Globalization, Culture and Inequality in Asia*, edited by Timothy J. Scrase, Todd Joseph, Miles Holden, and Scott Baum, 168–190. Melbourne: Trans Pacific Press, 2003.

Nisbet, E. C. "Public Diplomacy, Television News, and Muslim Opinion." *Harvard International Journal of Press/Politics* 9, no. 2 (2004): 11–37.

Norris, Pippa. *Digital Divide: Civic Engagement, Information Poverty, and the Internet Worldwide*, Communication, Society, and Politics. New York: Cambridge University Press, 2001.

Norris, Pippa. "Internet World: Parties, Governments and Online Democracy." In *International Political Science Association World Congress*. Quebec, 1–6 August 2000.

Nour, Samia Satti O. M. "ICT Opportunities and Challenges for Development in the Arab World." In *WIDER Discussion Paper Series*, 15. Helsinki: United Nations University, World Institute for Development Economics Research, 2002.

Nyabuga, George, and Okoth Fred Mudhai. "Misclick on Democracy: New Media Use by Key Political Parties in Kenya's Disputed December 2007 Presidential Election." In *African Media and the Digital Public Sphere*, edited by Okoth Fred Mudhai, Wisdom J. Tettey, and Fackson Banda, 41–56. New York: Palgrave MacMillan, 2009.

Obot, David, Fredrick Kintu, and Laurent Elder. "The Uganda Knowledge and Information Society: Early Lessons from ICT Projects." In *At the Crossroads: ICT Policy Making in East Africa*, edited by Florence Eba Etta and Laurent Elder. Ottawa: International Development Research Center, 2005.

Ogan, Christine L., and Kursat Cagiltay. "Confession, Revelation and Storytelling: Patterns of Use on a Popular Turkish Website." *New Media & Society* 8, no. 5 (2006): 801–823.

Ogola, George, Anne Schumann, and Michael Olutayo Olatunji. "Popular Music, New Media, and the Digital Public Sphere in Kenya, Cote d'Ivoire, and Nigeria." In *African Media and the Digital Public Sphere*, edited by Okoth Fred Mudhai, Wisdom J Tettey and Fackson Banda, 125–142. New York: Palgrave MacMillan, 2009.

Okwori, Jenkeri Zakari, and Akeem Adeyanju. "Nigeria: Reseach Findings and Conclusions." In *African Media Development Initiative*, edited by Gerry Power. London: BBC World Service Trust, 2006.

Opennet.net. "Country Profiles." Toronto: University of Toronto, www.opennet.net, 2006.

Opennet.net. "Tunisia Country Profile." Toronto: University of Toronto, www.opennet.net, 2006.

Palmer, J. J. "Internet Access in Bahrain: Business Patterns and Problems." *Technovation* 20, no. 8, 451–458 (2000).

Pax, Salam. *Salam Pax: The Clandestine Diary of an Ordinary Iraqi:* New York: Grove Press, 2006.

Paxton, Pamela, Melanie Hughes, and Jennifer Green. "The International Women's Movement and Women's Political Representation, 1893–2003." *American Sociological Review* 71, no. 6 (2006): 898–920.

Peled, Alon. "Debunking the Internet Myth: Technological Prophecies and Middle East Politics." *The Middle East Quarterly* 7, no. 3 (2000).

Peterson, S. "Iran's Newest Revolution: Holy Texts Go on Computer." *Christian Science Monitor*, 1996, 1–3.

Pew Global Attitudes Project. "The Great Divide: How Westerners and Muslims View Each Other." http://pewglobal.org/reports/pdf/253.pdf.

Pollack, David. "Slippery Polls: Uses and Abuses of Opinion Surveys from Arab States." The Washington Institute for Near East Policy, http://www.washingtoninstitute.org/templateC04.php?CID=290.

Poynder, Richard. "Malaysia (International Report)." *Information Today* 21, no. 3 (2004): 1–28.

Press, Larry. "Against All Odds, the Internet in Bangladesh." In *The Global Diffusion of the Internet Project*. Omaha: University of Nebraska, 1999.

Privacy International and the GreenNet Educational Trust. "Silenced: An International Report on Censorship and Control of the Internet" http://www.privacyinternational.org/survey/censorship/Silenced.pdf.

Quandt, William B. "Algeria's Uneasy Peace" *Journal of Democracy* 13, no. 4 (2002): 15–23.

Ragin, Charles. *Redesigning Social Inquiry: Set Relations in Social Research*. Chicago: University of Chicago Press, 2009.

Rahimi, Babak. "Cyberdissident: The Internet in Revolutionary Iran." *Middle East Review of International Affairs* 7, no. 3 (2003). Retreived from: http://www.gloria-center.org/meria/2003/09/rahimi.html.

Rahman, M. Golam. "Bangladesh: Much Scope for Alternative Media, but Is There Political Will?" In *Media Pluralism in Asia: The Role and Impact of Alternative Media*, edited by Kalinga Seneviratne, 1–27. Singapore: Nanyang Technological University, 2007.

Rahman, Sayeedur. "Bangladesh: Mobile Telephony = Social Good + Good Business." In *Asia Unplugged: The Wireless and Mobile Media Book in the Asia-Pacific*, edited by Lunita Mendoza and Madanmohan Rao, 407–412. New Delhi: Response Books, 2005.

Ramey, Corinne. "At Election Time It's Mobile Phone Journalism in Kenya." http://mobileactive.org/mobile-phone-journalism-kenya.

Rao, Madanmohan. "India." In *News Media and New Media*, edited by Madanmohan Rao, 301–311. Singapore: Eastern Universities Press, 2003.

Riverbend. *Baghdad Burning: Girl Blog from Iraq*. New York: The Feminist Press at the City University of New York, 2005.

Riverbend. *Baghdad Burning II: More Girl Blog from Iraq*. New York: The Feminist Press at the City University of New York, 2006.

Rogers, Everett M. *Diffusion of Innovations*. 5th ed. New York: Free Press, 2003.

Rogers, Richard. "'Internet & Society' in Armenia and Azerbaijan? Web Games and a Chronicle of an Infowar." *First Monday* 5, no. 9 (2000), http://firstmonday.org/issues/issue5_9/rogers/index.html.

Rozen, Laura. "Forums Point the Way to Jihad." Wired Magazine, June 2003. http://www.wired.com/culture/lifestyle/news/2003/08/59897?currentPage=all.

Rugh, William. *Arab Mass Media: Newspapers, Radio, and Television in Arab Politics*. Westport, CT: Praeger, 2004.

Saeed, Hamid, Muhammad Asghar, Muhammad Anwar, and Muhammad Ramzan. "Internet Use in University Libraries of Pakistan." *Online Information Review* 24, no. 2 (2000): 154.

Sardar, Ziauddin. "Paper, Printing and Compact Disks: The Making and Unmaking of Islamic Culture." *Media Culture Society* 15, no. 1 (1993): 43–59.

Sarkar, Partha Pratim. "Bangladesh." In *News Media and New Media*, edited by Madanmohan Rao, 243–253. Singapore: Eastern Universities Press, 2003.

Saunders, Robert A. "Virtual Irredentism? The Redemption and Reification of the Albanian Nation in Cyberspace." *Albanian Journal of Politics* 1, no. 2 (2005): 137–165.

Sawe, David. "The E-Thinktank and ICT Policy Making in Tanzania." In *At the Crossroads: ICT Policy Making in East Africa*, edited by Florence Eba Etta and Laurent Elder. Ottawa: International Development Research Center, 2005.

Schmitt, Eric, and Thom Shanker. "U.S. Adapts Cold-War Idea to Fight Terrorists." *New York Times*, 18 March 2008.

Schuler, Ian. "SMS as a Tool in Election Observation (Innovations Case Narrative: National Democratic Institute)." *Innovations: Technology, Governance, Globalization* 3, no. 2 (2008): 143–157.

Schwirtz, Michael. "An Overflowing of Islamic Fervor in Russia." *International Herald Tribune*, Monday, December 17, 2007, 2.

Seck, Ibrahima. "Senegal: Reseach Findings and Conclusions." In *African Media Development Initiative*, edited by Gerry Power. London, UK: BBC World Service Trust, 2006.

Sen, Ashish. "India: Regulations Need to Catch up with Technology." In *Media Pluralism in Asia: The Role and Impact of Alternative Media*, edited by Kalinga Seneviratne, 28–52. Singapore: Nanyang Technological University, 2007.

Seneviratne, Kalinga. "Malaysia: Alternative Media … Only on the Internet." In *Media Pluralism in Asia: The Role and Impact of Alternative Media*, edited by Kalinga Seneviratne, 86–131. Singapore: Nanyang Technological University, 2007.

Sevdik, Ayisigi B., and Varol Akman. "Internet in the Lives of Turkish Women." *First Monday* 7, no. 3 (2002).

Shapiro, Samantha M. "Revolution, Facebook-Style." *New York Times Magazine*, January 22, 2009.

Shariff, Zulfikar Mohamad. "Fateha.com: Challenging Control over Malay/Muslim Voices in Singapore." In *Asian Cyberactivism*, edited by Steven Gan, James Gomez, and Uwe Johannen, 318–371. Bangkok: Friedrich Naumann Foundation, 2004.

Siong, Tong Yee. "Malaysiakini: Threating a Tightrope of Political Pressure and Market Factors." In *Asian Cyberactivism*, edited by Steven Gan, James Gomez, and Uwe Johannen, 270–317. Bangkok: Friedrich Naumann Foundation, 2004.

Sisler, Vit. "The Internet and the Construction of Islamic Knowledge in Europe." *Masaryk University Journal of Law and Technology* 1, no. 2, 205–217 (2007).

Slavin, Barbara. "Internet Blogging Boom Alters Political Process in Iran." *USA Today*, 12 June 2005.

Sluma, Ephraim, Daniel Brode, and Nicky Roberts. "Internet Para as Escolas in Mozambique." In *Information and Communication Technologies for Development in Africa*, edited by Tina James. Ottawa: International Development Research Center, 2004.

Souri, Helga Tawil. "The Political Battlefield of Pro-Arab Video Games on Palestinian Screens." *Comparative Studies of South Asia, Africa and the Middle East* 27, no. 3 (2007): 536–551.

Sreberny-Mohammadi, Annabelle, and Ali Mohammadi. *Small Media, Big Revolution: Communication, Culture, and the Iranian Revolution*. Minneapolis, MN: University of Minnesota Press, 1994.

Stevens, Tim, and Peter R. Neumann. *Countering Online Radicalisation: A Strategy for Action*. London, UK: International Centre for the Study of Radicalisation and Political Violence, 2009.

Stohl, Cynthia, and Michael Stohl. "Networks of Terror: Theoretical Assumptions and Pragmatic Consequences." *Communication Theory* 17, no. 2 (2007): 93–124.

Stowasser, Barbara. "Old Shayks, Young Women, and the Internet: The Rewriting of Women's Political Rights in Islam." *The Muslim World* 91, no. 1, 99–120 (2001).

Sylla, Fatimata Seye. "ICT as an Instrument for Participation: The Regional Perspective from Africa, Examples of the Internet Use at the Grassroots Level." 12. Seoul, Korea: Division for the Advancement of Women, United Nations, 2002.

Tabaar, Mohammad Ayatollahi. "Who Wrote the Koran?" *New York Times Magazine* (5 December 2008): 24.

Taifur, S. A. S. M. *Comprehensive Study of E-Government Initiatives in Bangladesh: Final Report*. Dhaka: Government of Bangladesh, 2004.

Talbi, Mohamed, and Zerxes Spencer. "A Record of Failure." *Journal of Democracy* 11, no. 3 (2000): 58–68.

Tam-Bryoh, David. "Sierra Leone: Reseach Findings and Conclusions." In *African Media Development Initiative*, edited by Gerry Power. London: BBC World Service Trust, 2006.

Tarrow, Sidney. *The New Transnational Activism*, Cambridge Studies in Contentious Politics. New York: Cambridge University Press, 2005.

Tarrow, Sidney. *Power in Movement: Social Movements and Contentious Politics*, Cambridge Studies in Comparative Politics. New York: Cambridge University Press, 1998.

Teitelbaum, Joshua. "Dueling for Da' Wa: State vs. Society on the Saudi Internet." *The Middle East Journal* 56, no. 2 (2002): 222–236.

Tekwani, Shyam, and Kavitha Shetty. "Two Indias: The Role of the Internet in the 2004 Elections." In *The Internet and National Elections: A Comparative Study of Web Campaigning*, edited by Nicholas Jankowski, Randolph Kluver, Kirsten Foot, and Steven Schneider, 150-62. New York: Routledge, 2007.

Thioune, Ramata Molo Aw, and El Hadj Habib Camara. "Youth Cyber Clubs in Senegal." In *Information and Communication Technologies for Development in Africa*, edited by Tina James, 127-169. Ottawa: International Development Research Center, 2004.

Thompson, Kenneth. "Border Crossings and Diasporic Identities: Media Use and Leisure Practices of an Ethnic Minority." *Qualitative Sociology* 25, no. 3 (2002): 409-418.

Tizireen, Hassan. "Brunei Darussalam." In *News Media and New Media*, edited by Madanmohan Rao, 254-271. Singapore: Eastern Universities Press, 2003.

Tolbert, C., and K. Mossberger. "The Effects of E-Government on Trust and Confidence in Government." *Public Administration Review* 66, no. 3 (2006): 354-369.

Torenli, Nurcan. "From Virtual to Local Realities: Access to ICT and Women Advocacy Networks in Turkey." *Perspectives on Global Development and Technology* 4, no. 2 (2005): 169-96.

Torenli, Nurcan. "The 'Other' Faces of Digital Exclusion: ICT Gender Divides in the Broader Community." *European Journal of Communication* 21, no. 4 (2006): 435-454.

UNCTAD. "Exports of Computer and Information Services by Country, 2000-2003." 2005.

UNESCO. "Data Center." UNESCO, 2007. Retrieved from: http://stats.uis.unesco.org/unesco/tableviewer/document.aspx?ReportId=143.

UNESCO. "Measuring Linguistic Diversity on the Internet." Paris, France: UNESCO, 2005.

van Dijk, Michiel, and Adam Szirmai. "Industrial Policy and Technology Diffusion: Evidence from Paper Making Machinery in Indonesia." *World Development* 34, no. 12 (2006): 2137-52.

Vodaphone. "Africa: The Impact of Mobile Phones." In *The Vodafone Policy Paper Series*, 71. London: Vodaphone, 2005.

Waema, Timothy Mwololo. "E-Local Governance: A Case Study of Financial Management System Implementation in Two Municipal Councils in Kenya." *International Journal of Electronic Governance* 2, no. 1 (2009): 55-73.

Wallsten, Scott. "Regulation and Internet Use in Developing Countries." *Economic Development and Cultural Change* 53, no. 2 (2005): 501-523.

Warf, Barney, and Peter Vincent. "Multiple Geographies of the Arab Internet." *Area* 39, no. 1 (2007): 83-96.

Warschauer, Mark, Ghada R. El Said, and Ayman Zohry. "Language Choice Online: Globalization and Identity in Egypt." *Journal of Computer-Mediated Communication* 7, no. 4 (2002).

Watson, Ivan. "Film Comedy Highlights Turkish-Kurdish Tensions." National Public Radio, http://www.npr.org/templates/story/story.php?storyId=7092745.

Wax, Emily. "The Mufti in the Chat Room." *Washington Post*, July 31, 1999.

Websense. "Master Database—URL Categories." Websense, http://www.websense.com/global/en/ProductsServices/MasterDatabase/URLCategories.php.

Weiffen, Brigitte. "Liberalizing Autocracies in the Gulf Region? Reform Strategies in the Face of a Cultural-Economic Syndrome." *World Development* 36, no. 12 (2008): 2,586–2,604.

Weimann, Gabriel. *Terror on the Internet: The New Arena, the New Challenges.* Washington, DC: United States Institute of Peace, 2006.

Welch, E., C. Hinnant, and J. Moon. "Linking Citizen Satisfaction with E-Government with Trust in Government." *Journal of Public Administration Research and Theory* 15, no. 3 (2005): 371–391.

West, Darrell M. *Digital Government: Technology and Public Sector Performance.* Princeton, NJ: Princeton University Press, 2005.

West, Darrell M. "Improving Technology Utilization in Electronic Government around the World, 2008," pp. 1–30 Washington, DC: Brookings Institution, 2008. Retrieved from: http://www.brookings.edu.

Wheeler, Deborah L. "Blessings and Curses: Women and the Internet Revolution in the Arab World." In *Women and the Media in the Middle East: Power through Self-Expression,* edited by Naomi Sakr, 138–61. London: I. B. Taurus, 2004.

Wheeler, Deborah L. "Gender Sensitivity and the Drive for It: Lessons from the Netcorps Jordan Project." *Ethics and Information Technology* 8, no. 3 (2006): 131–142.

Wheeler, Deborah L. *The Internet and the Middle East: Global Expectations and Local Imaginations in Kuwait,* Suny Series in Computer-Mediated Communication. Albany: SUNY Press, 2006.

Wheeler, Deborah L. "New Technologies, Old Culture: A Look at Women, Gender and the Internet in Kuwait." In *Culture, Technology, Communication: Towards an Intercultural Village,* edited by Charles Ess and Fay Sudweeks, 187–212. New York: SUNY Press, 2001.

Wheeler, Deborah L. "Working around the State: Internet Use and Political Identity in the Arab World." In *The Handbook of Internet Politics,* edited by Andrew Chadwick and Philip N. Howard. London: Routledge, 2008.

Wilson, Ernest J. "Senegal: Internet Emergence Diffusion and the Emergence of Internet Markets." In *CIDCM Working Research Paper Series,* 9. College Park: Univesity of Maryland, Center for International Development and Conflict Management, 2004.

Winn, Jane. "Islamic Law, Globalization and Emerging Electronic Commerce Technologies." In *Strengthening Relations with Arab and Islamic Countries through International Law: E-Commerce, the WTO Dispute Settlement Mechanism and Foreign Investment,* edited by International Bureau of the Permanent Court of Arbitration. The Hague: Kluwer Law International, 2002.

Wolcott, Peter. "The Diffusion of the Internet in the Islamic Republic of Pakistan." In *The Global Diffusion of the Internet Project.* Omaha: University of Nebraska, 1999.

Wolcott, Peter. "The Diffusion of the Internet in the Kingdom of Saudi Arabia." In *The Global Diffusion of the Internet Project.* Omaha: University of Nebraska, 1999.

Wolcott, Peter. "The Diffusion of the Internet in the State of Israel." In *The Global Diffusion of the Internet Project.* Omaha: University of Nebraska, 1999.

Wolcott, Peter, and Kursat Cagiltay. "Telecommunications, Liberalization, and the Growth of the Internet in Turkey." *The Information Society* 17, no. 2 (2001): 133-141.

Wolcott, Peter, and Seymour Goodman. "The Internet in Turkey and Pakistan: A Comparative Analysis." 145. Palo Alto, CA: Center for International Security and Cooperation, Stanford University, 2000.

World Bank. *World Bank Annual Report.* Vol. 20060211_164900.pdf. Washington, DC: World Bank, 2001.

World Bank. "World Bank Development Indicators." World Bank. Retrieved from: http://web.worldbank.org/WBSITE/EXTERNAL/DATASTATISTICS/0,content MDK:21725423~pagePK:64133150~piPK:64133175~theSitePK:239419,00.html.

World Resources Institute. "Earthtrends Database." World Resources Institute, 2007-2010. Retrieved from: http://earthtrends.wri.org/

Worth, Robert F., and Nazila Fathi. "Results Spur Charge That Leaders Stole Presidential Vote." *New York Times,* June 14, 2009.

Xu, Wu. *Chinese Cyber Nationalism: Evolution, Characteristics, and Implications.* Lanham, MD: Lexington Books, 2007.

Yang, Kenneth. "Exploring Factors Affecting the Adoption of Mobile Commerce in Singapore." *Telematics and Informatics* 22, no. 3 (2005): 257-277.

Yavuz, M. Hakan. "Media Identities for Alevis and Kurds in Turkey." In *New Media in the Muslim World,* edited by Dale F. Eickelman and Jon W. Anderson, 180-200. Bloomington: Indiana University Press, 2003.

Yesil, Bilge. "Internet Cafe as Battlefield: State Control over Internet Cafes in Turkey and the Lack of Popular Resistence." *Journal of Popular Culture* 37, no. 1 (2003): 120-127.

Youngs, Gillian. "Closing the Gaps: Women, Communications and Technology." *Development* 45, no. 4 (2002): 23-28.

Zayani, Mohamed. "The Challenges and Limits of Universalist Concepts: Problematizing Public Opinion and a Mediated Arab Public Sphere." *The Middle East Journal of Communication and Culture* 1, no. 1 (2008): 60-79.

Zeitlyn, David, and Francine Barone. "Small Ads as First Steps to Internet Business: A Preliminary Survey of Cameroon's Commercial Internet Usage." *First Monday* 9, no. 9 (2004).

Zhou, Yuqiong, and Patricia Moy. "Parsing Framing Processes: The Interplay between Online Public Opinion and Media Coverage." *Journal of Communication* 57, no. 1 (2008): 79-98.

Index

Abtahi, Mohammad Ali, 5
Accidental censorship, 174–175
Afghanistan, 40, 206
  blogs in, 38
  censorship, 177
  civil society online, 139
  as crisis state, 74, 190, 228
  foreign military intervention
    in, 40
  government offices online, 69
  information infrastructure for
    political parties, 99
  jihadist media sources in, 128
  police payroll systems in, 41
  population practicing Islam, rate
    of ICT diffusion, and countries
    experiencing anarchy, 213
  remittances, ICT-led growth, state
    capacity, and policy
    effectiveness, 79
  state media ownership and online
    journalism, 125
  support for democratic
    governance, 189
  Taliban in, 30
  telecommunications reform and
    ICT policies, 65
Africa, journalistic practices in, 120
Aga Khan Foundation, 136
Al Ahram, 110
Al Arabiya, 117
Albania, 37, 39, 207, 209

censorship, 176
civil society online, 138
democratic transition, 220
government offices online, 68
information infrastructure for
  political parties, 98
population practicing Islam, rate
  of ICT diffusion, and
  democratic transition, 209
remittances, ICT-led growth, state
  capacity, and policy
  effectiveness, 78
state media ownership and online
  journalism, 124
telecommunications reform and
  ICT policies, 64
Al-Fajr Media Institute, 128
Algeria, 41, 54, 55, 122, 126, 190,
  207
censorship, 176
civil society online, 138
democratic transition, 220
government offices online, 68
information infrastructure for
  political parties, 98
media concentration, 121
population practicing Islam, rate
  of ICT diffusion, and
  democratic transition, 209
remittances, ICT-led growth, state
  capacity, and policy
  effectiveness, 78

Algeria (*continued*)
   state media ownership and online
      journalism, 124
   telecommunications reform and
      ICT policies, 64
Al-Hayat, 120
Al Jazeera, 110, 117
   online debate, 143
   research on, 119
Al-Nasir, Jamal 'Abd, 133
Al-Qaeda, 38
Al Quran Seluler, 150
American Standard Code for
    Information Interchange
    (ASCII), 158
Amnesty International, 134
Ansar al-Sunnah, 128
"April 6 Youth Movement," 135–136
Arabic language, 159
Arab League, 22, 169
Argentina, 127
Arrests, of bloggers, 113–116
   for debating public policy
      options, 112
   for violating cultural norms, 112
ASCII. *See* American Standard Code
    for Information Interchange
    (ASCII)
Authoritarian regimes, 69, 72–74
   competitive political participation
      in, 72–73
   constitutional monarchies, 73
   Islamic republics, 73
   media regulation in, 72
   religious practices in, 72
   ruling elites in, 71–72
   vs. democracies, 72
Azerbaijan, 112, 156
   authoritarianism, 190, 225
   blogger arrests in, 115
   censorship, 177
   civil society online, 139

government offices online, 69
information infrastructure for
   political parties, 99
lack of technology diffusion, 54
news in, 112
open political discourse in, 152
party websites in, 100
population practicing Islam, rate
   of ICT diffusion, and countries
   remained authoritarian, 212
remittances, ICT-led growth, state
   capacity, and policy
   effectiveness, 79
state media ownership and online
   journalism, 125
telecommunications reform and
   ICT policies, 65

Bahrain, 43, 56, 73, 85, 140, 152,
   172, 195, 207, 216
   censorship, 176
   civil society online, 138
   democratic transition, 220
   government offices online, 68
   information infrastructure for
      political parties, 98
   open political discourse in, 152
   population practicing Islam, rate
      of ICT diffusion, and
      democratic transition, 209
   remittances, ICT-led growth, state
      capacity, and policy
      effectiveness, 78
   state media ownership and online
      journalism, 124
   telecommunications reform and
      ICT policies, 64
Baku, 129
Bangladesh, 22, 71, 127, 158, 182,
   187, 190, 216
   censorship, 176
   civil society online, 138

democratic entrenchment, 223
government offices online, 68
information infrastructure for
political parties, 98
media concentration, 121
population practicing Islam, rate
of ICT diffusion, and
democratic entrenchment, 211
remittances, ICT-led growth, state
capacity, and policy
effectiveness, 78
state media ownership and online
journalism, 124
telecommunications reform and
ICT policies, 64
BBC, research on journalistic
practices, 120
Benin, 54, 61
censorship, 176
civil society online, 138
democratic entrenchment, 223
government offices online, 68
information infrastructure for
political parties, 98
population practicing Islam, rate
of ICT diffusion, and
democratic entrenchment, 211
remittances, ICT-led growth, state
capacity, and policy
effectiveness, 78
state media ownership and online
journalism, 124
telecommunications reform and
ICT policies, 64
Berg, Nick, 16
Bloggers, 112–117
arrests, 112, 113–116
harassment of, 117
Blogs, 110, 112, 117
Book production/consumption,
161–163
Bosnia, 52, 54, 97, 189, 206, 207, 216

censorship, 176
civil society online, 138
democratic transition, 220
government offices online, 68
information infrastructure for
political parties, 98
population practicing Islam, rate
of ICT diffusion, and
democratic transition, 209
remittances, ICT-led growth, state
capacity, and policy
effectiveness, 78
state media ownership and online
journalism, 124
telecommunications reform and
ICT policies, 64
Broadcast licenses, 118
Brunei, 61, 158, 204, 207, 216
authoritarianism, 225
censorship, 177
civil society online, 139
government offices online, 69
information infrastructure for
political parties, 99
population practicing Islam,
rate of ICT diffusion, and
countries remained
authoritarian, 212
remittances, ICT-led growth, state
capacity, and policy
effectiveness, 79
state media ownership and online
journalism, 125
telecommunications reform and
ICT policies, 65
Bulgaria, 189, 204, 206, 207, 216
censorship, 176
civil society online, 138
democratic entrenchment, 223
government offices online, 68
information infrastructure for
political parties, 98

Bulgaria (*continued*)
  population practicing Islam, rate
    of ICT diffusion, and
    democratic entrenchment, 211
  remittances, ICT-led growth, state
    capacity, and policy
    effectiveness, 78
  state media ownership and online
    journalism, 124
  telecommunications reform and
    ICT policies, 64
Burkina Faso
  censorship, 177
  civil society online, 139
  crisis states, 228
  government offices online, 69
  information infrastructure for
    political parties, 99
  population practicing Islam, rate
    of ICT diffusion, and countries
    experiencing anarchy, 213
  remittances, ICT-led growth, state
    capacity, and policy
    effectiveness, 79
  state media ownership and online
    journalism, 125
  telecommunications reform and
    ICT policies, 65

Calibration, 27–28, 35–36. *See also*
    Fuzzy calibrations
  defined, 203
  population example, 203–204
Cameroon, 206
  authoritarianism, 225
  censorship, 177
  civil society online, 139
  government offices online, 69
  information infrastructure for
    political parties, 99
  population practicing Islam, rate
    of ICT diffusion, and countries
    remained authoritarian, 212

  remittances, ICT-led growth, state
    capacity, and policy
    effectiveness, 79
  state media ownership and online
    journalism, 125
  telecommunications reform and
    ICT policies, 65
CAR. *See* Central African Republic
    (CAR)
Cassette tapes, 133
Causal sets
  necessary causes, 216–217
  selecting, 214–215
  for sufficient causes, 215–216
Censorship, 8–9
  accidental, 174–175
  cultural and spiritual
    information, 167–169
  filtering services, 172–173
  gender politics and, 165–167
  ISP regulation and, 170
  language and, 158–159
  market for, 172–173
  by non-Muslim
    governments, 173–174
  online libraries, 168–169
  overview, 157
  self-censorship, 174–175
  strategies, 171–172
  and surveilling political culture
    online, 169–172
Central African Republic
    (CAR), 207, 213
  authoritarianism, 225
  censorship, 177
  civil society online, 139
  government offices online, 69
  information infrastructure for
    political parties, 99
  lack of technology diffusion, 54
  population practicing Islam, rate
    of ICT diffusion, and countries
    remained authoritarian, 212

remittances, ICT-led growth, state capacity, and policy effectiveness, 79

state media ownership and online journalism, 125

telecommunications reform and ICT policies, 65

Central Asia, domestic news in, 119

Chad
  authoritarianism, 225
  censorship, 177
  civil society online, 139
  government offices online, 69
  information infrastructure for political parties, 99
  population practicing Islam, rate of ICT diffusion, and countries remained authoritarian, 212
  remittances, ICT-led growth, state capacity, and policy effectiveness, 79
  state media ownership and online journalism, 125
  telecommunications reform and ICT policies, 65

Chechnya, 197

Chechnyan insurgents, 24

Citizen journalism, 110

Citizen journalists, 112

Civic debate/discourse online, 142–144

Civil society, 132–136. *See also* Online civil society, in Muslim countries
  cyberactivism, 145–147
  defined, 134
  hactivism, 145–147
  learning online, 148–150
  scholarly research infrastructure and, 144–145
  social interaction, 135–136
  state response to, 147–148
  virtual communities, 133

wired citizenship, 152–154

Civil society groups, 182–183
  defined, 132
  organizational capacity, 135
  public Internet access and, 136–137
  as surrogate organizations, 133–134
  telecommunications standards, 137

CNN, 134

Collective action, 12, 17, 21, 137, 148–149, 175, 178–179, 199, 200

Collective identity, 33, 155–156
  of political culture, 168
  shared grievances, 169

Commercial cybercafés, 45

Committee for the Defense of Legitimate Rights, 134, 137

Comoros, 55, 214
  censorship, 176
  civil society online, 138
  democratic transition, 220
  government offices online, 68
  information infrastructure for political parties, 98
  population practicing Islam, rate of ICT diffusion, and democratic transition, 209
  remittances, ICT-led growth, state capacity, and policy effectiveness, 78
  state media ownership and online journalism, 124
  telecommunications reform and ICT policies, 64

Comparative method, use of, 26–28

Compound annual growth rate, 37

Computer training courses, for journalists, 118

Consistency, defined, 192

Constitutional monarchies, 73

Contagion effect, 149

Contemporary democratization,
    defined, 106
Coptic Christians, 133
Coverage, defined, 192
Crisis states, 69
    countries as, 74
    information infrastructure
        in, 74–75
    Muslims living in, 74
Cultural production and
    consumption, 161–164
    books, 161–163
    censorship and. *See* Censorship
    Internet user and host, 161–163
Cyberactivism, 145–147
Cybercafés, in Tehran, 16
Cyberterrorism, 14, 30, 145
Cyberwar, 145
Cypriot separatists, 146
Cyprus, 206, 207, 216
    censorship, 176
    civil society online, 138
    democratic entrenchment, 223
    government offices online, 68
    information infrastructure for
        political parties, 98
    population practicing Islam, rate
        of ICT diffusion, and
        democratic entrenchment, 211
    remittances, ICT-led growth, state
        capacity, and policy
        effectiveness, 78
    state media ownership and online
        journalism, 124
    telecommunications reform and
        ICT policies, 64

Dagestan, 197
Darfur, 197
Davos World Economic Forum, 63
Debate/discourse online, 142–144
Delta Force, 41

Democracies
    causal conditions, 183–184
    entrenched, 68, 70–71
    technological theory of, 184–197
    transition, 67, 68, 70
Democracy, Islam and, 13
Democratization
    causal conditions, 183–184,
        192–195
    contemporary trend, 197–201
    contextual factors, 184–188
    foreign policy and, 196–197
    ICT diffusion, 48–56, 198–201
    institutional consequences,
        189–190, 192
    political outcomes, 188–189
    regime hybridity, 195–196
    sufficient causes, 192–194
Developing countries, media
    in, 122–123
Developing indicators, 14–15
Diaspora, 111, 128, 200
    communities, 81, 85, 168
    Muslim in West, 40
    Persian, 5
    Turkish, 169
Diasporic communities, 118
Digital communications
    infrastructure, 16
Digital divide, 14–16, 46, 60
Digital revolution, 3–12
Digital transition, 140
Djibouti, 24, 186, 216
    censorship, 176
    civil society online, 138
    democratic transition, 220
    government offices online, 68
    information infrastructure for
        political parties, 98
    population practicing Islam, rate
        of ICT diffusion, and
        democratic transition, 209

remittances, ICT-led growth, state
   capacity, and policy
   effectiveness, 78
state media ownership and online
   journalism, 124
telecommunications reform and
   ICT policies, 64
Doubling time, 37

EBRD. *See* European Bank for
   Reconstruction and
   Development (EBRD)
Economic wealth, and ICT
   diffusion, 46–48
E-democracy tools, 66
E-government programs, 181
Egypt, 3, 45, 58, 67, 70, 71, 95, 110,
   117, 126, 127, 133, 135, 140, 163,
   168, 190, 195, 214
   blogger arrests in, 113, 114, 115
   bloggers in, 112
   censorship, 176
   civil society online, 138
   democratic transition, 190, 220
   Facebook in, 135
   government offices online, 68
   information infrastructure for
      political parties, 98
   media concentration, 121
   population practicing Islam, rate
      of ICT diffusion, and
      democratic transition, 209
   remittances, ICT-led growth, state
      capacity, and policy
      effectiveness, 78
   state media ownership and online
      journalism, 124
   surveilling bloggers, 112
   telecommunications reform and
      ICT policies, 64
E-jihadis, 30
El Fattah, Alaa Abd, 112

Email, 133
England, governance in, 73
English languages news media, 30
Entrenched democracies, 68,
   70–71
Entrepreneurial Muslim
   businesses, 150–151
Eritrea, 52, 64
   authoritarianism, 225
   censorship, 177
   civil society online, 139
   government offices online, 69
   information infrastructure for
      political parties, 99
   population practicing Islam, rate
      of ICT diffusion, and countries
      remained authoritarian, 212
   remittances, ICT-led growth, state
      capacity, and policy
      effectiveness, 79
   state media ownership and online
      journalism, 125
   telecommunications reform and
      ICT policies, 65
Ethiopia, 59, 171, 187, 207, 216
   authoritarianism, 225
   censorship, 177
   civil society online, 139
   government offices online, 69
   information infrastructure for
      political parties, 99
   population practicing Islam,
      rate of ICT diffusion, and
      countries remained
      authoritarian, 212
   remittances, ICT-led growth, state
      capacity, and policy
      effectiveness, 79
   state media ownership and online
      journalism, 125
   telecommunications reform and
      ICT policies, 65

European Bank for Reconstruction
 and Development (EBRD), 44,
 62

Facebook, 41, 135
 in campaigning, 5
 in Egypt, 45, 135
 in Iran, 5, 7, 8, 16, 41, 148
Filtering software, 172–173, 174–175
Firewall, 44, 164
Flikr, 74, 135
France, 38, 41
 governance in, 73
Free-trade economic zones, 85
Fund-raising, 134
Fuzzy calibrations
 contextual conditions, 206–207
 information infrastructure,
  205–206
 institutional outcomes, 207–209
 membership, 203–204
Fuzzy sets, 28, 124
 calibrations. *See* Fuzzy
  calibrations
 overview, 203
 theory of, 184

Gambia, 12, 207
 authoritarianism, 225
 censorship, 177
 civil society online, 139
 government offices online, 69
 information infrastructure for
  political parties, 99
 population practicing Islam, rate
  of ICT diffusion, and countries
  remained authoritarian, 212
 remittances, ICT-led growth, state
  capacity, and policy
  effectiveness, 79
 state media ownership and online
  journalism, 125

telecommunications reform and
  ICT policies, 65
Gay and Lesbian Arabic Society, 133
Gaza, Israel's attack on, 117, 136
Gender gap, in Internet use, 45
Gender politics, 165–167
Georgia, 24, 46, 54, 70, 97, 145, 149,
  186, 190, 195, 207, 216
 censorship, 176
 civil society online, 138
 democratic transition, 220
 government offices online, 68
 information infrastructure for
  political parties, 98
 population practicing Islam, rate
  of ICT diffusion, and
  democratic transition, 209
 remittances, ICT-led growth, state
  capacity, and policy
  effectiveness, 78
 state media ownership and online
  journalism, 124
 telecommunications reform and
  ICT policies, 64
Gforce Pakistan, 146
Ghana, 59, 206, 207
 censorship, 176
 civil society online, 138
 democratic transition, 220
 government offices online, 68
 information infrastructure for
  political parties, 98
 population practicing Islam, rate
  of ICT diffusion, and
  democratic transition, 209
 remittances, ICT-led growth, state
  capacity, and policy
  effectiveness, 78
 state media ownership and online
  journalism, 124
 telecommunications reform and
  ICT policies, 64

Gini coefficients, 185
Global Islamic Media Front, 128
Google, 7, 135, 174
    language offerings, 159
Google Maps, 172, 174
Government offices online, 66–76.
        See also Wired states
    in authoritarian regimes, 71–74
    in crisis states, 74–75
    in democratic entrenchment,
        70–71
    investment in infrastructure,
        75–76
    remittances, 76–77
    state capacity, 76–77
    in transition states, 67, 70
Government(s)
    branches of, 66–67
    online. *See* Government offices
        online
Guardian, 110
Guinea
    authoritarianism, 225
    censorship, 177
    civil society online, 139
    government offices online, 69
    information infrastructure for
        political parties, 99
    population practicing Islam, rate
        of ICT diffusion, and countries
        remained authoritarian, 212
    remittances, ICT-led growth, state
        capacity, and policy
        effectiveness, 79
    state media ownership and online
        journalism, 125
    telecommunications reform and
        ICT policies, 65
Guinea-Bissau, 206, 207, 214
    censorship, 176
    civil society online, 138
    democratic entrenchment, 223

government offices online, 68
information infrastructure for
    political parties, 98
population practicing Islam, rate
    of ICT diffusion, and
    democratic entrenchment, 211
remittances, ICT-led growth, state
    capacity, and policy
    effectiveness, 78
state media ownership and online
    journalism, 124
telecommunications reform and
    ICT policies, 64

Hackers, 145–146
Hactivism, 145–147
Hakerz Club, 146
Hanzi language, 159
Hezbollah, 16
Hosting services, 67

Identity management, politics
    of, 176, 178–179
Identity news, 127–129
    digital information
        infrastructure, 129
    types of, 128
IMF. *See* International Monetary
    Fund (IMF)
Income inequalities, 22, 207
Independent journalists, 108
Index, of ICT diffusion, 46–48, 77
India, 22, 45, 47, 127, 141, 146, 186,
    187, 189, 203, 203, 204, 206,
    207, 214
    blogger arrests in, 114
    censorship, 176
    civil society online, 138
    democratic entrenchment, 223
    government offices online, 68
    information infrastructure for
        political parties, 98

India (*continued*)
  media concentration, 121
  media outlets in, 87
  political parties online, 97
  population practicing Islam, rate
    of ICT diffusion, and
    democratic entrenchment, 211
  population size, 186, 187
  remittances, ICT led growth, state
    capacity, and policy
    effectiveness, 78
  state media ownership and online
    journalism, 124
  telecommunications reform and
    ICT policies, 64
Indic language, 159
Indonesia, 3, 13, 22, 27, 38, 52, 54,
  56, 71, 88, 89, 97, 122, 127, 133,
  141, 145, 150, 154, 182, 186, 187,
  195, 197, 203, 213
  censorship, 176
  civil society online, 138
  democratic transition, 220
  government offices online, 68
  information infrastructure for
    political parties, 98
  media concentration, 121
  population practicing Islam, rate
    of ICT diffusion, and
    democratic transition, 209
  remittances, ICT-led growth, state
    capacity, and policy
    effectiveness, 78
  state media ownership and online
    journalism, 124
  telecommunications reform and
    ICT policies, 64
Information and communication
  technologies (ICT)
  diffusion, 46-56
  index of, 46-48
  Islamic political culture and, 39-42

Muslim communities and, 42-46.
  See also Muslim countries
  policies in Muslim countries. *See*
    Policy reforms
Information infrastructure
  for business but not politics, 80-81
  for Islamic but not Western
    Culture, 82
  for personal but not public
    communications, 81-82
Ingushetia, 197
International Monetary Fund
  (IMF), 44, 62
International Telecommunications
  Union, 15, 63
Internet, in Muslim countries.
  See also Muslim countries
  political impact, 39-42
Internet exchange points, 10, 171,
  175
  administrative control of, 87
  political battles for, 136
Internet jihad, 30
Internet population, 37
Internet Protocol Packets, 67
Internet service provider
  (ISP), 122, 137, 145
  and censorship, 170, 171, 175
  local entrepreneurs and, 196
  NGOs and, 182
Iran, 22, 34, 38, 39, 73, 117, 122,
  126, 127, 128, 129, 146, 148, 158,
  165, 169, 171, 172, 175, 186, 206
  authoritarianism, 225
  blogger arrests in, 113, 114, 115,
    116
  blogs in, 38
  campaigning, 5
  censorship, 8-9, 177
  civil society in, 4
  civil society online, 139
  digital revolution in, 3-12

domestic politics in, 3
Facebook in, 5, 7, 8, 16, 41, 148
government offices online, 69
ICT, 4
information infrastructure for
    political parties, 99
media concentration, 121
media in, 122
Persian-language content, 119
population practicing Islam,
    rate of ICT diffusion, and
    countries remained
    authoritarian, 212
presidential election 2005, 3
protests in, 6–8
remittances, ICT-led growth, state
    capacity, and policy
    effectiveness, 79
state media ownership and online
    journalism, 125
surveilling bloggers, 112
telecommunications reform and
    ICT policies, 65
voting, 6
Iraq, 52, 102, 110, 117, 122, 127, 128,
    169, 174, 189, 190, 206
blogs in, 38
censorship, 177
civil society online, 139
as crisis state, 74, 228
government offices online, 69
information infrastructure for
    political parties, 99
jihadist media sources in, 128
media concentration, 121
media in, 122
population practicing Islam, rate
    of ICT diffusion, and countries
    experiencing anarchy, 213
remittances, ICT-led growth, state
    capacity, and policy
    effectiveness, 79

state media ownership and online
    journalism, 125
support for democratic
    governance, 189
telecommunications reform and
    ICT policies, 65
Iraq war, 110
Islam, and democracy, 13
Islamic civil society online,
    136–142. See also Civil society;
    Online civil society, in Muslim
    countries
Islamic political culture, ICT
    and, 39–42
Islamic republics, 73
Israel, 40, 97, 115, 127, 136, 206,
    214, 216
censorship, 176
civil society online, 138
democratic entrenchment, 223
government offices online, 68
information infrastructure for
    political parties, 98
population practicing Islam, rate
    of ICT diffusion, and
    democratic entrenchment, 211
remittances, ICT-led growth, state
    capacity, and policy
    effectiveness, 78
state media ownership and online
    journalism, 124
telecommunications reform and
    ICT policies, 64
Israel, attack on Gaza, 117, 136
Itiraf.com, 135
Ivory Coast, 136, 206
censorship, 177
civil society online, 139
crisis states, 228
government offices online, 69
information infrastructure for
    political parties, 99

Ivory Coast (*continued*)
  population practicing Islam, rate of ICT diffusion, and countries experiencing anarchy, 213
  remittances, ICT-led growth, state capacity, and policy effectiveness, 79
  state media ownership and online journalism, 125
  telecommunications reform and ICT policies, 65

Jihadist media sources, 128
Jordan, 43, 45, 89, 102, 108, 172, 205, 216
  authoritarianism, 225
  censorship, 177
  civil society online, 139
  government offices online, 69
  information infrastructure for political parties, 99
  population practicing Islam, rate of ICT diffusion, and countries remained authoritarian, 212
  remittances, ICT-led growth, state capacity, and policy effectiveness, 79
  state media ownership and online journalism, 125
  telecommunications reform and ICT policies, 65
Journalism, 182. *See also* Media ownership
  blogging and. *See* Bloggers
  challenges of, 118–120
  changing work and forms of, 108–110
  news diets, 110–112
  overview, 108
Journalism 2.0, 110

Journalists, 182. *See also* Journalism; Media ownership
  in crisis, 111
  professional associations of, 108
  professional ethics, 109

Kazakhstan, 3, 38, 129, 216
  authoritarianism, 225
  censorship, 177
  civil society online, 139
  government offices online, 69
  information infrastructure for political parties, 99
  population practicing Islam, rate of ICT diffusion, and countries remained authoritarian, 212
  remittances, ICT-led growth, state capacity, and policy effectiveness, 79
  state media ownership and online journalism, 125
  telecommunications reform and ICT policies, 65
Kenya, 59, 207
  censorship, 176
  civil society online, 138
  democratic transition, 221
  government offices online, 68
  information infrastructure for political parties, 98
  population practicing Islam, rate of ICT diffusion, and democratic transition, 209
  remittances, ICT-led growth, state capacity, and policy effectiveness, 78
  state media ownership and online journalism, 124
  telecommunications reform and ICT policies, 64
Kenya, 2007 elections in, 117

Khamenei, Ayatollah, 9
Khurdish separatists, 146
Koran, 40, 73
Koranic interpretation, 40, 73, 119,
     142–143
"FatwaBase," 151
Kranzberg, Melvin, 16
Kurds, 133, 146, 147
Kuwait, 52, 59, 101, 117, 140, 154,
     158, 173, 186, 190, 216
  blogger arrests in, 114
  censorship, 176
  civil society online, 138
  democratic transition, 190, 221
  government offices online, 68
  information infrastructure for
     political parties, 98
  population practicing Islam, rate
     of ICT diffusion, and
     democratic transition, 209
  remittances, ICT-led growth, state
     capacity, and policy
     effectiveness, 78
  state media ownership and online
     journalism, 124
  telecommunications reform and
     ICT policies, 64
Kyrgystan, "samizdat," 117
Kyrgyzstan, 56, 70, 129, 147, 158, 216
  censorship, 176
  civil society online, 138
  democratic transition, 221
  government offices online, 68
  information infrastructure for
     political parties, 98
  population practicing Islam, rate
     of ICT diffusion, and
     democratic transition, 209
  remittances, ICT-led growth, state
     capacity, and policy
     effectiveness, 78

  state media ownership and online
     journalism, 124
  telecommunications reform and
     ICT policies, 64

Language, 151, 158–159
Lebanon, 41, 97, 127, 132, 214, 216
  censorship, 176
  civil society online, 138
  democratic transition, 221
  government offices online, 68
  information infrastructure for
     political parties, 98
  population practicing Islam, rate
     of ICT diffusion, and
     democratic transition, 209
  remittances, ICT-led growth, state
     capacity, and policy
     effectiveness, 78
  state media ownership and online
     journalism, 124
  telecommunications reform and
     ICT policies, 64
Libel laws, 118
Liberia, 55, 61, 137, 206, 207, 216
  censorship, 176
  civil society online, 138
  democratic transition, 221
  government offices online, 68
  information infrastructure for
     political parties, 98
  population practicing Islam, rate
     of ICT diffusion, and
     democratic transition, 209
  remittances, ICT-led growth, state
     capacity, and policy
     effectiveness, 78
  state media ownership and online
     journalism, 124
  telecommunications reform and
     ICT policies, 64

Libraries, 144–145
Libya, 27, 57, 133, 140, 206, 214
    authoritarianism, 225
    censorship, 177
    civil society online, 139
    government offices online, 69
    information infrastructure for
        political parties, 99
    population practicing Islam, rate
        of ICT diffusion, and countries
        remained authoritarian, 212
    remittances, ICT-led growth, state
        capacity, and policy
        effectiveness, 79
    state media ownership and online
        journalism, 125
    telecommunications reform and
        ICT policies, 65
Linguistic diversity, 158–159

Macedonia, 96
    censorship, 176
    civil society online, 138
    democratic transition, 221
    government offices online, 68
    information infrastructure for
        political parties, 98
    population practicing Islam, rate
        of ICT diffusion, and
        democratic transition, 209
    remittances, ICT-led growth, state
        capacity, and policy
        effectiveness, 78
    state media ownership and online
        journalism, 124
    telecommunications reform and
        ICT policies, 64
Madrassa, 45, 186. See also
    Schools
Malawi, 207, 216
    censorship, 176
    civil society online, 138

    democratic entrenchment, 223
    government offices online, 68
    information infrastructure for
        political parties, 98
    population practicing Islam, rate
        of ICT diffusion, and
        democratic entrenchment, 211
    remittances, ICT-led growth, state
        capacity, and policy
        effectiveness, 78
    state media ownership and online
        journalism, 124
    telecommunications reform and
        ICT policies, 64
Malaysia, 3–4, 22, 41, 71, 80, 86, 97,
    110, 150, 163, 168, 182, 186,
    190, 214
    blogger arrests in, 114, 115, 116
    censorship, 176
    civil society online, 138
    democratic entrenchment, 223
    government offices online, 68
    information infrastructure for
        political parties, 98
    population practicing Islam,
        rate of ICT diffusion, and
        democratic entrenchment,
        211
    remittances, ICT-led growth, state
        capacity, and policy
        effectiveness, 78
    state media ownership and online
        journalism, 124
    telecommunications reform and
        ICT policies, 64
Maldives, 24, 204, 207, 216
    censorship, 176
    civil society online, 138
    democratic transition, 221
    government offices online, 68
    information infrastructure for
        political parties, 98

population practicing Islam, rate
  of ICT diffusion, and
  democratic transition, 210
remittances, ICT-led growth, state
  capacity, and policy
  effectiveness, 78
state media ownership and online
  journalism, 124
telecommunications reform and
  ICT policies, 64
Mali, 45, 46, 206
  censorship, 176
  civil society online, 138
  democratic entrenchment, 223
  government offices online, 68
  information infrastructure for
    political parties, 98
  population practicing Islam, rate
    of ICT diffusion, and
    democratic entrenchment, 211
  remittances, ICT-led growth, state
    capacity, and policy
    effectiveness, 78
  state media ownership and online
    journalism, 124
  telecommunications reform and
    ICT policies, 64
Maluku conflict, 109
Market for censorship, 172–173
Mauritania, 67, 166, 207, 214, 216
  censorship, 176
  civil society online, 138
  democratic transition, 221
  government offices online, 68
  information infrastructure for
    political parties, 98
  population practicing Islam, rate
    of ICT diffusion, and
    democratic transition, 210
  remittances, ICT-led growth, state
    capacity, and policy
    effectiveness, 78

state media ownership and online
  journalism, 124
telecommunications reform and
  ICT policies, 64
Mauritius, 61, 214
  censorship, 176
  civil society online, 138
  democratic entrenchment, 223
  government offices online, 68
  information infrastructure for
    political parties, 98
  population practicing Islam, rate
    of ICT diffusion, and
    democratic entrenchment, 211
  remittances, ICT-led growth, state
    capacity, and policy
    effectiveness, 78
  state media ownership and online
    journalism, 124
  telecommunications reform and
    ICT policies, 64
Media ownership, 120–127
  assets concentration, 120–121
  critical information
    infrastructures, 121–122
  state dominance of, 122
Mindinao, 197
Mobile phone cameras, 117
Mobile phones, 19. *See also*
    Information and
    communication technologies
    (ICT); Muslim countries
  and revolution, 38
Mobile Syariah Banking, 150
Modular political phenomena, 149
Montenegro, 97, 189, 205, 207
  censorship, 176
  civil society online, 138
  democratic transition, 221
  government offices online, 68
  information infrastructure for
    political parties, 98

Montenegro (*continued*)
  population practicing Islam, rate
    of ICT diffusion, and
    democratic transition, 210
  remittances, ICT-led growth, state
    capacity, and policy
    effectiveness, 78
  state media ownership and online
    journalism, 124
  telecommunications reform and
    ICT policies, 64
Moore, Barrington, 200
Morocco, 52, 70, 96, 122, 126, 190
  authoritarianism, 190, 226
  blogger arrests in, 115, 116
  censorship, 177
  civil society online, 139
  government offices online, 69
  information infrastructure for
    political parties, 99
  media concentration, 121
  population practicing Islam,
    rate of ICT diffusion, and
    countries remained
    authoritarian, 212
  remittances, ICT-led growth, state
    capacity, and policy
    effectiveness, 79
  state media ownership and online
    journalism, 125
  telecommunications reform and
    ICT policies, 65
Morocco, media industry in, 122
Motalebi, Sina, 112
Movement for Islamic Reform in
  Arabia, 134, 137
Mozambique, 45, 59, 166, 216
  censorship, 176
  civil society online, 138
  democratic entrenchment, 224
  government offices online, 68
  information infrastructure for
    political parties, 99

  population practicing Islam, rate
    of ICT diffusion, and
    democratic entrenchment, 211
  remittances, ICT-led growth, state
    capacity, and policy
    effectiveness, 78
  state media ownership and online
    journalism, 125
  telecommunications reform and
    ICT policies, 64
MOs, 146
Multimedia commercial news
  organizations, 109
Multipurpose community center, 45
Muslim Brotherhood, 133
Muslim countries, 20–25. *See also*
  specific countries
  access to, 42–46
  censorship in. *See* Censorship
  diversity, 22
  echnology diffusion in, 25
  economic wealth and, 22–23
  homologous, 23
  in Indian subcontinent, 22
  online civil society. *See* Civil society
  online governments in. *See*
    Government offices online
  online news sources, 29
  policies. *See* Policy reforms
  political impact, 39–42
  political leaders in, 29
  political parties in. *See* Political
    parties online
  political structures and, 23
Muslim extremists, 134
Muslim households, 18–20
  Internet users per, 19–20
Muslim politics online, 14
Myspace, 110

News consumption, 129
News diet, 110–112
  in military crisis, 111

in political crisis, 111–112
News managers, 118–119
News organizations, 109
  in Arab countries, 109
  multimedia commercial
    organizations, 109
Newsrooms, 109
News sources, 110
News websites, 117
New York Times, 110, 134
Niger, 61, 207, 213, 216
  censorship, 176
  civil society online, 138
  democratic transition, 221
  government offices online, 68
  information infrastructure for
    political parties, 98
  population practicing Islam, rate
    of ICT diffusion, and
    democratic transition, 210
  remittances, ICT-led growth, state
    capacity, and policy
    effectiveness, 78
  state media ownership and online
    journalism, 124
  telecommunications reform and
    ICT policies, 64
Nigeria, 37, 59, 122, 127, 137, 141,
    166, 186, 207
  blogger arrests in, 116
  censorship, 176
  civil society online, 138
  democratic transition, 221
  government offices online, 68
  information infrastructure for
    political parties, 98
  media concentration, 121
  population practicing Islam, rate
    of ICT diffusion, and
    democratic transition, 210
  remittances, ICT-led growth, state
    capacity, and policy
    effectiveness, 78

state media ownership and online
    journalism, 124
  telecommunications reform and
    ICT policies, 64
Nigeria, media in, 122

Ocalan, Abdullah, 133
OECD countries, media industry
    in, 122
Oman, 140, 171, 173, 205, 214
  authoritarianism, 226
  censorship, 177
  civil society online, 139
  government offices online, 69
  information infrastructure for
    political parties, 99
  population practicing Islam,
    rate of ICT diffusion, and
    countries remained
    authoritarian, 212
  remittances, ICT-led growth, state
    capacity, and policy
    effectiveness, 79
  state media ownership and online
    journalism, 125
  telecommunications reform and
    ICT policies, 65
Online Arab newspapers, 117
Online civil society, in Muslim
    countries, 136–142. *See also*
    Civil society
  citizenship, 152–154
  cost of Internet access,
    140–141
  digital transition, 140
  infrastructure investments,
    141–142
  learning online, 148–150
  state response to, 147–148
  World Bank and, 141–142
Online cultural tools, 74
Online debate/discourse, 142–144
Online journalism. *See* Journalism

Online news. *See also* Journalism;
    Media ownership
  consumption, 111
  sources, 110
  state dominance, 123–127
Online publication, 38
Online public opinion, 127
OpenNet Initiative, 172
Open Society Institute, 136
Opportunity structure, 28, 132, 149,
    180, 197

Pakistan, 22, 34, 52, 67, 70, 87,
    97–98, 110, 111, 122, 127, 140,
    141, 146, 168, 171, 172, 182,
    203, 206, 213, 214, 216
  authoritarianism, 226
  blogger arrests in, 114
  censorship, 177
  civil society online, 138, 139
  government offices online, 69
  information infrastructure for
    political parties, 99
  media concentration, 121
  media outlets in, 87
  population practicing Islam,
    rate of ICT diffusion, and
    countries remained
    authoritarian, 212
  remittances, ICT-led growth, state
    capacity, and policy
    effectiveness, 79
  state media ownership and online
    journalism, 125
  telecommunications reform and
    ICT policies, 65
Pakistan, media in, 122
Participatory journalism, 110
Personal computers, 18–19
PKK, 133
Policy reforms, 59–65
  comparative analysis of, 62–63

depoliticizing regulatory
    authorities, 61–62, 63
  liberalizing domestic
    markets, 61–62
  making telecommunications
    regulator independent, 62, 63
  privatization and, 60
  privatizing national
    telecommunications
    provider, 62, 63
  on remittances, 76
  separating regulatory authority
    from executive branch, 61, 62,
    63
  types of, 60–61
Political conflict online, 146
Political culture, 159–164. *See also*
    Cultural production and
    consumption
  as cognitive and material
    schema, 160
  concept of, 159–160
  Internet hosts, 161
  material frames and, 160
Political economy of online
    journalism, 129–131
Political engagement online, 14
Political parties, 41, 205–206
  competitiveness, 181–182
Political parties online, 84–106
  economic strategies, 85–87
  growth of, 89–95
  in Gulf countries, 84
  homepage, 85
  infrastructure, 96–100
  logistics and, 87–88
  media information
    technologies, 87–88
  political discourse online, 96–100
  public opinion, 100–104
  websites, 84–85
Political systems, range of, 66

Pornographic websites, 172
Professional community, of
    journalists, 118
Public opinion, construction
    of, 100–104
    political leaders and, 101
    Western news agencies and,
        102–103

Qatar, 25, 140, 186, 206, 207, 216
    authoritarianism, 226
    censorship, 177
    civil society online, 139
    government offices online, 69
    information infrastructure for
        political parties, 99
    population practicing Islam, rate
        of ICT diffusion, and countries
        remained authoritarian, 212
    remittances, ICT-led growth, state
        capacity, and policy
        effectiveness, 79
    state media ownership and online
        journalism, 125
    telecommunications reform and
        ICT policies, 65

Remittances, 76–77
Remittances, and policy reforms, 76
Republics, defined, 73
Robot.txt, 174
Russia, 22, 24, 97, 126, 127, 187, 206,
    216
    authoritarianism, 226
    censorship, 177
    civil society online, 139
    government offices online, 69
    information infrastructure for
        political parties, 99
    population practicing Islam, rate
        of ICT diffusion, and countries
        remained authoritarian, 212

    remittances, ICT-led growth, state
        capacity, and policy
        effectiveness, 79
    state media ownership and online
        journalism, 125
    telecommunications reform and
        ICT policies, 65

Said, Edward, 29
"Samizdat," 117
Saudi Arabia, 34, 43, 53, 56, 57, 59,
    73, 80, 89, 103, 122, 126, 127,
    134, 146, 156, 167, 170, 172, 173,
    190, 214
    authoritarianism, 226
    blogger arrests in, 114, 115
    censorship, 177
    civil society online, 139
    government offices online, 69
    information infrastructure for
        political parties, 99
    media concentration, 121
    population practicing Islam, rate
        of ICT diffusion, and countries
        remained authoritarian, 212
    remittances, ICT-led growth, state
        capacity, and policy
        effectiveness, 79
    state media ownership and online
        journalism, 125
    telecommunications reform and
        ICT policies, 65
Schools, 43, 86, 166–167, 186
Secure Computing, 173
Self-censorship, 174–175
Senegal, 41, 46, 166
    censorship, 176
    civil society online, 138
    democratic transition, 222
    government offices online, 68
    information infrastructure for
        political parties, 98

Senegal (*continued*)
  population practicing Islam, rate
    of ICT diffusion, and
    democratic transition, 210
  remittances, ICT-led growth, state
    capacity, and policy
    effectiveness, 78
  state media ownership and online
    journalism, 124
  telecommunications reform and
    ICT policies, 64
Separatist movement, 24, 146
September 11 attack, 111
Service attacks, 146
Sexuality, 14, 166
Sexually transmitted diseases, 166
Shared grievances, 32, 40, 102–103,
    165, 169
Sharia law, 73, 134
Sierra Leone, 88, 123, 206, 207,
    216
  censorship, 176
  civil society online, 138
  democratic transition, 222
  government offices online, 68
  information infrastructure for
    political parties, 98
  population practicing Islam, rate
    of ICT diffusion, and
    democratic transition, 210
  remittances, ICT-led growth, state
    capacity, and policy
    effectiveness, 78
  state media ownership and online
    journalism, 124
  telecommunications reform and
    ICT policies, 64
Silicon Valley, 173
Singapore, 42, 43, 52, 67, 80, 140,
    156, 172, 173, 190, 206
  authoritarianism, 227
  blogger arrests in, 113

censorship, 177
civil society online, 139
government offices online, 69
information infrastructure for
    political parties, 99
population practicing Islam, rate
    of ICT diffusion, and countries
    remained authoritarian, 212
remittances, ICT-led growth, state
    capacity, and policy
    effectiveness, 79
state media ownership and online
    journalism, 125
telecommunications reform and
    ICT policies, 65
Smartfilter, 174–175
Social interaction, 135–136
*The Social Origins of Dictatorship
    and Democracy*, 200
Somalia, 36, 54, 74, 123, 128, 206,
    207
  censorship, 177
  civil society online, 139
  as crisis state, 74
  crisis states, 228
  government offices online, 69
  information infrastructure for
    political parties, 99
  jihadist media sources in, 128
  population practicing Islam, rate
    of ICT diffusion, and countries
    experiencing anarchy, 213
  remittances, ICT-led growth, state
    capacity, and policy
    effectiveness, 79
  state media ownership and online
    journalism, 125
  telecommunications reform and
    ICT policies, 65
Spain, 111
Special Force, 41
State capacity, 76–77

State media ownership, 120–127.
  See also Media ownership
  and online journalism, 124–125
Stories, 109–110
Sudan, 140, 171, 173, 174, 207, 216
  authoritarianism, 227
  censorship, 177
  civil society online, 139
  government offices online, 69
  information infrastructure for
    political parties, 99
  media concentration, 121
  population practicing Islam, rate
    of ICT diffusion, and countries
    remained authoritarian, 213
  remittances, ICT-led growth, state
    capacity, and policy
    effectiveness, 79
  state media ownership and online
    journalism, 125
  telecommunications reform and
    ICT policies, 65
SurfControl, 173
Suriname, 24, 204
  censorship, 176
  civil society online, 138
  democratic transition, 222
  government offices online, 68
  information infrastructure for
    political parties, 98
  population practicing Islam, rate
    of ICT diffusion, and
    democratic transition, 210
  remittances, ICT-led growth, state
    capacity, and policy
    effectiveness, 78
  state media ownership and online
    journalism, 124
  telecommunications reform and
    ICT policies, 64
Syria, 37, 43, 102, 140, 158, 171, 172
  authoritarianism, 227

  blogger arrests in, 113, 114, 115,
    116
  censorship, 177
  civil society online, 139
  government offices online, 69
  information infrastructure for
    political parties, 99
  population practicing Islam, rate
    of ICT diffusion, and countries
    remained authoritarian, 213
  remittances, ICT-led growth, state
    capacity, and policy
    effectiveness, 79
  state media ownership and online
    journalism, 125
  telecommunications reform and
    ICT policies, 65

Tajikistan, 85, 123, 129, 204, 207,
    216
  authoritarianism, 227
  censorship, 177
  civil society online, 139
  government offices online, 69
  information infrastructure for
    political parties, 99
  population practicing Islam, rate
    of ICT diffusion, and countries
    remained authoritarian, 213
  remittances, ICT-led growth, state
    capacity, and policy
    effectiveness, 79
  state media ownership and online
    journalism, 125
  telecommunications reform and
    ICT policies, 65
Tanzania, 41, 43, 57, 59, 70, 97, 154,
    195, 205, 206, 207
  censorship, 176
  civil society online, 138
  democratic transition, 222
  government offices online, 68

Tanzania (*continued*)
  information infrastructure for
    political parties, 98
  population practicing Islam, rate
    of ICT diffusion, and
    democratic transition, 210
  remittances, ICT-led growth, state
    capacity, and policy
    effcctiveness, 78
  state media ownership and online
    journalism, 124
  telecommunications reform and
    ICT policies, 64
Technologies of freedom, 13
Technologies of oppression, 13-14
Telecenters, in Muslim
    countries, 44-46
  civic, 45
  franchises, 44-45
  madrassas and, 45
  in rural marginalized areas, 44
Telecommunications, 43
  licenses, 58
  policy reforms and. *See* Policy
    reforms
  privatization and, 60
Television, 110
Terrorists. *See also* Cyberterrorism
  organizations, 135, 143
  websites, 39
Terror online, 30
Text messaging, 38
Togo, 206
  authoritarianism, 227
  censorship, 177
  civil society online, 139
  government offices online, 69
  information infrastructure for
    political parties, 99
  population practicing Islam, rate
    of ICT diffusion, and countries
    remained authoritarian, 213

  remittances, ICT-led growth, state
    capacity, and policy
    effectiveness, 79
  state media ownership and online
    journalism, 125
  telecommunications reform and
    ICT policies, 65
Transition democracies, 67, 68, 70
Tulip Revolution, 117
Tulip Revolution, of Kyrgyzstan,
    38
Tunisia, 3, 41, 56, 97, 140, 172, 173,
    174, 190, 216
  authoritarianism, 190, 227
  blogger arrests in, 113, 114, 116
  censorship, 177
  civil society online, 139
  government offices online, 69
  information infrastructure for
    political parties, 99
  population practicing Islam,
    rate of ICT diffusion, and
    countries remained
    authoritarian, 213
  remittances, ICT-led growth, state
    capacity, and policy
    effectiveness, 79
  state media ownership and online
    journalism, 125
  telecommunications reform and
    ICT policies, 65
Turkey, 3-4, 22-23, 27, 56, 59, 71,
    80, 89, 96, 97, 110, 117, 122, 127,
    133, 145, 147, 163, 168, 182, 189,
    197, 206, 214, 216
  blogger arrests in, 116
  censorship, 176
  civil society online, 138
  democratic entrenchment, 224
  government offices online, 68
  information infrastructure for
    political parties, 99

media concentration, 121
population practicing Islam, rate
   of ICT diffusion, and
   democratic entrenchment, 211
remittances, ICT-led growth, state
   capacity, and policy
   effectiveness, 78
state media ownership and online
   journalism, 125
telecommunications reform and
   ICT policies, 64
Turkey, media in, 122
Turkmenistan, 27, 52, 53, 158, 206
authoritarianism, 227
censorship, 177
civil society online, 139
government offices online, 69
information infrastructure for
   political parties, 99
population practicing Islam,
   rate of ICT diffusion, and
   countries remained
   authoritarian, 213
remittances, ICT-led growth, state
   capacity, and policy
   effectiveness, 79
state media ownership and online
   journalism, 125
telecommunications reform and
   ICT policies, 65
Twitter, 9, 11, 12, 117, 135
in campaigning, 5
in protests, 7–8

UAE, 25, 36, 59, 110, 137, 140, 158,
   171, 172, 173, 206
authoritarianism, 227
censorship, 177
civil society online, 139
government offices online, 69
information infrastructure for
   political parties, 99

population practicing Islam,
   rate of ICT diffusion, and
   countries remained
   authoritarian, 213
remittances, ICT-led growth, state
   capacity, and policy
   effectiveness, 79
state media ownership and online
   journalism, 125
telecommunications reform and
   ICT policies, 65
Uganda, 45, 166, 186, 190
censorship, 176
civil society online, 138
democratic transition, 190, 222
government offices online, 68
information infrastructure for
   political parties, 98
population practicing Islam, rate
   of ICT diffusion, and
   democratic transition, 210
remittances, ICT-led growth, state
   capacity, and policy
   effectiveness, 78
state media ownership and online
   journalism, 124
telecommunications reform and
   ICT policies, 64
United Kingdom, 32, 111
United States, 30, 32, 46, 62, 67, 75,
   90, 110, 111, 112, 126, 129, 174
Urdun al Jadid Research Center in
   Jordan, 108
Uyghurs, 24
Uzbekistan, 129, 158, 171, 172, 173,
   207
authoritarianism, 227
censorship, 177
civil society online, 139
government offices online, 69
information infrastructure for
   political parties, 99

Uzbekistan (*continued*)
  media concentration, 121
  population practicing Islam, rate
    of ICT diffusion, and countries
    remained authoritarian, 213
  remittances, ICT-led growth, state
    capacity, and policy
    effectiveness, 79
  state media ownership and online
    journalism, 125
  telecommunications reform and
    ICT policies, 65

Video games, political impact
  of, 41–42
Virtual environments, 41

Wahhabist Islam, 167–168
Washington Post, 174
Websense, 173
West Bank & Gaza, 24, 88, 146, 158,
  205, 209, 214, 215
  censorship, 177
  civil society online, 139
  crisis states, 228
  government offices online, 69
  information infrastructure for
    political parties, 99
  population practicing Islam, rate
    of ICT diffusion, and countries
    experiencing anarchy, 213
  remittances, ICT-led growth, state
    capacity, and policy
    effectiveness, 79
  state media ownership and online
    journalism, 125
  telecommunications reform and
    ICT policies, 65
Western news media, 29
Western Sahara, 24, 204, 205, 207,
  209, 214, 215

  censorship, 177
  civil society online, 139
  crisis states, 228
  government offices online, 69
  information infrastructure for
    political parties, 99
  population practicing Islam, rate
    of ICT diffusion, and countries
    experiencing anarchy, 213
  remittances, ICT-led growth, state
    capacity, and policy
    effectiveness, 79
  state media ownership and online
    journalism, 125
  telecommunications reform and
    ICT policies, 65
Wired citizenship, 152–154. *See also*
  Civil society
Wired political parties, 104–106.
  See also Political parties online
Wired states, 77, 80. *See also*
  Government offices online
  for business but not politics,
    80–81
  for Islamic but not Western
    culture, 82
  for personal but not public
    communications, 81–82
Women's suffrage movement, 38
World Bank, 141–142
World Trade Center, 111

Yahoo, 84, 135, 174
Yemen, 52, 88, 158, 171, 173, 190,
  206, 214
  authoritarianism, 190, 227
  censorship, 177
  civil society online, 139
  government offices online, 69
  information infrastructure for
    political parties, 99

population practicing Islam, rate
  of ICT diffusion, and countries
  remained authoritarian, 213
remittances, ICT-led growth, state
  capacity, and policy
  effectiveness, 79

state media ownership and online
  journalism, 125
telecommunications reform and
  ICT policies, 65
YouTube, 5, 8, 12, 74, 110, 112, 135,
  142, 178, 179